An
Un-American
Childhood

An Un-American Childhood

. . . .

ANN KIMMAGE

The University of Georgia Press

Athens and London

Published by the University of Georgia Press
Athens, Georgia 30602
© 1996 by Ann Kimmage

Designed by Betty Palmer McDaniel
Set in ten on thirteen Electra
by Tseng Information Systems, Inc.
Printed and bound by Thomson-Shore, Inc.
The paper in this book meets the guidelines for
permanence and durability of the Committee
on Production Guidelines for Book Longevity
of the Council on Library Resources.

Printed in the United States of America

00 99 98 97 96   C   5   4   3   2

Library of Congress Cataloging in Publication Data
Kimmage, Ann, 1942–
An un-American childhood / Ann Kimmage.
    p.   cm.
ISBN 0-8203-1768-3 (alk. paper)
1. Kimmage, Ann, 1942–. 2. Communists
—United States—Biography. 3. Anti-communist
movements—United States—History—20th century.
I. Title.
HX84.K56A3   1996
321.9'2'092—dc20
[B]   95-13229

The poem "Abe" was originally published in
Nightmare Begins Responsibility by Michael S.
Harper. Reprinted by permission of Michael S.
Harper and the University of Illinois Press.

British Library Cataloging in Publication Data available

my father, a man with a far-reaching vision, a shaper of ideas, who loved life with a passion and for whom each day was a chance for new experiences

my mother, who used to say jokingly that if she ever wrote a book about her life, she would be arrested in all the countries we lived in, but who nonetheless one day turned to me saying, "You know, Ann, I think you should write," which I thought was crazy

my sister, who helped me get through my childhood

In 1984 my husband and I and our two sons, aged eleven and fourteen, took our first trip to Europe as a family. My sons, who grew up in Plattsburgh, New York, with American-born parents, were not prepared for the transformation in their mother, who switched into fluent Czech when we arrived in Prague. My older son, Daniel, was amazed to discover a part of me he had never seen come to life until this return to Prague brought it out of me. When I accidentally addressed him in Czech, forgetting in the excitement that he couldn't speak this language and that he had never been part of that "other" life I had once lived in Czech only, he gave me a new name, *naše češka*, "our Czech." I wrote this book so that my sons would know why their American mother had a mysterious past with roots in Prague instead of New York City, where I was born, and what circumstances in America in the 1950s led to my changed identity. Here is that story of my un-American childhood.

Contents

Acknowledgments

For me this book has been a journey from darkness to light, from fears and confusions to awareness, from haunting memories to the chronological sequence of events that created my story. I could never have recorded events of my childhood without the prodding, exchanges, instruction, and support of others. In my imagination the real and unreal were troubled partners. Did I imagine what I lived or did I live what I imagined? The act of remembering was private, but the act of writing what I remembered opened up new relationships with people who became participants in the act of creation.

Without the investment of time, energy, and skill by the following people, this book would have remained a private story. Each contribution fueled my drive and strengthened my ability to complete it. I am deeply indebted to those who believed in the worth and importance of this project and who helped me overcome the obstacles I encountered along the way.

This manuscript was written on a Macintosh computer loaned to me by Plattsburgh State University of New York. I want to thank reference librarians Tim Hartnett, Carla List, Gordon Muir, and Michael Miranda, who answered strange questions such as what the hat was called that men wore in the 1950s (fedora) or what instrument in "Peter and the Wolf" represented the bird. I am grateful to the staff at the Academic Support Center, Raney Ellis, Jeannette Mammano, John Bradley, and Bernard Grabczewski, who helped me at panicked moments.

Ben Morreale, a history professor at Plattsburgh State, said to me at a dinner party, "If you don't turn this story into a book I will. You must do it, Ann. This is important history." He told me to sit at my desk, not let life interfere (how does one do that?), and write (where do I start, as a child or an adult?). Ben Morreale, Fran Straight, and Janice Beach read individual chapters early on, and their critical response forced me to clarify, refocus, and develop my thoughts. The supportive interest and encouraging editorial comments and criticisms of my editor Malcom L. Call to improve the style and flow of the narrative made the revising of the book a positive experience. The final copy of the manuscript was edited with sensitivity and skill by copyeditor Trudie Calvert. She showed me that saying less says more, while maintaining my own narrative voice, and that the use of the comma is an art.

When I had written only 120 pages and lacked the time to do more, I was accepted at Hedgebrook, a writer's retreat for women on Whidbey Island. I was a guest for a month. At Hedgebrook I was treated as a writer, and my other roles in life disappeared. There I met writers who became my first audience at informal after-dinner readings in the farm living room. Jean Brody sat with a pad and pencil in hand, Christian McEwen listened carefully curled up on a large cushion under the window, Eileen Hennessy sat neatly on the couch listening to the rhythm of my words, and Marguerite Bouvard's intelligent eyes remained fixed on my lips as I read the text I had written that day in my secluded cottage. Responses and criticisms from these poets and fiction and nonfiction writers were long-awaited rain on parched soil.

Jean helped me understand that I was the character in this story who had to have a faithful voice, and she discussed the intricacies of the writing craft with me. Eileen, eager for me to start reading, would call into the kitchen: "Come on everybody. Ann is going to read about living in China now." Christian left a copy of an essay she wrote about her own family background and the circumstances she grew up in to show me how she distilled the final powerful thirty pages from multiple drafts. And Marguerite, on long walks in the hot sun and drizzle and later during visits in her Wellesley home, pulled the story out of me with skilled questions and patiently edited redundancies while praising the passages that worked.

Early readers of the manuscript were Anne Mitchell, Emily Burde, Saba Weisner, Mary Kimmage, Cerise Oberman, Harvey Cohen, Helenka Richards, George Gibian, Margaret Engelhart, Diana Anhalt, and Laurie Bergamini, who sent edited chapters by express from her Lake Placid home so I could work without interruption. Close friends Jim and Jan Chingos weathered the years of ups and downs in writing this book, sharing experiences, cocktails, gourmet meals, and restorative long walks on the beach near their home. A line-by-line edit that started at the kitchen table of the Plattsburgh home of Margaret and Carl Engelhart and continued when Carl marked up my pages in their Vinalhaven home in Maine made the text readable. With a pot of tea on the table and a pen in hand, Carl read each sentence aloud, making me aware of the language rhythms that needed work. Each editing session with Carl was at the same time a lesson on the wonders of the English language.

While working on my book I read *The Strangest Dream* on the Canadian communists, the spy trials, and the Cold War written by journalist and documentary film writer Merrily Weisbord. Her book stirred deep emotions in me, which I expressed in a letter that started a correspondence and became a friendship. Merrily's astute editorial suggestions and critical comments made me dare what I had never tried before.

My sons Daniel and Michael have been an inspiration and encouragement. They read portions of the manuscript and investigated sources that contributed to the context in which my story took place. My Czech friends Vladimír and Kitty Munk were a valuable source of Czech historic events and figures. The historian Ronald Radosh read a near final version and encouraged me to seek a publisher. Irving Howe read an early version and commented: "I have read the pages you sent me, sometimes with a good deal of sadness, as I thought of the waste of hope and energy they reflect. But that is part of the history of our time and there is nothing we can do about it." Tobias Wolff graciously responded to my request to read the manuscript for a critical commentary, and he encouraged me to persevere and rewrite to preserve the cultural and family history I had set down. These critical comments on my work in progress gave me direction to make the necessary changes.

In the early stages of writing, discussions with Larry Soroka forced me to define my focus. He edited beginning chapters of the text that needed major rewriting and clarification at a time when he had a new baby to care for and stacks of student papers to correct. His patient finding of worthwhile passages in the midst of unnecessary digressions disclosed some of my most pressing themes. When we went over the revisions, he would point to a sentence asking, "What did you mean by this?" I would start explaining, and he would calmly say, "Well, why don't you say it the way you did now?" My little friend Tova, now four years old, provided the playful distraction from the frustrations of writing that I needed to return to the computer screen with a smile on my face and in my fingertips.

This book would have never come together without the devoted support of my husband, Dennis Kimmage. As a librarian, he helped me search for sources on the McCarthy period. He read and discussed eye-witness accounts of individuals who lived through the years I was writing about. He was always willing to dash up to Montreal with me to see a film such as the Chinese film *The Blue Kite* that relates to my story or visit the Boston bookstores in search of materials. In frequent stimulating discussions about the ramifications of the political events on the lives of the participants, he contributed to my growing knowledge and challenged me to learn more about the American scene. With a red pen and a sharp eye, he launched a campaign against my addiction to long sentences and demanded that I substantiate the context for my memories. Most important, he sustained my spirit with exquisite meals and consistent faith in the importance of preserving my personal history. His loving contributions made this book a reality.

Introduction

In those days one didn't ask questions about people who "disappeared." I assumed he [Abe Chapman] was in Czechoslovakia not because he wanted to live there but that he had been sent there directly or indirectly by the party leadership.

This was a time of frenetic persecution of Communists and other progressives that began even before McCarthy came on the scene. Some party members were sent out of the country either to become part of the party underground apparatus or to preserve them from arrest so that they might continue their activity in the future. These decisions were based on an estimate that fascism in the U.S. was advancing and almost inevitable. In the late fifties the party recognized that this estimate was exaggerated and many of the decisons based on it were wrong.

—From a 1994 letter from A. B. Magil, former correspondent for the *Daily Worker*

On a drizzly fall night in 1987 my husband and I went to a dance sponsored by ethnic Hungarians in Montreal, slightly over an hour from our home in Plattsburgh, New York. That night I witnessed a chance encounter between strangers that resurrected the memory of a deep and lasting cultural division between my parents and me. By chance we were seated at a table with a family that spoke several languages. The father was Hungarian and his wife was French Canadian. Neither the wife nor the children spoke Hungarian. The father addressed his children in a heavily accented English while his wife spoke to them in French. I knew from personal experience what it was like to speak one language with my parents and another with my sister and those around me.

A red-nosed old man started the cultural program, narrating a story in

Hungarian. His Hungarian listeners, who filled the hall, responded to the rising and deepening tones of his booming voice with alternating expressions of happiness and sadness. The Hungarian father seated across the round table from me was engrossed in the narrative. His children, however, fidgeted restlessly. His oldest daughter, no more than eight years old, complained to the mother, between yawns, about putting up with this Hungarian story she could not follow.

Suddenly, smiling young people in colorful costumes filled the dance floor. The intricate footwork of the twirling dancers, performed to the accompaniment of Hungarian tunes, brought an enormous smile to the father's face. He shifted his eyes from the dancers to his daughter, hoping she would share his excitement. But instead of watching the dancers, she sat with her back toward them, a sour expression on her face. After asking her to turn around, which she refused to do, he brusquely picked up her chair and turned her so that she would have to face the performers. His daughter defiantly persisted in looking away from the flushed dancers. Slowly, the hand with which the father was holding his daughter's chair slipped back to his lap. His shoulders drooped. He averted his saddened eyes from his slouching daughter. Alienated from her, he no longer took delight in the movements of the dancers. Within seconds, father and daughter became strangers to each other, inhabiting separate worlds.

Although I never spoke to this man, I felt his pain and disappointment. I saw my own father trying to make me respond to the American culture that defined him but from which I had been torn by the circumstances of our lives. These subtle gestures between a father and daughter stirred painful memories of the summer of 1950 in New York City, when I was eight years old. My father and I shared the same language and culture until that point in my life. After that, a new language, culture, and homeland distanced me from the one to which my father belonged. From then on, we each responded to the sounds of our respective languages, failing to bridge the gap it created.

My father and mother's political commitments forced our family into an exile that affected each of us differently but profoundly changed our individual lives and interrelationships. The cultural rift separating the Canadian daughter from her Hungarian father touched me deeply. The unresolved conflicts that started in my childhood evoked intense memories that had been deeply buried within me but were still powerful enough to sting. Though my parents are no longer alive, our shared past and the consequences of their political radicalism continue to live within me. I wondered, that night, if I was ready, after thirty-seven years, to untangle the strands of my own identity and explore the events that threw our family into turmoil and divided us culturally, linguistically, and politically.

I was born in New York City in 1942, the second of two daughters of Jewish-American parents, Abraham and Belle Chapman. Since the 1930s both of my parents had been politically active communists. In 1950 the four of us left America in haste and secrecy. We returned in 1963 as a family of three, leaving my sister Laura, by then married, in Europe. History books refer to those years as the McCarthy era: for me, they were the years of my childhood.

In a recent conversation, Renah, one of my Chicago cousins, recalled the suddenness of our mysterious disappearance from Queens, where my family had been living during that late spring of 1950:

> I can still vividly remember how hysterical my mother, Fanny [my father's oldest sister], was when she could not reach your family in New York City. Nobody answered the repeated phone calls at your home. There were no messages or clues as to your whereabouts. The entire Chapman family was frantic with worry. They tried every means possible to get some information about your disappearance. When relatives in New York City searched your residence, they found records and books on the shelves, beds made, plants in their places, closets full, but the rooms silent and empty. For years there was no information about your family—all four of you vanished—just like that!

During the thirteen years we were away from the United States, my father sent only one message to his family, consisting of a single sentence: "The four of us are alive." The message was delivered by a Communist Party (CP) courier via Egypt (to disguise our whereabouts), and in the interests of our safety it carried no return address. Family needs were secondary to the party commands and the absolute secrecy it demanded to protect the cause. By the time my father returned to the United States, his mother and his sister Fanny had died, never learning about our concealed lives. Family relationships were broken, leaving a void that could not be overcome easily and that was made more painful by lost years.

My mother's relationship to her strictly Orthodox Jewish family also suffered irreparable harm. After Belle's disappearance, her family moved to a new community and into anonymity to avoid uncomfortable questions from neighbors and harassing visits from the FBI, in search of my mother and father. In a new community my mother's family resumed life as a mother, a father, and a son, but no longer with a daughter, son-in-law, and grandchildren. Irreconcilable differences over religion and politics made it ultimately impossible for my mother to ease the pain her disappearance and political commitments created.

When we returned to New York City in 1963, she made telephone contact with her parents for the first time in thirteen years. Her father, who answered the phone, informed her that he no longer had a daughter. Helpless and at a loss for words, she dropped the telephone receiver. Her body crumpled forward, and she sobbed uncontrollably. Years of pent-up emotions, deliberately concealed from me behind her iron exterior, poured out. Although gradually she did reestablish a relationship with her parents and younger brother, it remained strained and distant. The ties between me and my grandparents, already disconnected by our political exile, were permanently broken by my eventual marriage to a non-Jew. I could never accept the severing of my once active relationship with my grandparents, which faded to a longing memory and ultimately a void.

I have always found it upsetting that my parents refused to reveal the specific reasons for our secretive departure from the United States. Their loyalty to the party committed them to silence about the true nature of their party involvements, and they maintained this secrecy to the end of their lives. My parents claimed it was for our protection that my sister and I had not been told why we left the United States so abruptly. They insisted that what we didn't know could not be revealed to others.

I have still not found a definitive answer. Reading about the 1940s and 1950s has made me better equipped to speculate about the reasons for our departure. I still wonder if our flight and subsequent exile were the result of something dangerous, worthy, noble, ignoble, or trivial. Was it perhaps related to something specific and illegal that my parents had done for the party and against the government, or was it just a result of the political climate of McCarthyism and the Cold War? Or were my parents part of some espionage network that required secrecy and escape? Or was it the general paranoia among the top ranks of the American Communist Party that led to decisions to send some functionaries underground in the United States and others, like my parents, abroad? And was our exile intended to last thirteen years?

Speculation is not a satisfying substitute for facts or an explanation from my parents about what led to the upheaval in our lives. Much will always remain unknown. I sometimes wonder whether knowing the truth today would be any compensation for the price my parents paid for their loyalties.

The story of our family is integrally connected to the witch-hunts and political polarization that affected the American Communist Party in the late 1940s and early 1950s. In 1949 eleven communist leaders were imprisoned for violating the Smith Act by allegedly advocating the violent overthrow of the government. The spread of McCarthysim made it dangerous to be a communist or to associate with communists. The outbreak of the Korean War only intensified anticommunist hysteria, and in 1950 Julius Rosenberg (and later his wife, Ethel) was arrested and accused of espionage. It was at this time that the American party ordered some of its functionaries and potential future leaders to go underground and, in some cases, to leave the country. For some American communists Mexico became a haven or a stop along the escape route. On August 16, 1950, Morton Sobell was kidnapped by the FBI in Mexico City in connection with the Rosenberg case and brought back to the United States for prosecution. The Rosenbergs themselves had secured passport photos and were allegedly preparing to escape behind the Iron Curtain via Mexico when Julius was arrested.

I do not know if our disappearance had any direct relation to the Rosenberg case. We slipped out of the country when American communists were mistrusted, harassed, fired from jobs, and in some instances arrested (rightly or wrongly) for their activities and beliefs. Children of known communists were followed by the FBI and humiliated in school for their parents' communist affiliations. It was an oppressive, politically hostile atmosphere for the American Left and active communists who were the main target. Yet the timing of our departure paralleled the Rosenberg arrests and other escapes, such as those of Morton Sobell,

Morris and Lena Cohen (American communists accused of playing a role in the American espionage ring, which according to a 1992 article in the *New York Post* was confirmed by the KGB spymaster Anatoly Yakovlev) and the scientist Joel Barr. I know the decision to flee was based on party instructions. Those instructions directed us along the familiar Mexican route to the communist bloc.

It was by accident that, in preparation for writing this book, I found in the records of congressional hearings evidence of my father's activities that targeted him for investigation. It was an eerie feeling to realize, several years after the death of my parents, that my father was one of the many characters in the McCarthy drama being played out in America's legislative chambers. Reading those portions of the Senate hearings in which my father's name was mentioned was fascinating, mysterious, and disturbing. It brought me face to face with a chapter of his life that might have contained the key (or one of the keys) to understanding what happened to our family.

In 1950–51 congressional hearings were held to investigate the alleged infiltration of the Institute of Pacific Relations (IPR) by communists and to determine their influence on and manipulation of American foreign policy. A broad goal of the hearings was to learn how sensitive information about the Far East was being passed to Soviet agents to undermine American policies in China, the Philippines, and other strategic areas. The immediate purpose was to expose communists in the IPR and thus destroy any influence they might try to exert on American public opinion.

My father had published reviews and articles on the Philippines and developments in other Pacific islands in *Far Eastern Survey* and *Pacific Affairs*, both of which were IPR publications. The 1950 IPR hearings revealed that my father had written a study titled "Philippine Nationalism" scheduled for publication that year in *Pacific Affairs*. The political premise of the article reflected precisely the sort of influence the hearings were designed to curtail. One of the exhibits at the hearings was a letter by the secretary-general of the IPR, William Holland, written May 17, 1950. In it he defends the policies of the IPR, whose publications were under attack not for the quality of their scholarship but because some of the published authors were known communists. As an example he used my father's article "Philippine Nationalism." William Holland's letter addresses the core of the conflict between the American government, his own position, and the position of the IPR with regard to censorship, all brought to a head by my father's scholarship and communist affiliations:

The Chapman study has also been delayed. He promised to submit the complete manuscript at the end of 1949. I phoned him the other day and he told me that the report is about 90 percent finished and that he will definitely submit the whole manuscript before the middle of June. It's quality is hard to predict but I expect it will contain (besides historical background) a great deal of accurate and hitherto not generally available information on Philippine politics and parties. He knows a lot about the Philippine political situation.

Chapman is under attack because, as he readily states, he was elected in 1945 as a member of the New York State Committee of the Communist Party. I think it is almost certain that he is still a communist. As far as I know this is the only case in the IPR research program involving a study by a communist party member. It thus constitutes a good test case of whether we should follow our traditional practice of judging a study on its merits, in the light of comments from qualified critics, or of deciding in advance whether to accept or reject it in the light of the author's communist membership. My own policy, and the one I would recommend despite its unpopularity these days, is to decide on the basis of the manuscript. I've informed Chapman and have also told him that the manuscript will undoubtedly be read with a very critical eye and that I can give him no assurance it will be accepted for publication. To me it would seem absurd and cowardly at this late date for us to disown the study in advance after it's been on our lists for several years.

Admittedly it will be easier to form an opinion on this after we see a few sample chapters, which I may receive in about two weeks. However, the question is complicated by the fact that last January, the American I.P.R. at Clayton Lane's strong insistence rejected (but paid for) an article by Chapman on Philippine politics today, which had previously been requested by the editor of the *Far Eastern Survey*, and which in quality and essential accuracy was judged by all who read it, including Mr. Lane, as acceptable. The ground given for rejection, was Chapman's membership on the executive committee of the Committee for a Democratic Far Eastern Policy, New York, an organization which was listed as "subversive" last year by the Attorney General. The Survey editor was unaware of this fact when she originally requested the article. The American I.P.R. Executive Committee which was asked to rule on this point of policy was divided in its views, but left it to Mr. Lane to decide.

Mr. Lane still feels that no manuscript should be accepted by the IPR from a writer who is a Communist or a member of a policy committee of an organization listed as subversive by the Attorney General. Undoubtedly several other members of the American IPR Board of Trustees share Mr. Lane's view, though the matter was never put to a vote. Mr. Lane and they would of course respect the views of the international officers and other members of the Pacific Council, but would probably point out that since Chapman is an American, and since the study began under American IPR auspices with a grant from Field's American Fund, the publication report, even under International Secretariat auspices, would provide further ammunition to those who are already attacking the IPR. On the other hand it seems to me unlikely that cancellation of the project now and suppression of the report would do much to make our critics end their attacks, especially when the project has been included on our lists for the last five years, and when both *Pacific Affairs* and *Far Eastern Survey* have previously (in 1946) published articles by Chapman.

By late May or June we were already out of the country. Was there something related to these hearings that set things in motion? My father's activities up to 1950 indicate that the scope of his party work was broad and influential. He was chairman of the Upper West Side Section Communist Party of America, a member of the New York State Committee of the Communist Party, contributor to the *Daily Worker* and other communist publications, an editor of the Communist Jewish daily *Morning Freiheit*, and a Communist Party authority on Jewish problems. He lectured at Communist Party clubs and the Jefferson School of Social Science and taught at the National Maritime Training Communist Party School. He was also executive officer of the International Worker's Order (IWO) and editor of *Fraternal Outlook*, an IWO publication. The IWO was founded in 1930 to provide insurance benefits and to advance the recreational, cultural, and educational interests of working people. In 1947 it was listed as a "subversive" organization. As William Holland points out, my father was also a member of the board of directors of the Committee for a Democratic Far Eastern Policy, a communist front organization. In a 1951 memorandum of the McCarran Subcommittee describing "subversive" activities I learned for the first time that my father was also known as John Arnold and John Gordon, aliases he used to conceal his political connections, as was common among party members and leaders at this time.

In the July 25, 1951–June 20, 1952, hearings on the Institute of Pacific Relations affair I learned that "nineteen individuals connected with the IPR who were by evidence involved in subversive activity, including seven staff members were either out of the country or otherwise unavailable for committee subpoena, namely . . . Abraham Chapman" and a long list of others.

In this atmosphere of harassment and arrests, the American CP sent numerous people, like my father, underground to preserve its intellectual leadership for the future. Reading the hearings made me wonder if there was a connection between my father's activities, the IPR, and the Rosenbergs that made it too dangerous for him and other party members to appear at the hearings and stay in the United States. Our sudden and inexplicable departure suggests that my father knew it would be dangerous to remain. His insistence on taking the entire family with him, moreover, leads me to believe he expected we would be gone for a long time. Although I have no hard facts to explain why we were uprooted from family, friends, and country, I have memories that make a new history, my history and the history of other communist children who also share parts of this story.

Countless books provide evidence that the period of political repression known as McCarthyism took a heavy toll on many American intellectuals, disrupting careers and in some cases ruining lives. The execution of the Rosenbergs was the most brutal and inhuman expression of McCarthyism. Owen Lattimore, who was accused of espionage when he was chairman of the Institute for Pacific Relations, introduces his book *Ordeal by Slander* with the following words: "This book is an account of what happened to me and my family when I was suddenly accused, without warrant or warning, of being 'the top Russian espionage agent in this country.' It is not written in self-defense. . . . My most important purpose has been to give a clear and consecutive account of what happened, because I believe that the story shows clearly the danger to which we are all exposed. It might have happened to you."

There is a difference, however, between the McCarthy period in America and the political purges of the 1950s in the countries under communist rule. For instance, Owen Lattimore, as evidenced by his book, was able to clarify his own position and publicly defend himself. As an American citizen, he could secure legal counsel and make his voice heard. It was a very different situation for the victims of communist regimes, whose opponents and onetime supporters were treated with equal contempt when it suited party politics. In the 1950s in Czechoslovakia, where we ultimately settled, opponents of the government, loyal supporters who fell out of favor with the regime, and other "traitors" disappeared in unmarked graves, work camps, or prisons, often after forced confessions of guilt. The scale of McCarthyite repression, despite the personal suffering and tragedy it brought to thousands of Americans, bears no comparison to the magnitude of the repression suffered over decades by millions in the Soviet Union and in the countries of Eastern Europe, China, and Cuba.

There is, nevertheless, a bond between the victims of both sides of the Cold War that was pointed out to me by a Czech immigrant friend of mine, Helenka. Her family left Czechoslovakia shortly after the communist coup in 1948. They owned a small business that was confiscated, and, like most immigrants, they left to seek a better future for their children in a free and democratic society. Ironically, when thousands of such immigrants were fleeing their homelands for the West, out of fear of persecution by the communists, a handful of Americans was seeking in communist countries protection from democratic governments that suspected their loyalty and political motives.

Helenka commented on how sad it was that in 1950, when these two groups of people were passing each other in their flight, each going in a different direction, political differences made them blind to their common plight. The fall of communism may now make it possible for us to be more compassionate and less judgmental about the winners and losers of the Cold War and more conscious of the twisted lives left in its wake. Our family lived in a world divided between communist and noncommunist visions of society. But the division was more than a philosophical difference. Ultimately it played havoc with our lives, as it did with the lives of millions of others who could not escape the intrusion of politics into the personal sphere.

For my parents, the political adventure was initially a wild, intoxicating, passionate rollercoaster ride, with unbelievable highs, but it also brought them nightmarish lows. My story is about what it was like for a child growing up in the midst of turbulent political forces that swept away my American origins and introduced me to a very different world that was foreign to my parents but that I made my own.

I had to penetrate the bitter lines that tightened around my mother's mouth in the later years of her life whenever she thought about the past.

I had to make English work for me as a means of expression rather than an enemy of Czech.

I had to find a way to identify with a past worthy of the passions it evoked rather than the losses it created.

I had to write this book for myself and for my parents, who loved my sons.

An
Un-American
Childhood

Chapter 1
. . . .
America

BROKEN WINGS

After the crash
broken wings.

Out of memories of flying,
the immensity of the search
for whatever life's search is
the distances to the
near and the immediate

I learn to fly
with broken wings

—Poem by Abraham Chapman, 1976

The workers have no country . . . they
have nothing to lose but their chains.

—Karl Marx, *The Communist Manifesto*

At birth my native country was America; my native language was English, and my name was Ann. I had a large extended family of grandparents, aunts, uncles, and cousins in addition to my parents and my older sister, Laura. In the spring of 1950 our family lived in a small row house in Queens. I was a wild tomboy, happiest outdoors either on the playground or running between and behind the small row houses. I was in second grade and I loved school. That year I wrote my first poem. In it I described the trees and bushes that had burst into life after the long winter, a change I had noticed on a recent outing our family had taken into the country. The teacher was excited about my poem, and she wrote it out in large, neat black letters on a posterboard so it could be displayed in our classroom. Each time I reread the poem, I wondered how I could have created those neatly written words. The poem kept alive the spring images that inspired it. How well I still remember the thrill of learning a new word for a new concept while on that family outing. The new word I connected with a specific image that day was *view*. The English language was beginning to obey my commands and excite my imagination. The world of experiences and sensations reflected in words fascinated me.

Perhaps I also remember that particular day so well because it was one of the last calm days spent with my parents and some of their close friends before everything changed. It was a sunny day. The air was full of spring fragrances. We left behind the city heat for a long hilly walk along a bubbling stream in the woods. Unconcerned about slowing down the grown-ups, who wanted to continue walking, I stopped along the way to play with the slippery flat rocks in the stream. I was aware of their conversation as it merged with the sound of the water rushing through the rocks. I dipped my hand in the cold water, intrigued by the force with which the water flowed through my fingers. My parents and their friends continued to argue about issues I was not interested in while I collected the smooth, wet rocks from the stream. My father encouraged me to move along by telling me that when we got to the top of this path, there would be a beautiful view. I tried to visualize what a *view* would look like, but I could not picture what sight would open up to me. I persistently questioned the experienced adults, "What is a view? What will I see when we get there? Is this it? Are we there yet?" Amused by my curiosity and impatience, they gently repeated, "You'll see when you get there. We can't describe it to you. It's something you have to see for yourself."

To curb my impatient anticipation, I created my own image of what a *view* might be like. In my mind I saw floating trees and brooks flowing into wide rivers, mountains shrinking to the size of rocks with spotted mushrooms growing on them and cows licking giant scoops of ice cream. That was something I would want to see! My fantasizing was interrupted when I heard my father say, "Here we are, Ann; what you see in front of you is the *view* we promised you." Instead of what I had imagined, I saw in the valley beneath me the hills we had climbed and green patchy fields with farmhouses encircled by white fences. They looked like dollhouses with miniature cows grazing lazily in the fields. The trees were no larger than oversized flowers, and the stream was a thick, silvery snake shining in the sun. I had seen sights like this before without making the connection between what I was seeing and the word that named it.

I was seven years old when I was standing on top of that hill taking in every last detail—the houses, the cows, the stream, and the strip of field, each with its own name identifying its uniqueness. Yet that day I realized that the individual parts also combined into something larger captured by the newly mastered word, *view*. This realization excited me because of the powerful magic of a single word to create new concepts. I loved what words could do when I created my poem. I felt powerful when I could get words to recreate feelings and moments I did not want to forget. I whispered the word *view* before falling asleep, recalling the image of what I had seen that afternoon, scanning in my memory the details of the landscape associated with those sounds and sights.

Only a few weeks were left before the end of the school year. I was looking forward to the summer days when I could play for hours on the front stoop and run around the neighborhood. And I was almost certain I would spend some time in my grandparents' home in the country, in Monsey, as I had done last summer. In my own neighborhood, I loved to play hide and seek behind our house, where there were thick lilac bushes. That spring, when all still seemed normal in our lives, I looked forward to the summer, when there would be more time to blow bubbles and watch them float through the air until they burst. Now that I was almost eight, I had been given permission to go as far as the corner drugstore with my friends for a treat at the soda fountain and the latest comic books. Once the school year was over, there would be more time to jump rope with my friends to see who could last the longest before giving up, or to play marbles to test who could get them into the hole first. I cherished my collection of multicolored shiny marbles stored in a large tin box. More than anything else I looked forward to washing my doll's clothes in a basin and preparing elaborate meals for her on my set of plastic miniature dishes with my friends. The summer of 1950 I eagerly anticipated was not far off.

Lately, however, disturbing incidents puzzled and frightened me, interfering with my happy dreams of carefree summer days. Most of them took place at the school playground or on my way home from school. Certain neighborhood children whose parents disapproved of my parents would push or taunt me shouting, "Commie, commie, go home. We don't want to play with you. Your parents are communists!! We don't want any Reds on the playground!" Sometimes the neighborhood bullies who instigated the attacks to beat me up were joined by others unknown to me. Their punches, which were unjustified by anything I had done, added to the bruises I had already acquired from falling off swings or scraping against walls.

One day I ran into the safety of my home, escaping from my attackers and certain that my mother would scold them and protect me. I asked her what was so terrible about being a communist. I thought my parents were the best, the wisest, and by far the most caring people and that they could do nothing wrong. I could not understand why everybody did not love them as I did. I was attached to their communist friends who played with me and brought me tasty treats and surprises when they came to our house. What I loved more than anything was that some of them were wonderful storytellers. In my home the word *communist* was said with pride and respect. It meant something special, something wonderful. I wanted to understand what made the neighbors think otherwise, dividing *us* from *them*, the bad from the good, the rejected from the accepted. Why was I being singled out? What did I do to deserve the torments of those classmates and playmates who despised communists?

To my surprise, instead of protecting me, my mother wanted me to fend for myself and to stand up to my attackers. She explained that I had nothing to be ashamed of. She wanted me to show my attackers that I was proud to belong to my family and that I was not afraid of them. (It was the first time I had to rely on my own resources, forced to realize that these daily problems were my own.) The beliefs of the adults intruded into our child's play, changing the game of Cowboys and Indians into a battle between Korean Reds and Americans. In these games adult fears and hostilities were translated into the insults that we yelled at each other, words like "dirty commie," "filthy Reds," which we heard on the news or at dinner. Since many of these taunts were directed at me, I demanded an explanation from my mother. I wanted to understand what my parents were doing that made me an object of scorn in these neighborhood games. My mother reassured me that one day I would understand. But I wanted it to make sense then, at that very moment. My mother told me to have faith in my parents' wisdom and judgment. She explained that there was injustice in the world and not all people were treated fairly. She told me about the important things communists did with such firm conviction that I could not doubt that she and my father were fighting to make the world a better place for all who were oppressed. They believed in asserting dignified rights for poor blacks, workers, and farmers. She asked me to be patient, for she was certain that truth and justice were on their side. I wanted to be strong because I believed implicitly in my parents' goodness.

I knew from my friends that some of their mothers warned them not to play with me because I was the daughter of "those communists." They were told to stay away from *a family like that*. I sensed the growing intensity of this hostility. Not everybody on the block smiled when I walked by as they used to. There was nothing I could do to ease the hurt of not being invited to my classmate Kathy's birthday party. Just last year she loved the animal picture book I gave her as a present. My mother assured me it had nothing to do with me personally, but when I saw my friends running home with birthday balloons and faces smudged with ice cream, I knew it was me who missed the party and not some imaginary daughter of communists.

I began to look over my shoulder on my way home from school, frightened that I would be followed and beaten. At night ugly monsters with long horns and twisted tails pursued me, yelling, "Commie! Commie! Go home. We don't want you here!" I would wake up to the sound of my own screams and try to make sure none of the monsters had entered my room. When my nighttime fears lingered into the daylight hours, I started to wet my bed, something I had not done since I was a toddler. How could I escape these troublesome demons who made it hard to be carefree, to laugh, run, and play? More than anything, I desired to wake up in the morning excited about what I would learn or discover that day. To have such a simple wish come true was getting harder and harder.

I arrived home from school one hot spring day in 1950, eager to tell my mother about my day in school. She was folding clothes in her bedroom. As soon as I glanced at the lively purple bedspread with white dots, I could not resist the temptation to jump on the bed, flinging my schoolbag to the floor. To my surprise, the bed felt different. It was hard and unyielding to the touch instead of soft and bouncy. Curious, I looked under the bed and noticed some suitcases and bags I had never seen before. My mother was strangely unwilling to explain why they were in such an unusual place. Her face remained stony and unresponsive when I questioned her persistently. Casually, even indifferently, she finally admitted that we might be taking a trip but told me it was a secret not to be mentioned to anyone. I was honored to be entrusted with this important "secret." I was certain that if the hidden suitcases were part of a surprise, I would eventually be rewarded for my ability to wait and see what would happen. Surprises, after all, had to be special and involved fun.

At the time, we lived in a small apartment in an attached row house. I was comfortable in our modest home. The two bedrooms, kitchen, and living room were tight but cozy. The tables and some of the chairs were covered with books and huge piles of newspapers. My father worked at his desk in my parents' bedroom late into the night. I often went to sleep to the sound of his typewriter keys. These cramped rooms always accommodated the extensive circle of my parents' friends and comrades. People of many backgrounds, black, white, Americans, Chinese, Filipinos, Russians, and others came to our home on a regular basis. If in my grandparents' home there were fixed religious practices and a distinct Jewish presence, in my parents' home there was a bohemian flair and categorical rejection of "bourgeois" traditions and formalities. "Family" took on a broader meaning, involving friendships that were international and based on political (rather than religious or ethnic) solidarity. Although I loved the excitement and stimulating atmosphere created by my parents and their intellectual friends, I was also drawn to the stability and calm reflected in my grandparents' way of life. It was an atmosphere clearly absent in our Queens home. We had lived in this neighborhood just long enough for me to know most of its secret pathways. In the past we had moved from apartment to apartment with a suddenness and frequency that hinted that my parents had been forced to leave, either as a result of their political activities, party work, or conflicts with landlords. My mother was a master at fighting with landlords for fair rents for herself and her large circle of progressive friends. I was fond of my new neighborhood. I thought it was so nice here that we would stay for a long time. There was plenty of grass between the houses, a spacious playground, and, despite the recent upsetting trouble with the neighborhood bullies, I liked my home and close friends who chose to play with me.

The day I discovered the suitcases under my parents' bed was no different from any other day. I spent the evening the same way I spent most evenings. First, I played my favorite "Peter and the Wolf" record and hummed the familiar tunes. The high tones of the flute announced the bird Sasha's arrival and the deep sounds of the horns let me know the wolf was approaching. I felt sorry for the duck as it was swallowed by the wolf, the rich oboe sounds expressing its helplessness. When I closed my eyes, the musical sounds helped me see the animals and Peter in the woods. Then I reread the rhymes from the worn pages of my Winnie the Pooh books. I kept bothering my sister, who had heard me recite these lines day after day:

The more it snows
(Tiddely pom),
The more it goes
(Tiddely pom),
The more it goes
(Tiddely pom),
On snowing.
And nobody knows
(Tiddely pom),
How cold my toes
(Tiddely pom),
How cold my toes
(Tiddely pom),
Are growing.

Trying hard to get her to smile, I exclaimed, "Listen, Laura, isn't this funny?" before I once again repeated the verse. She just gave me one of those older sister looks that said, "Oh, please, not again!"

The small room I shared with my sister contained all the treasures that mattered to me: my books, records, coloring pads, dolls, miniature dishes, and clothes; it also had my first poem that was no longer hanging in my classroom but right over my bed. In my room I played with the friends who were not afraid or forbidden to come to our home. This room sheltered me from the playground and school hallways where someone might push me, beat me up, or call me names. Here I could forget about frightening things I could not control.

Later that night Laura and I were awakened by our parents and told to get dressed quickly. I put on the powder blue cotton dress with little geometric designs that I was going to wear to school the next day. Two small suitcases were by the door. Within minutes, all four of us were in a cab on the way to Grand Central Station. I was still sleepy, leaning my head on my father's shoulder, when the cab made its way through the busy downtown Manhattan streets. My parents acted as if it were perfectly normal to be wakened in the middle of the night and to slip out of the house without forewarning or explanation. Aside from the few small pieces of luggage we had with us, everything in the house remained in its place. I tried to figure out where this surprise trip would take me. "How far are we going? For how long?" I kept asking my unresponsive parents. Judging by the modest amount of luggage, this had to be a short trip. The presents my sister recently received for her twelfth birthday and my favorite books, records, and my new curly-haired blond doll remained in our bedroom. I was convinced that we had to be back soon because there were still a few weeks left before the end of the school year, and my parents knew how much I loved school.

Almost awake by now, I was distracted by the lively nightlife in the city and at the train station. The four of us stood in the center of this bustle united by our silence. My parents' faces were serious. I held on to my mother's hand so I would not get lost. The sharp glare of the artificial lights made me forget it was the middle of the night. The frenetic activity of the crowds entertained me. We walked through passageways and underground tunnels until we reached the platform for our train. My father, who had left us for a short while, returned with a little bag. There were two treats for me: a maple candy, a favorite of mine, and a hand-sized plastic box with little metal ball bearings that had to be maneuvered through an obstacle course. I tilted the box gently, watching the balls glide through the obstacles and make their way to the other side.

A male voice announced the train departures and arrivals over the loudspeaker. In one hand I rattled the small ball bearings from one side to the other; in the other hand I held the large maple candy figurine that I was saving until we boarded the train. I thought about all the times my father had returned from his mysterious trips with beautifully shaped maple candies. The sweet aroma of maple sugar was all that was on my mind as I stepped on board. The maple candy slowly melted in my mouth, becoming inseparably wedded to my last sights of New York City.

Many times I have recalled the sounds, smells, sights, and smallest details of those final moments on the train platform at Grand Central Station. They remained the only demarcation between my previous life and the one the train carried me toward. Shortly before we left on our mysterious journey, I placed a sweet potato to sprout in our dark coat closet. It had been part of a second grade class project. Long after we started our journey, I had a recurrent dream about my deserted plant withering in the closet without my care. My impatience to see the potato bloom was intensified by the mysterious process itself, which originated in darkness but required sunlight to flower. When I had still been at home, I asked my mother almost daily when I could move the potato from the dark closet to the bright living room. Because of our sudden departure, I never saw the sweet potato blossom. Unlike the sweet potato waiting in the darkness to sprout and be moved into the light, I was being moved from the known to the unknown, from a (relatively) ordinary free and established childhood existence to concealment, isolation, and strangeness.

Chapter 2

· · · · · · · · · · ·

Hiding

In connection with Abraham Chapman who has been a writer for the Institute of Pacific Relations, we have made extensive efforts to reach him. We have asked the Justice Department to assist us in finding him. We have had four different addresses. We have had several subpoenas out, and all of them have been unavailing, and · nobody apparently knows where Abraham Chapman is now. It may be that a public announcement would turn him up, but the Department of Justice—and I presume they got in touch with the FBI— were not able to find where Chapman is at the present time.
—Congressional Hearings, Washington, D.C., 1951–52

The night train we boarded in New York City took us to Mexico. All I remember is boarding the train. The trip itself and our arrival are obliterated from my memory. I recall that we settled into a house in a crowded section of Mexico City. We spent our days aimlessly roaming the streets and watching the noisy crowds. I saw, tasted, heard, and felt how different everything was around me. The Spanish language had a musical rhythm that made English sound flat. I watched the expressions on people's faces and followed the movements of their hands to try to figure out what they were saying. Hand-painted pottery and thick woven rugs and blankets with strong pinks and greens decorated the stalls at the marketplace. My mother bought me a Mexican doll with long braided black hair and tan skin. To my delight, she also got me a set of toy clay dishes decorated with painted red flowers and colorful chickens. The doll did not resemble my blue-eyed blond-haired one left at home, and my favorite Winnie the Pooh poems did not seem quite right whispered into her ear.

Vendors flashed strings of rainbow-colored beads and long silver necklaces to attract customers. Hundreds of arms and legs filled the streets with action and sound. There was music and rhythm in the movements of the bodies as they pushed and dragged me along. Bright colors, loud sounds, and strong smells of frying food seduced me. The weeks we spent in Mexico City are a blur of sounds, colors, sights, and smells. At night I dropped into bed overwhelmed by these accumulated impressions.

There is, however, one particular night I remember with absolute clarity—the night I was awakened by agitated voices filling the house we were temporarily occupying. Still groggy, I walked to the staircase landing and leaned over the banister to see what was going on in the room below me. I tried to decode the rapid flow of words that were not an extension of my unfinished dream as I had originally thought they were. The voices of my father and mother were intermingled with those of strange men who spoke English with thick accents. The intense tempo of their speech frightened me. I could only grasp individual words as they rose to the ceiling: "arrests, searches, FBI agents, escape," and names of people I did not know.

I watched my parents and their three night visitors huddled in a tight circle, fascinated by what I was witnessing. Abe and Belle's cigarette ashes were falling to the floor, both too absorbed in the conversation to use the ashtray. The Mexican men had dark, unruly hair, thick mustaches, and olive skin, and when they spoke they waved their arms wildly. Their hair and complexion resembled those of the new doll that was on my bed. Their voices had an urgent power that went through me. I pulled my nightgown closer to my body to protect myself from the ill-defined danger I sensed was closing in on us.

For a brief moment their voices quieted. My father paced back and forth, and I could see deep folds of wrinkled skin form on his forehead. My mother's face was tightly drawn and her body movements were slow but determined. I called out, "What is going on?" expecting to be sent back to bed, but to my surprise my mother announced impatiently without exposing her emotions, "Get ready, Ann, we're leaving. Now, right now!" Still in our nightgowns, my sister and I were ushered into a car that was waiting behind the house. From the window of the moving car I watched the last flickers of the city lights vanish. We sped into the dark countryside. In the unexpected haste of our flight, I had left my new Mexican doll tucked into the covers of my deserted bed. Sad that my doll was not with me, I buried my head in my mother's lap. It was hard to stay awake and yet hard to fall asleep. Troubled by the anxiety of the adults, I closed my eyes, letting their conversation fade into the background as I fell in and out of consciousness.

The driver spoke almost no English. He maneuvered the car on the narrow mountain roads with skill and daring. Hours later the car stopped when we entered a small settlement in a remote area. The heavy darkness was beginning to break up. The car slid through the gates of an isolated farm. Our arrival must have been anticipated because the gates were flung open in front of our car. Before the gates closed, I got a quick glimpse of the dirt path that led to the farm. That was the only and last chance I had to see what was on the other side of the farm walls. Once the gates closed behind us, I was never let out beyond the farm's courtyard, and even that was restricted to the darkness of night when no outsiders were around the farm.

This farm, run by a poor Mexican family and enclosed by high stone walls, became our hideout. Upon our arrival, we were hurried into the house, and it was not until we were in the kitchen that I got a chance to see our host family of five. The father was short. His face was framed with dark, curly hair, and a thick mustache concealed his lips. His wife, who wore a simple dress, had large hands that were constantly moving, feeding the chickens, making tortillas, or washing the dishes. Busy with her chores, she spoke little. The three sons, close in age, loved to joke around, and they pushed and shoved each other with great energy and frequency. Every once in a while they would break into loud laughter as they swung their hands and arms in the air. We could not talk with them because we had no common language.

It did not take me long to realize that this farm was my prison. My mother, father, sister, and I shared a cramped room with whitewashed walls, two beds, and two cots. There was hardly space to walk. This room that belonged to one of the sons before we came had never been meant to accommodate a family of four. Now that we were there, the three boys had to share a room down the hall.

My freedom to play outside or to go anywhere at all had come to a sudden halt. Emptiness claimed me, filled me, surrounded me. Monotonous days became formless weeks and shapeless months. Days and nights merged, barely distinguished from each other. The isolation terrified me. I could smell the ever-present farm animals, their food and excrement. The large, grassless courtyard was dusty and drab. There were no flowers to decorate the yard or house. Day and night sickly looking dogs roamed through the enclosed courtyard. Everybody on the farm was too busy to lavish any attention on them. The small dogs looked funny next to the larger ones, who paraded back and forth on skinny legs. Some of the dogs had intestines protruding between their legs like clumps of tangled spaghetti, most likely the result of disease. The sight of them made my stomach turn.

I spent my days staring out of the bedroom window that overlooked the courtyard. I did a lot of dreaming about what my life had been like just a few weeks earlier, and I wondered what would happen next, anxiously awaiting a change. I so yearned to roam freely outside and to have playmates. Throughout the day I watched the dogs, as trapped and unhappy as I was. They sniffed the tortillas that were tossed into their dented pails, the same tortillas we ate at the kitchen table for dinner. The lethargy of the courtyard dogs was mirrored in my gradual loss of energy. Only in colorful memory could I step outside of the bleakness that surrounded me. What I remembered grew larger and larger in my dreams. Questioning my parents about tomorrow and the day after yielded no answers.

I can hardly remember sharing meals with the Mexican family at the kitchen table; mainly I recall our bedroom—my private prison, the neglected dogs, the noise of farm equipment, Spanish-speaking voices, the loud banter of the young sons, and my parents' subdued voices in their corner of the bedroom. I recall waking up many mornings in a tangle of urine-soaked sheets and, above all, with a pressing, ever-present sadness. I felt as if I was in a dark tunnel from which I could not escape, much like Winnie the Pooh when he ate too much honey and could not get out of the hole in which he was trapped. Pooh's predicament made me laugh when I read about it, but now I was too sad to find it funny that I was actually living in a place I could not get out of by myself. I had never before spent so much time crowded into one room with my family yet feeling absolutely alone for the first time in my life. I did not know how to discuss these overpowering fears with my parents.

My sole distraction came from the courtyard activities. I watched the chickens strut back and forth, pecking at the kernels of corn the farm wife scattered on the ground every morning. The chickens fought over the corn the way my friends and I fought at the playground to be first, to jump the farthest, to be the best or the most popular kid on the street.

But that was in the past. Now in this ghostlike existence I withdrew into myself, succumbing to the monotony of the long days, each just like the other. Anxiety twisted its way into our small room. It was not something I could touch or taste, yet it had a presence that firmly clasped and pulled all four of us into a tight web, isolating us from our previous lives.

The Mexican family's three sons, whose names I cannot remember, were older than my sister and me. Unable to figure out what they were saying, I invented my own meanings. Their badgering and teasing, however, made me uncomfortable, even frightened. Sometimes the oldest tried to brush against my sister's body when we passed them in the hall. She clung to me, pushing me ahead until we reached the safety of our bedroom. Their stares made her turn her eyes away. I absorbed her concern, and when I heard them in the barn or in the kitchen, I tried to avoid them. Today I know that this Mexican farm family must have had a strong commitment to the communist cause to be brave enough to hide us. In doing so, they undoubtedly jeopardized their own safety and imposed a heavy burden of silence on their sons. At the time, however, they were my prison wardens.

Laura, with her round, freckled face, golden-red hair, and warm, loving smile, was my sole companion and comfort. I wanted her to be all the playmates I had lost. I watched her skilled hand sketch the trees and flowers that she imagined were on the other side of the farm wall, making more real a world that was now alive only in memory. Her loving eyes and reassuring voice were my anchor in this void. I trusted that she would never leave me or betray me. I clung to her fiercely.

After a few weeks on the farm, Laura became indifferent to events around her. She could not tolerate the Mexican farm diet. Each day she ate less. She spent more and more time resting and sleeping. I watched her escape into sleep, and I worried that she might not wake up. I needed to look into her eyes and to hear the sound of her voice to feel safe. As long as Laura was there, I had some flicker of hope; without her existence was unimaginable. But every day she slept for longer stretches. Everything became an effort for her. She was sinking deeper and deeper into a world far away from me. Desperately frightened, I sat on the edge of her bed, holding her hand, watching every movement of her pale, tired face.

In that spartan farm room I learned about fear, sadness, and longing. I wanted my home, my school, my friends, and my grandparents back. If only I could once again run in the park behind our home or walk to the corner drugstore for an ice cream and bubble gum. Did my grandparents know where I was? Could they come find me, rescue me? I repeated to myself stories my grandmother used to tell me, and if I tried hard enough, I could practically smell the aromas of her kugel and chicken soup with matzo balls. I wanted to know if my grandparents still remembered and loved me. What kind of a summer were my friends having, and what did they think happened to me? What did happen to me?

My only link to my former schoolroom was the second grade reader my mother packed for me. Trying to make the time pass, I neatly copied the words from the reader into my lined notebook:

The peeping chick said,
"Who will be my chum?"
A big red hen rushed up and said,
"I will be your chum.
Your mom will be your chum!"

My mind a blank, I copied for an entire morning without giving my hand a rest:

A mouse once found
a wishing well.
"Now all of my wishes
can come true!"
She cried.

She threw a penny
into the well
and made a wish
"OUCH!"
said the wishing well.

The black letters that filled the pages of my notebook reminded me of the classroom I longed to be in. I feared that if I stopped writing these words I would forget or, worse yet, never return to school and my neighborhood friends. The sound of my classmates' voices jumped out of the pages, but when I tried to answer them their voices vanished. It was a mirage, a vision true only in my daydreams. Inside I felt hollow. In this crowded, stuffy farm room there were no new or exciting images to evoke the flow of words that could become a poem like the one left behind on my bedroom wall. Only the routine act of copying what was in front of me helped pass the time and keep a tie to my past alive.

The days on the farm dragged, interrupted only by occasional night visits from party couriers bringing messages to my parents. At times these men spent long hours talking in broken English with my parents around the kitchen table. On occasion their excited voices sounded as loud and powerful as approaching thunder. My own fears had been forcing me to escape into imaginary regions inhabited with creatures I'd never seen before—witches and wizards whose words were magic. I asked the goblins, ghosts, knights, princes, and princesses of my faraway kingdoms and hidden underworlds who visited me at night to take me with them into their world. In that isolation they were my closest companions, and I grew accustomed to them spending the night with me. In the daytime hours I was on my own.

One night (they always came at night) three tall men appeared speaking halting English with my parents and brisk Spanish with the farm husband and wife. From my cot, where I lay trying to fall asleep, I could see their heads move back and forth through a crack in the bedroom door. The agitated tone of their voices and the frequent movements of their hands told me that their message was urgent and disturbing. I wrapped my blanket tightly around my body in hopes of shielding myself. An escape into my own world of inventions did not remove me from what I was hearing and seeing. Gradually, their authoritative voices took over, filling me with panic.

Before I was able to fall asleep, my parents told Laura and me that we would be leaving the farm. I knew only that they had been instructed to move on, not why or how we would get to our next destination. Either it was no longer safe for us to stay or the signal to move on to a more permanent arrangement had arrived from the comrades in charge of our fate. That night we drove along serpentine mountain paths until the early morning. My eyes were overwhelmed by the colorful variety of the landscape. Hungrily I took in each detail, the curve in the road, the trees, and the scattered villages we passed. Having lost track of how long we were on the farm, I studied the passing landscape from the car window. I hoped the trees and vegetation would give me an idea of how long we had been in captivity. The lush countryside revived my listless sister, and she sketched the huge flowering cacti in the distance. Her colorful pictures were more beautiful than the growing cacti. My parents' tense gestures and voices reminded me that the invisible danger pursuing us was still there. Leaving the farm did not end the fears that lived within me. No one I knew was waiting to see me or to welcome me back. No one in the car would name our destination. No one said anything about returning to New York, returning home.

Eventually we reached the airport, where my mother told me my father would be traveling to an unnamed destination on his own. Our paths parted. My mother, sister, and I were scheduled to take a plane the day after my father's solitary departure. In tears, I repeatedly whispered, "Why isn't father coming with us?" One more tight hug, one more kiss, and I was watching his plane spiral toward the clouds until swallowed by the vast expanse of space above me. Not knowing when or where we would be reunited, I clung even more tightly to my silent mother, to my sallow and equally speechless sister.

The three of us continued our journey. The airplane we boarded had luxurious berths with crisp white sheets and soft blankets. My sister spent the entire flight curled up on a berth, too sick to talk with me about the fluffy clouds beneath us. Smiling stewardesses gave us smooth, sweet chocolates in the shape of windmills and miniature wooden clogs. It was no longer a secret that we were flying to Holland. At the airport we were met by a comrade who was expecting us and who must have informed my mother of the subsequent arrangements and gave her some money. (Only in fairy tales can one go from country to country without currency or reservations.) He delivered us to a train station, and we continued our journey through picturesque villages and neatly arranged towns. A charming room was waiting for us in a secluded lodge. Our windows faced a thick forest. I stared into the forest, hoping to see what lay beyond. Images and sounds of the Mexican farm were still on my mind. Here, in an unknown place in the Dutch countryside it was peaceful and magically beautiful. The sudden silence wrapped its firm arms around me.

[*Once we were settled in our newly reconstructed lives my sister and I were forbidden ever to talk to anyone about our stay in Mexico or flight to Holland. It was one more secret we had to live with. Only a few stark images remained intact, but a heavy, deeply sad feeling about those days has never left me. To write about them I had to break the taboo of secrecy to which I had been bound. Giving those suppressed experiences a voice was painful, nightmarish, and liberating at the same time. In these pages I tried to recreate a sequence of events as accurately as I could, but ultimately what mattered to me was not the details of what happened but how it felt to be trapped in a situation that made no sense to me at all.]*

Laura's health was rapidly deteriorating. She was unable to eat, and she spent most of her time sleeping. Her eyes turned a strange yellow. She looked small in the large bed we shared. My worried mother hovered around my sister's bed until a doctor arrived to examine her. Because we were in hiding and could not leave our Dutch refuge, the doctor had to be either a party member or a sympathizer who could be trusted not to reveal our presence. After carefully examining Laura, he spoke to my mother in a soothing voice. When my mother turned the lights out for the night, I could hear her whisper between soft sobs: "Abe, Abe, my darling." The next day, regaining control of herself, Belle told me Laura would be sick for a long time and that I had to leave her alone as much as possible so she could rest. In a few days we left the country lodge. We spent a couple of dreary nights in a hotel in Amsterdam, where sounds of dance music, shrill, drunken voices, and seductive laughter rose up from the hotel lounge. The music continued into the early morning hours and followed me as I escaped from the present to a more comforting world of fairyland characters. These friendly creatures accompanied me on phantasmagoric journeys in search of lost treasures and a magical homeland. They had been my faithful playmates since the months on the Mexican farm, my sole travel companions.

At last, the three of us left the restless hotel nights behind and flew to a country, I was promised, that was closer to our final destination. We landed during the night. From the airplane window I could see the long strip of the runway and the lights of a small airport terminal. When I stepped onto the airplane stairway, I was greeted by piercing winter winds that penetrated my light summer jacket—a reminder of the suddenness with which we had departed from our home in Queens, where my winter clothes still hung in the closet. Those days were far away. The change in the seasons was the only way I could estimate how much time had passed since we had left New York City. I calculated we had been in hiding for approximately six months. Alien sounds from the conversations I overheard at the airport terminal interrupted my thoughts. Words I could not understand enveloped me and increased the panic growing within me.

During the car ride from the airport, the magically beautiful buildings of an ancient city came into view. What I saw took away my breath. High up on a hill, overlooking the city, was a most amazing medieval castle. Until now I had seen castles only in storybooks. But this one was real, and it was right before my eyes in all its splendor. Who lived in it, a king and a queen perhaps? Would I get to see them? What part of the world had I landed in? The jerky movements of the car maneuvering on cobblestone-paved streets shook my exhausted body. The car practically brushed against the buildings that lined the narrow streets. We stopped at a hotel building on a wide boulevard in the center of town in which a room with three beds was waiting for us.

The hotel had the smell of antiquity. The three of us spent only one night together. The next day, my mother and my sick sister disappeared for a large part of the day. I remained alone in this old, crumbling building with long carpeted halls and portraits of dignitaries decorating the wallpaper. When Belle returned, she was pale and her hand trembled when she lit a cigarette. Still dressed in her coat, she collapsed in the cushioned chair under the window. "Laura won't be with us for a long time, Ann. You will have to be a big girl and manage on your own as much as possible," she said in a weak, discouraged voice. Over the next few weeks I spent my days in this hotel room while my mother maneuvered between my hospitalized sister and our temporary residence. Years later, Laura told me that Belle bought her a pocket dictionary so that she could communicate her basic needs to the nurses, who, of course, knew no English. Laura's condition was ultimately diagnosed as hepatitis, and she needed a long period to recuperate. With my sister gone and my father at some faraway undisclosed location, I hoped only that my mother would not leave me. I desperately desired a family reunion, a home, and a return to my childhood existence. Alone in that hotel room I could only imagine what had been taken from me because I had no idea when or how things would change in the immediate future. And there was nothing I wanted more than for what was happening to turn out to be a bad dream that had never happened.

Chapter 3

· · · · · · · · · · · ·

Passionate
Convictions

An absolute had first to be established in the minds of the comrades so that they could measure the success or failure of their deeds by it. There was no mysticism, no invoking of God, merely a passionate identification of all present with a will to right wrongs. It was a simple, elemental morality. Communism had found a moral code that could control the conduct of men, yet it was a code that stemmed from practical living, and not from the injunctions of the supernatural. . . . With the exception of the church and its myths and legends, there was no agency in the world so capable of making men feel the earth and the people upon it as the Communist party.

—Richard Wright, *American Hunger*

Before I continue with my own story it is important to introduce my parents, the actual movers of this narrative, and their family backgrounds. The things that happened to me are hardly comprehensible without some discussion of the ideas and ideals dominating the world that shaped them. In their early youth, my parents exchanged the religious background to which their parents adhered for their own equally passionate faith in a politically radical and atheistic vision of life. I grew up in the midst of these strong convictions.

Unfortunately, my knowledge of my parents' families is incomplete. I am still cut off from my mother's family and could not interview any of them. I was fortunate a few years ago to have a chance to visit a Chapman cousin who showed me old family photographs and recounted family history that I was unaware of. My mother's parents, the Shulmans, were devout Orthodox Jews. My father's parents, the Chapmans, were also Orthodox but with Chassidic roots. The more worldly, Zionist Chapmans were not as pious as the Shulmans, who lived strictly by the commands of the Torah. As a small child I had frequent contact only with my mother's parents, who lived within an hour from us in a close-knit Jewish community. My grandfather, Harry Chapman, died before I was born, and my grandmother, Chassi, lived far from us, dividing her time between Chicago and Palestine. She is merely an exotic name, a person I can barely picture from family stories and photographs.

The conflicting but intensely passionate beliefs of my parents and grandparents created barriers and distances that neither could overcome. My parents gave themselves to the communist cause with the same religious fervor their parents and ancestors reserved for God. While my grandparents found meaning in their religious heritage, my parents looked to a future based on a blueprint for building a perfect society. By separating themselves from their parents spiritually, and after we left the United States physically, Abe and Belle unintentionally cut me off from any religious influence my grandparents and their Old World thinking and traditions might have exerted on me. The communist vision I was raised to believe in remained uncontested.

My strong-willed parents subordinated their personal lives to the dogmas of the party, initially by choice and later by necessity. The party demanded undivided devotion from its active members: time, energy, talents, faith, obedient compliance to orders, and absolute loyalty. I sometimes wonder if there was room to accommodate the demands of a family life and children under such revolutionary circumstances. Memoirs written by husbands, wives, and children of former communists show that the conflict between the demands of the party and the personal needs of family members often seriously damaged family relationships.

[*One example of loyal obedience to party orders and its tragic outcome is the Eugene Dennis family. Eugene became general secretary of the American CP in 1956 after he and his wife, Peggy, spent decades in the communist movement and several years in the Soviet Union as Comintern members. When they were about to return to the Untied States just before World War II, the Soviet leaders informed them that their son Tim, then five years old, was to stay in the Soviet Union. The Soviet comrades felt it was too risky for the American party's image to have Dennis seen with a five-year-old who spoke only Russian. Tim went on to be educated at special schools for the Comintern members, but he was never reunited with his parents and a younger brother who grew up in the United States. He still lives in Russia with his Russian wife and children, denied*] *a chance to be part of his family as a result of international politics and his parents' utter devotion to the communist cause.]*

My parents' love affair with what ultimately turned out to be an idealized social experiment led to a fragmented existence and discontinuity in the values that were transmitted to my sister and me. The process of change that severed ties from one generation to the next began with my parents' break from religious structures and culminated in disillusionment with the secular ideal that replaced those structures. During the years I was growing up, however, the belief that communism was the wave of the future prevailed in our home. The communist values were the ones I lived by and believed in during my youth.

It is ironic that my parents' forebears left Russia seeking religious freedom and opportunity in America whereas my parents followed a path leading back to that world, assuming that under communism they would find the protection and freedom they needed. My Jewish forebears deliberately started a new life when they embarked for America, but my parents unintentionally uprooted their own family when they committed themselves to the communist experiment.

With neither a religious nor a political credo left intact, I have come to identify with those who feel a spiritual and moral void in the aftermath of the failed communist ideology. In some ways, our family history, though somewhat extreme, resembles the clash of values several generations of twentieth-century families have had to deal with. The differing convictions from one generation of Chapmans and Shulmans to the next introduced such drastic changes in lifestyle and thinking that the family relationships could not be sustained. My personal family relationship was with my parents and my sister. All else is distant history, which I never experienced for myself. My family connection to my ancestors did not survive.

Chapter 4

· · · · · · · · · · ·

Belle: Family

Background—

the Shulmans

TO BELLE

who has always been herself
helped me become myself
warm in her understanding of others
independent in her critical judgement

the pull, polarities, and tensions of our
shared lives
worlds to grow in
—Fragments of poems by Abe Chapman written in the Intensive Care Unit, Wisconsin, 1976

In 1982, my mother, Belle, was a young, spirited sixty-six-year old. For three years she had defied a growing, deadly cancer, outliving the doctor's prediction that she would live a year at best. But for an experienced fighter like Belle, cancer became a cause against which to rally all her strategic skills, much as she had done in the past against the class "enemy." The cancerous cells temporarily retreated in the face of her powerful will, giving her two additional years of life. Though the disease was debilitating, Belle had the same victorious exhilaration at outsmarting the cancer as I had seen in her in the old days when her radical spirit gave her the strength and courage to try the impossible.

She was no longer able to leave her bed in the hospital room during that last winter of her life in 1982, when her younger and only brother, Avi, came to see her. At this point Belle was clinging to the last vestiges of fading strength. She looked diminutive in the large white bed, surrounded by pillows, covers, and a network of tubes leading to and from her arms, which were hidden in giant white bandages. The technological web merely added hours, perhaps days, to her futile struggle. Belle grew up as a single child because her brother was born when she was eighteen years old, by which time she was married and no longer living at home. This long-awaited miracle, the birth of their son Avi, fulfilled his parents' hopes for a continuity of the religious values their firstborn, Belle, rejected. (My mother was most grateful that her parents had a son who brought them happiness and who cared for them in their old age in a way her chosen lifestyle made impossible for her. Though brother and sister were worlds apart, my mother respected him for being a dutiful son.) I knew my uncle only through the visits I made to my grandmother's house as a child before we left the United States. As adults we were complete strangers. The two of us—my uncle and I—stood awkwardly at my mother's deathbed.

With great curiosity, I studied the face and body movements of my uncle. I had not expected to find facial features and speech patterns that resembled my mother's. I knew hardly anything about his present life and nothing at all about his personality or interests, yet he was my mother's brother. He belonged to that part of her private life she had never shared with me. Silently I watched as brother and sister exchanged pleasantries. He stood in his coat and hat by the foot of her bed. He had driven five hours to see her, but he remained miles away from her, a distance no journey could bridge.

With a voice weakened by illness, she asked, "How is mama?" "Fine, mama and papa are fine," he answered politely, offering no further information. She reassured him that she had obeyed his request that her elderly parents be shielded from any knowledge about her illness and approaching death. It was the price she owed him for the life she had chosen. While my mother was unavailable to her family, Avi lived beside his parents within walking distance of the shul. This was a time for final accounts, and Belle accepted the terms set by her brother.

I could see no intimacy between brother and sister, merely a formal observance of decency between the living and the dying. Her brother, a rabbi, educator, and scholar, knew the importance of such rituals. At this final moment of her defiant and turbulent life, he was kind and concerned, though he had disapproved of her lifestyle. Moreover, she readily mocked and rejected his. While he chose to become a rabbi, his sister remained an inveterate rebel.

Over the years brother and sister remained sealed off from each other. By this time, the hurt was too deep, the pride too strong, the minds too inflexible to change. Many unanswered questions raced through my mind while I silently watched the two carry on their conversation: What was he like? What did he know about our past? Was he curious about what his sister's life had been like? Was he at all like my mother? In this sterile hospital room, where we both felt the tragedy of my mother's fast-approaching death, the estrangement from my uncle highlighted the incongruities of her life. When my mother became too exhausted to talk, my uncle prepared to go. I walked with him to his car in the hospital parking lot. I wanted to talk about how difficult these last few weeks had been for Belle and me. Words caught in my throat. I felt silence was preferable to a revelation of raw, painful feelings before someone with whom I had no intimate connection. It was all too complicated, too incomprehensible, too late. For my uncle there was no future for our relationship because of my marriage to a non-Jew. How can you start to know someone when the beginning is an end in itself?

"What kind of funeral arrangements did your mother make?" he asked, breaking the heavy silence and revealing one of the purposes of his long drive to the hospital. "No final decisions have been made, except for my mother's wish to be cremated." Avi sighed and shook his head in disapproval. "She knows that Orthodox Jews only accept a burial. She is defiant to the very end, remaining the last actor on an empty stage without an audience left to witness the final performance. If she gets cremated I will not be able to attend the funeral." I asked no further questions. We parted in the parking lot without a handshake, without a hug. One final phone call informing him my mother had died was the last time I spoke with him.

Instead of attending my mother's funeral, he wrote a letter in which he explained he had to "struggle through my own emotions." He shared his thoughts about the life my mother had chosen and the source of strength his own faith has been to him:

But I am perplexed by the tremendous void of religious values that permeated the lifestyle of your father and mother. As open-minded as they were about all other areas of their life . . . they denied themselves and you the one area of life that could have added as much meaning to all of life.

Obviously many years ago something happened to "turn them off" from any religious values. . . . It pained me to see how a life of a wonderful person could have been even greater, more rewarding, and so much more fulfilling had she allowed herself to enjoy a Jewish and religious frame of reference. . . .

The ending of life of any person — especially a person with

such rare personality as your mother—brings every thinking person head to head with real gut questions, such as: What is life all about?

On the third page of the letter he expressed a hope that I would not dismiss the significance of my rich Jewish heritage:

> In spite of the fact that your father and mother chose to ignore religion from their life . . . this does not change the fact that we, as Jews, do enjoy a special mandate and purpose in life. We, the Jewish nation, were privileged to be given a set of Jewish values by which to live, values that are as relevant in our modern society as on the day that they were given—if not even more so!
>
> I wonder if you consider exploring and exposing yourself and children to a way of life that would offer them the solidarity, reassurance, and dynamism that Jewish life offers?
>
> Judaism is a treasured heritage cherished generation after generation. While your parents might not have placed great value on it, millions of people were and are ready to preserve this heritage at great cost . . . so don't be too quick to arbitrarily wave it away with the comment "We are not religious."

At the time, I did not have the knowledge or the strength to deal with a family conflict of this magnitude, one I inherited and one which even that master strategist, my mother, could not overcome. Belle's wish to be cremated was a final message to her family and an important symbolic gesture telling them: "I have no regrets." I knew she was dying in excruciating mental anguish, but at this late time, to comply with the predetermined rules of her Orthodox family for a burial rather than a cremation would not have softened or mitigated the rift. Belle's indescribable pain was solitary and unrelenting.

A few days before her death, Belle, barely capable of holding a pen in her frail hand, asked me to buy a birthday card. When I asked who the card was for, she said briskly: "Never mind, just do what I am asking," in her determined but unyielding tone. The next day I brought the card to her bedside and handed her a pen she held for the last time. On the card she wrote with a shaky hand: DEAR MAMA, I AM FINE, HAPPY BIRTHDAY, YOUR DAUGHTER BELLE. I did not know it was my grandmother's birthday. I did not know Belle had been writing her mother letters all these years. Two weeks later Belle's last words were, "MAMA, MAMA!" before she slipped into unconsciousness.

My mother was born a Shulman in 1915 on the Lower East Side of New York City, a Jewish community where the religious and political conflicts from the old country continued in a new American setting. Her family roots went back to Vilna, in Lithuania. Her Orthodox upbringing restricted contact outside the immediate religious community. My mother hardly ever talked about her childhood. I got the impression that the only life that mattered to her was the one she shared with Abe. On rare occasions she would allow herself to remember, "When I was a child I traveled to Palestine with my parents" or "My mother made the best blintzes." Just when I wanted to hear more, her lips would tightly clasp the cigarette in her mouth, leaving barely enough room for the small puffs of smoke to escape. Not only her family history but her thoughts and feelings about her family remained locked within her.

I had only seven childhood years to get to know my grandparents and to spend time in their home. My grandparents' home in Monsey, New York, was not far from New York City. I do not remember my grandfather, Israel, ever visiting our home in New York City, but on occasion my grandmother, Etia, would stop by when she came to the city to shop or to go to Radio City Music Hall with my mother for an afternoon show. She never ate in our home because my mother did not keep a kosher kitchen. My parents rarely lingered when they dropped my sister and me off at my grandparents' house. They were in a rush to return to their busy lives. At my grandparents' my sister and I played with my uncle Avi, who was only four years older than my sister. He never came to visit us in our home in New York.

Switching from one household to the other was as dramatic as a trip to a foreign country. The rules and daily rhythms differed in all respects. I watched my grandfather pray when we gathered at the table, something my father never did. In the living room I overheard my grandfather's long discussions with men who attended the synagogue services with him. The importance attached to these conversations reminded me of the animated discussions I heard in my parents' home. From the mixture of Yiddish, Hebrew, and English that reached my ears I sensed they were discussing matters very different from those my parents discussed. It took many years before I realized how irreconcilable those differences were, but I did not need to grasp the meaning of their words to sense the same passion in their voices I heard when my mother and father gathered with their companions. The meaning of what they discussed was beyond my comprehension, but the intensity of the feelings in both homes made a deep impression on me.

My grandmother was the reason I loved visiting Monsey. After the family meal was over, I stayed in the kitchen to talk with my grandmother, who, unlike my mother, never participated in the men's discussions. It was fun spending time in her kosher kitchen, where I watched or helped make delicate blintzes or crunchy mandelbrot while listening to her animated storytelling. My grandmother always made the time we spent together special. In heavily accented English, she told me about the different people she knew in the shul, her childhood, and the numerous members of our extended family. When the meal was ready, I helped her set the table according to the prescribed rituals of her household. At my home I could eat off any dish in the kitchen, whereas at my grandmother's, dairy foods had to go on the dishes from the cabinet above the stove, and meat dishes had to be served on the plates from the cabinet on the wall near the sink. I easily accommodated myself to the way they did things; it made me feel grown up and important. It was comforting to know that each time I visited, the patterns of daily life in my grandparents' house remained unchanged. In my grandmother's kitchen I felt free and playful. Under the probing gaze of my grandfather, who was too absorbed in his prayer to notice me, the dining room and living room were spaces in which I felt reserved and unimportant.

In the summertime my sister and I were sent to visit our grandparents for a few weeks so we could get out of the city. I looked forward to those visits in their large house and to playing on the beautiful grounds. In comparison with the tight living quarters in our New York apartment, their house was a mansion. Everything was done with a unique touch that in no way varied the pattern or disturbed the repetitive cycle. Every Friday night my grandparents lit the Shabbat candles and said a prayer over my grandmother's challah bread. On Shabbat work of any kind was forbidden. After sunset, cooking or even turning on the light was not allowed, and elaborate arrangements were made to assure the faithful adherence to this rule. In my grandparents' home something larger than my own will determined the way things were done. Here God set the rules, whereas in my parents' home they created the rules. My parents did not fear change; they engineered it. I knew what every Friday night in my grandparents' house was going to be like, but in my parents' home every Friday night was different and unpredictable.

After we left America, I missed those visits in my grandparents' home. The first few years I struggled to remember every detail of how the rooms were arranged in their house, the way they talked and laughed, the flavor of my grandmother's cooking; however, over the years the image of my grandmother's smile and the feel of her gentle embrace faded. She remained imprinted in my mind the way I saw her the last time we were together. I was always a small child sitting on her lap pleading for one more story and an extra piece of her marble cake. When my new friends talked about visits with their grandmothers, I felt a stabbing pain, a longing, which eventually became a dull but persistent sadness.

Not until recently did I learn that my grandfather owned a haberdashery in Valley Stream, Long Island, New York. Later he lost a considerable amount of money on the stock market, forcing him to alter his lifestyle. My grandfather was a small man with a soft voice whose religious life centered around prayer, study, and shul. I observed him from a distance like a painting on a wall or a clock that periodically reminded me that another hour has passed. Through him the rules and schedules of a religious lifestyle governed the household. These rules determined what one was allowed to eat, with whom one could associate, and how and when religious holidays were observed. My grandfather made sure his accounts with God were in order, while my grandmother's obligation was to maintain the practical aspects of an Orthodox Jewish home. She kept a kosher kitchen, observed the Sabbath, and lived by the commandments.

My mother was unwilling to accept the role designated to a female in an Orthodox household. Her mother's traditional role in the family was unacceptable for a woman with the political and intellectual interests of my mother. As a female in her father's Orthodox home she had no voice or power, but in the communist movement she could challenge the enemy with her sharp intellect and organize to institute change. Belle frequently commented that women in an Orthodox home were limited to raising the children and running the household so that men would be free to commune with God. Her parents were as determined not to compromise their beliefs as my mother was about her right to control the course of her own destiny.

Belle married in 1934 in Tel Aviv, where her family was visiting when she met Abe. As they told the story, their love was immediate and passionate. They were both eighteen when they were married in an Orthodox ceremony. My father, though a Jew, was a self-taught Marxist rather than a student of the Torah, which made it difficult for the Shulmans to rejoice in their daughter's match. Through marriage the Shulmans did not gain a son; they ultimately lost a daughter. Marrying Abe may have distanced Belle from her family, but it also liberated her to establish an independent and radically new life. After their marriage, Abe and Belle returned to the United States and settled in Chicago, the city where my father was born and where most of his family lived. Here they met people in the communist movement who introduced them to a political network through which they could channel their energy and shape their worldview. And that is when it all started, years before I was born.

Everybody called my mother Belle. The name given to her at birth was Isabelle, but she never used it because she disliked it. Unlike my friends, who addressed their parents as mom and dad, I always called mine Abe and Belle. The traditional mom and dad did not suit people who believed in creating a revolutionary future. Belle's petite figure did not reflect the largeness of her scope or the power of her will. Her gaze was straightforward and penetrating; her warm smile was charged with energy. She was an engaging conversationalist, and she had a wonderful sense of humor and a spontaneous laugh. She absorbed the spoken and unspoken messages in any conversation. It was not uncommon for me to come home from school to find my mother preparing dinner while engrossed in conversation with a friend sitting at the kitchen table. They discussed politics, personal problems, relationships, love, or family separations while the soup got made and the potatoes peeled. I took in the smell of food and drink, the flow of words, the smell of cigarette fumes.

Belle was tough and daring when making decisions and dealing with people. She would convey the idea that negotiating with her would be useless or at least extremely difficult. Once she set the rules, there was no way of getting around them. She was fair, demanding, loving, but unwaveringly firm. When my mother worked, which she did during most of my childhood and youth, my sister and I had to shop, clean house, iron, and wash dishes. She had high standards for how a job had to be done and, knowing she would inspect the floor I had just washed, I went over it twice so I could join my friends without delay. She praised me for a job well done, and her trust in my competency made me feel capable of any task. Early in the morning I loved to bring my parents, already engrossed in conversation or a book, hot coffee in bed.

Secretive about her deepest feelings, she preferred to talk about the lives of others rather than to reveal her own. Once she served some Czech friends a cake she made from an American cake mix brought by contacts from the West. These Czechs had never tasted such a smooth-textured cake. Pleased, and not a cake eater or baker herself, she smiled coyly, answering the proddings as to how she made such a spectacular cake, "I have my secrets." I so much wanted to tell them the truth.

For Belle life was a series of strategic moves which she handled with incredible dexterity. Almost everybody responded to her charm and wit. She was a masterful poker player, good at outguessing her opponent without revealing by the slightest twitch of her facial muscles if she was bluffing or not. For days, after a night of poker, Belle would be delighted with her triumph at guessing her opponent's hand and taking everybody by surprise. Her poker skills came in handy in the political arena, where the hand she played was not always a winning one and the stakes at times frighteningly high.

If a teacher wronged a child or a boss an employee, Belle rallied into action. She came alive when she had an enemy to fight. When in her sixties she flew to my home to stay with me after major surgery for her cancer, I worried how this dying, frail woman would manage the trip. When the passengers from her flight came out through the gates, she was not among them. I was frantic with fear that something terrible had happened to her. After all the passengers were gone, she appeared in a wheelchair, waving a sheet of paper in her hand. She was smiling as if she had won a major victory. It was an insurance claim for a minor rip in her worn suitcase, which had been damaged on the flight. Shocked that she had the desire to process the necessary insurance forms, I said, "Belle, why did you bother, the rip is so insignificant, don't you want to get to our home as soon as possible for a rest? You must be exhausted!" Pleased with herself, she said, "Who cares about the money. It's the principle of it. After all, I'm not dead yet." For someone as fiercely self-sufficient as Belle, the gradual loss of independence during her illness in the last years of her life was devastating.

More than once she had to leave everything behind: family, friends, jobs, familiar language, possessions, and a home she worked hard to set up without much money or help. If we planned an outdoor picnic with another family and it rained, she spread the beach blanket on the living room floor, transforming our disappointment into unexpected delight and excitement. When we least anticipated it, she came home after a long day at work with a bouquet of spring flowers, ready to prepare a delicious meal out of meager ingredients. She was admired for feasts she prepared for friends when it was virtually impossible to find food supplies. She was remarkably imaginative in substituting and recreating dishes that have never been tried before and never tasted so good. When she had a rough day or if life was particularly unmanageable, Belle was the first to pronounce, "I need a drink, how about you?"

Belle was a natural storyteller, and if the story was a bit short on excitement and dramatic detail, she helped it along for the listener's enjoyment with descriptive touches that stretched the excitement of the narrative. I loved listening to her soothing voice while watching her long, graceful fingers punctuate the climax of her story. The objective of her story was not to remain faithful to the mundane factual details but to make the story dramatic.

A story she told with great flare was that of my birth. Nine months pregnant and still keeping a busy schedule, she was on a subway when she felt the first signs that I was on my way. Since she was near her gynecologist's office (who, she never failed to add, was also a party friend), she got off the subway at the appropriate station and rang his doorbell ready to give birth on the doorstep. I cannot piece together the sequence of how my rapid birth took place, but she always concluded the story by saying, "It all happened so fast I really shouldn't have paid the doctor for delivering you. He didn't do anything, I did it all by myself." Motherhood was natural for her. She loved it. When asked by her friends which stage of her children's childhood was her favorite, she would answer without hesitation and with a glowing expression on her face, "All stages, each one was exciting and wonderful!" But of all her life's accomplishments she was proudest of keeping our family together when it was not always certain that would be possible.

She never liked formal flower arrangements, but she loved flowers, particularly gladioli. Every day I brought a handful of fresh flowers to the hospital during the last weeks of her life. One day, after a particularly frightening and anguished night, during which she thought she would die, she opened her eyes in disbelief that she was still alive. I was sitting by her bed holding her restless hand when she looked at the tall, bright red gladioli in the vase resting against the window. Still somewhat angry that her agony was not over, she said, "How can I not want to know what will happen tomorrow, what news you will bring me about my grandsons, what you are thinking and doing? How can I leave this world when a flower is so beautiful?"

Even though Belle was a radical nonconformist in her political life, she was a traditional wife. She did all the cooking by herself, managed the entire running of the household, typed for my father, and kept my sister and me occupied so that Abe could devote himself to his writing. Though she never had a formal education until much later in her life, she was a bright, well-read woman with unmatched survival skills. In her relationship with her husband she was a spiritual companion and equal. Frequently Abe jumped up from his typewriter to read her passages from his writings. Every few seconds she breathed in puffs of air because of the ever-present cigarette between her lips while her hands continued to peel and chop. Ashes slipped into the pot as she took in my father's flow of words.

Bourgeois thinking, imperialist aggression, reactionary, agents provocateurs, fascist crimes, Cold War mania, Marxism, inquisitions, witchhunts, literary renegades, and *McCarthyism* were terms my father frequently used in the weekly articles about the U.S. literary scene he wrote for the Czech press. After their discussion, Abe would rush back to the typewriter to incorporate her suggestions.

In their long-lasting partnership Abe and Belle worked one mind against the other, gaining from their different approaches. They were bound to each other and to their commitment to the communist cause, one inseparable from the other. Down to earth in her judgment, my astute mother saved our family from political dangers my father could not detect with the same sharpness and speed. My father was a dreamer, theoretician, and visionary. He needed my mother to balance the scope of his dreams and to keep us alive.

I can still picture my father as he so often was, sitting in the living room absorbed in a book with a lighted cigarette in one hand and a pencil hovering over the open page in the other. Every once in a while he would raise his head and look not at us but above us, neither seeing nor hearing what was happening around him. My mother greeted me, angry, when I came home from the playground late, my filthy clothes in disarray: "Ann, when are you going to get your chores done? You were supposed to be home more than an hour ago. And look at your hands and knees, how will you ever wash all that dirt off? This is the second time this week this has happened." My father, who was sitting in the same room, did not hear a single word.

Exasperated, my mother turned to him saying, "Abe, be a father, pay attention, say something to her! Can't you see what she looks like and how late it is?" He raised his head, trying to return from his inner journey. The more he tried to "be a father" the more I laughed. Now not only I was being disciplined, but so was my father. A guilty smile broke out on Abe's face. My mother shrugged her shoulders and sighed deeply, looking away from my father, whose pencil was already scanning his book. Meanwhile, she sent me to the bathroom to clean up, sternly reminding me, "You better get all that dirt off and come help me put dinner on the table." As soon as she left the room, I winked at my father, who momentarily looked up before he lost himself in his book again. We smiled at each other, sealing our partnership in the crime of disobeying the law established in my mother's reign.

Chapter 5

. . . .

Abe: Family Background— the Chapmans

I am rooted in crossings, exiles, broken
    memories.
I never saw my grandfather.

Memory is more than me:
Private I and history
Locked in the floes of time
I see beyond my time
The deepest concerns of my self
Remember lives I haven't lived

Memory is more than me
Singularity and ancestry
My tree
And humanity
Me and not me
Touching separately
—Fragments of poems by Abe Chapman writ-
ten in the Intensive Care Unit, Wisconsin, 1976

        My father died on a cold, wintry March
day in 1976 at the age of sixty in a hospital in Stevens Point, Wisconsin.
Within hours his body was transported to Chicago, where he was buried
in the Chapman family plot in an Orthodox Jewish cemetery, Nusachs-
faard. I was thirty-four years old and not ready for this final separation.
Life without his presence and our ongoing dialogue was unthinkable.
Over the years we had talked passionately about literature, politics, art,
and life in general, never touching on the secrets of his political past. A
great deal had been left unsaid, unexplored. But as of March 6, 1976, I
had to learn how to live without him.

On the way to the cemetery I was seated in the car that followed
the limousine carrying my father's coffin. The motion of the car made
me dizzy. Sadness penetrated every cell of my body. The voices of my
mother and aunt merged with the hum of the wheels. My thoughts
dwelled on what I could not come to terms with: where did Abe's vast
wealth of knowledge and remarkable ability to challenge and question

go? Was it floating somewhere in the universe, or was it about to be buried with his worn-out body? Limp and silent, I rested my head on my mother's small, bony shoulder. On his last journey through the streets of Chicago, my father and I were already separated physically: his reassuring gaze and firm hand were no longer tangible. A desire for a response from him filled me with a sharp pain; this was my first awareness of irretrievable loss. Once again I felt like that small child my parents took to the train station in the middle of the night when I was eight and taken from the known to the unknown. I trusted then, as I trusted those around me now to lead me through this terrifying experience. When we arrived at the cemetery, the cars slipped quietly through the heavy wrought-iron gates into the bleak snow-covered grounds.

The modern building in which the funeral service was held had shiny tile floors and wood-paneled walls. The foyer reminded me of the sterile hospital halls where I had spent so much time during my father's illness. For me, there was no connection between the man who was still alive yesterday in the intensive care unit and the one whose death brought us here today. My mother disappeared into the funeral director's office, leaving me in the care of my aunt and uncle. I was startled to see my father's presence displayed in capital white letters on one of the doors. I was used to seeing his name, ABRAHAM CHAPMAN, posted on lecture halls and in newspapers, but here the name announced the termination of a life, not the start of a lecture or an article.

Slowly people I had never met before started to gather for the funeral service. They stood in small groups apart from me and spoke in hushed voices. Soft whispers reached my ears: "That must be Abe's daughter, she looks like him, don't you think?" The people who gathered here knew my father at some point in his life, either as family members, former comrades, or colleagues. My aunt leaned over to whisper names and associations: "He is . . . and she is. . . . And years ago they worked together . . . and they knew each other in the movement when. . . ." I could not connect the faces with the names, the past with the present, America with our years of exile, my life with my father's.

The religious tradition that dictated the rituals at this funeral—the washing of the body, the white shroud within which his body was wrapped, the pine coffin, and the Hebrew prayers recited in his honor— were not ones I associated with my father. Expressions he used like *mazoltov, gesuntheit, shlemeil, chazerai,* along with his strong interest in Jewish history and culture, always made me feel the strength of his Jewish ties. His religious feelings or connections, remained private, however, uncommunicated. I mourned not only the loss of the man who was my father but our lost chance for a deeper spiritual unity and continuity. Too late to change the past, I concentrated on the memories of the life we shared together.

Despite the radical beliefs he once adhered to, my father had now chosen (after prolonged indecision during the last months of his life) to be buried as an Orthodox Jew. As he lay dying, the cause to which he had dedicated years of his life had nothing to offer him. When facing his own finality, he drew strength from his beginnings and from the faith that united him with his family and people. The phase of his life I knew as his daughter was absent at his Orthodox funeral service. I was isolated from my father's religious past, which had no connection to the family life we lived while I was growing up. This discovery made me wonder how many other hidden parts of his inner self were still unrevealed to me.

When the service was over, everyone accompanied the body to the family plot, where Abe's grandmother, sister, and parents were buried. The coffin was covered with an American flag because my father was a World War II veteran. Before the coffin was lowered into the ground, the flag was neatly folded and gently placed in the hands of the widow, my mother. I could tell from the surprised look on her face that she had not expected to receive it. After the service, my mother and I drove around the streets near the cemetery until we found a cozy-looking restaurant. We wanted time to realize what all this meant to us before she returned to her empty home and I flew back to my husband and children.

When my mother noticed there was a mailbox in front of the restaurant, she quickly returned to get something from the car. Resolutely, she held the flag up in the air saying, "Let the American government get it back. It should stay where it belongs. I don't want it after what we lived through!" and she dropped the flag into the mailbox, confirming her undefeated need to fight back. This was her first small victory over an unjust fate she was unwilling to accept; it was the first time she smiled as a widow. I have often wondered what the mailman thought when he found the large, neatly folded flag in the U.S. government mailbox the next day and if the flag ever made it to Washington.

My father was born in Chicago. The original family name, Chipiniuk, was changed at Ellis Island to Chapman. The Chapmans came from the town of Zhitomir in the Ukraine, near Kiev. My father, the fifth of six children, was born in 1915, the same year as my mother. My grandfather, Harry Chapman, was a collector of scrap rubber who did well enough during World War I to own two homes, one in Chicago and one in Palestine. My grandparents were Zionists and spent a considerable amount of time in Palestine. My grandfather was a kind, gentle man, who loved books and learning more than managing a business. His wife, Chassi, however, made sure her husband provided well for their large family.

My father's childhood was divided between two cultures. He lived in America until the age of eleven. In 1926 the Chapmans sold their scrap rubber business because my grandfather had developed a heart condition and sailed for Palestine with their daughters Belle and Adele and youngest son, Abe. In Palestine they lived on the family-owned orange grove outside of Jerusalem. Harry and Chassi Chapman traveled back and forth between their Chicago home and their home in Palestine. Abe and Adele were left with their married sister Belle whenever their parents were in Chicago. Belle, who had three small children, pretty much raised Abe during his teen years.

Abe completed his high school education in Hebrew, a language he loved. He also loved the sounds of Arabic that he heard spoken on the streets around him. These cultural images lingered in his memory for the rest of his life. The violent conflicts that erupted between Arabs and Jews on the streets of Jerusalem had a lasting impact on him. My father blamed his sister Belle's fragile emotional state on the frequent and disturbing clashes that took place in their Jerusalem neighborhood. The struggle for land and power between the Jews and the Arabs in Palestine taught Abe that world affairs are centered around conflict, that society is divided into the oppressors and the oppressed. Justice, he could see, was not automatic; one had to struggle to gain it. His exposure to Palestine's politically charged atmosphere overpowered his formal education.

Rather than just follow the assigned school readings, Abe undertook projects that excited his intellect. As a high school student he was one of the first to translate Longfellow's poetry into Hebrew. Throughout his life a love of literature and words and the poetic music of language sustained and recharged him. In his youth the world of politics attracted him as a platform for change because it was a direct way to do something about the injustices he saw around him. Always sensitive to the plight of the oppressed, he wanted to act on those sentiments. In his life experience human injustice was universal: in Russia, pogroms were behind the emigration of his parents and other Jews; in Palestine the Arabs and Jews fought to establish ancestral rights to the land; in America racism prevented blacks from riding the same buses or eating in the same restaurants as whites, bosses exploited immigrants and others in factories, mines, and mills. In his political and literary writings Abe's pen was his most powerful weapon, his sword against injustice.

He lived according to his beliefs. When his friend the writer Richard Wright came to New York City without a place to stay, my parents invited him to live with them, straining relations with their white neighbors, who objected to the presence of a black man in their apartment building. Michel Fabre in his biography, *The Unfinished Quest of Richard Wright*, notes that "Abraham Chapman, Howard Nutt, Lawrence Lipton and Nelson Algren were among his [Wright's] favorite companions because of their common and sincere interest in the underworld and the 'underdog.'" Fabre recounts that Wright left Chicago by the end of May 1937 and once in New York lived with his friend Abraham Chapman until mid-June.

Abe's friendship with Wright was based on their dual interest in literature and politics. The young Wright submitted to Abe for criticism the broad outlines of "Fire and Cloud," a work designed to show the development of political awareness among African-Americans. Although Abe found it "excellent," he suggested that Wright read a recent article by Abram Moiseevich Deborin, a Soviet philosopher who developed Marxist sociopolitical doctrines relating to philosophy and literature. Abe wanted Wright to apply Deborin's theories on genius and social consciousness to his story. My twenty-two-year-old father made no separation between politics, family life, and literature, and this was the case in his friendship with Wright as with his personal relationships during those years in New York City.

After their marriage in Palestine in 1934, Abe and Belle left for Chicago, where Abe still had a large family. He was particularly fond of his sister Fanny. Thirteen years older than Abe, Fanny had graduated with a degree in social work from the University of Chicago. Married to a poet and writer and concerned about the plight of her fellow humans, Fanny was involved in communist-related political activities. She introduced Abe and Belle to her circle of progressive and bohemian friends.

Before long both my parents joined the communist movement. Impatient to move to New York City to be closer to the center of political action, Abe never completed his degree at the University of Chicago, relying on his ability to learn on his own. In New York he worked for a variety of communist publications. Abe's older brother, Manny, already living in New York City, was the sibling who most closely replicated his search for a higher vision of life and social change.

Manny was the most accomplished member of the Chapman family. In a family photograph taken in 1929, my grandfather is seated in the center surrounded by his adult children and their spouses. Yet for me the photograph is dominated by Manny's presence, particularly his dreamlike gaze. His eyes, lifted slightly upward, hold the unearthly quality of the eternal dreamer. He projects a spiritual strength and intellectual power that reminds me of my father. This portrait, which my father was still too young to be in, links the destiny of the two brothers, each of whom had a powerful dream larger than life itself and was willing to devote his physical and intellectual energies to make it succeed.

Manny studied at the University of Chicago, Loyola University, and the University of Toronto, where he got his Ph.D. He attracted a large circle of friends who responded to his dynamic personality and his thoughts on philosophy, theology, and art. In 1926 he followed the path of many other intellectual Americans and moved to Paris to write a novel and to study with the Catholic theologian Jacques Maritain. Manny was a frequent visitor at Maritain's weekly theological discussions in his home. By the age of twenty-four Manny had published several articles in the *Chicago Post*'s art magazine and a book about the life, works, and philosophy of the Russian painter William Schwartz. He describes the artist as a "restorer of the lost who repairs the broken," honoring art with the power to transform life. The artist is the visionary who can recreate reality in new and radical ways, for Manny asserts, "What is tradition today was revolutionary yesterday. Much that is revolutionary today will be traditional tomorrow." Manny saw radical change occurring through art (and ultimately religion) rather than political Marxism as my father did, yet he displayed a similar concern for the inadequacies of the human condition and the need to make life conform to a higher ideal.

Manny hurt his parents deeply when he converted to Catholicism in the mid-1930s. When Abe and Belle moved to New York City, Abe maintained close ties with his brother, who taught psychology and philosophy at Hunter College until his premature death in 1948, at the age of forty-three. Both brothers shared a passionate love of ideas and a fierce nonconformity in expressing their radical views. The only Chapmans to attend his Catholic funeral in St. Patrick's Cathedral were Abe and Belle. The only Chapman to continue to live by his radical beliefs after Manny's death was Abe.

The obituaries in the *New York Times* and *Commonweal* highlight the characteristics that made Manny and my parents kindred souls despite their philosophical and political differences. The *Commonweal* obituary noted: "Few Americans have been as active in the battle against religious and racial hatred as Professor E. Chapman. . . . It can be said without hesitation that the vehemence with which this convert threw himself into the struggle, the way in which he spent himself, directly caused his untimely death. . . . His was a policy of presence. In his eagerness to join battle with evil his pronouncements at times reflected rash practical judgments." According to the *New York Times* obituary, Manny was dedicated to the struggle for human rights: "Dr. Chapman had also served as executive secretary of the Committee of Catholics to Fight Anti-Semitism, out of which grew the Committee of Catholics for Human Rights . . . to combat inter-racial and inter-religious hatred. His motive was to counteract hatred, which he regarded as more terrible than the atomic bomb."

Manny and Abe were bold, even daring, spirits motivated by a desire to improve the human condition. Abe's initial inspiration to struggle for a better world came from his Jewish past. In an article written in 1938, when he was twenty-three, for the magazine *Jewish Life* (a publication of the Communist Party of New York State) titled "Jewish Movements of Revolt," Abe presented the following interpretation of Jewish history: "The history of the Jews is rich with movements of revolt, of reaction to oppression, of aspirations for freedom and complete equality. The Jews were not only *acted upon* by powerful historic forces, passively accepting the scars inflicted by overwhelming social forces, but *reacted* in an attempt to live a better and more human life, free of tyranny and persecution." Manny's desire to make the world more humane and just may have been inspired by the same Jewish roots that nourished his brother, but he found fulfillment in Catholicism while his brother was drawn to communism. Manny's search for a meaningful life was spiritual; Abe found meaning in a structured political ideology. Neither, however, was interested in materialism as a way to achieve fulfillment in life. My father joined the Communist Party so he could make his ideals a reality. His passionate love of life and his ability to translate ideas into political platforms and to inspire people into action were all put to use in his party work.

Yet there remains a huge gap between this positive image I have of my father, the communist idealist, and the things he did as a party functionary, who vanished behind the Iron Curtain one day with his immediate family. Abe, the party functionary I never knew, came to life for me on the pages of the congressional hearings I accidentally came upon in the library while visiting my son in college at SUNY Binghamton. In the transcript of the 1952 hearings of the Internal Security Subcommittee of the Senate Judiciary Committee on the Institute of Pacific Relations, the following interchange took place with Louis Budenz, a former communist and editor of the *Daily Worker*. Budenz broke with communism in 1945 and began a career as a professional anticommunist, appearing as a witness in at least sixty congressional proceedings during the next several years. About Abe he said:

MR. MORRIS (assistant counsel): Mr. Budenz, did you know Abraham Chapman?

MR. BUDENZ: Yes, sir, he is a veteran Communist, also known as John Arnold.

MR. MORRIS: When you say "John Arnold" is that his party name?

MR. BUDENZ: Well, he wrote under these different names and was sometimes known in the party as John Arnold. It was a party name. He was on the editorial board in connection with "Freiheit," which is the Communist daily paper in New York, published in the same building as the "Daily Worker." Therefore I conferred with Mr. Chapman many times and know him, as a Communist. He has a very high position as far as the regard of the Communist Party leaders in the Communist movement.

Communists like my father who either wrote or functioned in a public capacity used aliases to maximize their influence in a hostile political climate. One popular party argument was that if people could not identify an author as a communist, they had to deal with an article's argument on intellectual grounds rather than undermine it with labels and smears. In addition, the hostile political environment justified paranoia and secretiveness among party members, promoting the use of aliases, codes, front organizations, and the like. Top party members in America, who were often trained for political combat by their Soviet comrades in Moscow, inherited the secret tactics of the party cells used in czarist Russia. During the harshest political repression of the McCarthy period, the American Communist Party took drastic measures to protect its interests and future. As a result, functionaries like my father came under pressure from both sides, from the American government seeking to destroy domestic communist activities and influences and from an American Communist Party seeking to conceal its Soviet ties and to preserve its most promising cadres for better days.

In the 1952 congressional report on the IPR hearings, Robert Morris comments on Abraham Chapman's disappearance: "I am just saying that the best efforts on the part of all the staff to find Mr. Chapman have been unavailing and I want to say that we have tried to reach him through the Department of Justice and several times through the United States marshal's office." Not only did Chapman leave the United States, but so too did John Arnold and John Gordon. They all came along, as did Belle and Ann and Laura.

The drama of which my father was a part in the United States before we disappeared into Mexico, revealed to me on the pages of the IPR hearings, came as a shock. This was not the man I knew. The man I knew loved life to its fullest and had an extraordinary talent for turning ordinary events into excitement and wonder. When inspired by a piece of music, he barged into my bedroom grabbing my foot to use it as an imaginary baton. When I least expected it, he would show me he could twist his legs into the shape of the number four, balancing himself on one leg and challenging me, "Ann, see if you can do this. How long can you hold on?" When I broke my collarbone in a serious accident at age nineteen, without asking, he lit a cigarette which he placed in my mouth to calm me down from the shock I had experienced. This was how, in a comradely fashion, he revealed he knew I had been smoking for two years behind his back.

Abe was a tall, large-framed man with a round, friendly face full of expression and feeling. He loved sharing his thoughts and impressions with people, whether it was his response to a beautiful landscape or the Marxist vision of a new world. When he worked, his mind wandered far from his present surroundings until he was ready to exclaim, "Can you believe that . . . ," or "What do you think of . . . ," involving us in his latest train of thought. The attraction to change and movement permeated his actions; he loved to get in the car, grip the steering wheel, press the accelerator, and race to meet the known or the unknown. The thrill was in getting there. A Czech joke about a seasoned traveler, who when asked which place of his travels was his favorite, answered, "I like the journey of getting there the best!" captures one dimension of my father's personality.

He loved the beat of jazz and the expressive melodies of folk songs. He was fully at home with the language of blues, which describes the pain of love, mingled with longing and desire, and contrasting moments of sadness and happiness. The sounds of Coltrane, Theloneus Monk, Vivaldi, or Hassidic melodies made his head sway and his eyes fill with emotion. The sounds of jazz could make him drop his book and pen, run into the kitchen, and clasp my mother tightly in his arms, dancing her through the apartment. Belle released the carrot or potato that was in her hand and followed his graceful movements in perfect harmony. He sang Yiddish songs with a strong, melodic voice and deep feeling, and with his comrades he sang "progressive" songs that confirmed their radical fellowship. When alone, he listened to the unaccompanied voice of cantorial chanting on records worn with age.

He lived at full speed at all times, whether he was debating serious ideas, sharing a meal with friends, walking barefoot on a sandy beach, or watching a sunset. Literature was his fellow traveler through the mysteries of life. As he lay dying of heart failure, literature made him want to stay alive, as these lines from his incomplete poem indicate:

All art, all literature
Is energy in form
Life's movement captured, frozen
    in the fire of the imagination
    the X-ray of the mind the intellect
    the crossfire of emotion
Pump, heart, pump

He was in awe of the immense power and unpredictable moods of the ocean. He invented games with tiny sand crabs as he played with my five-year-old son, treating them like friends and imagining elaborate skits my son thought were incredible. When my father was weakened by his repeated heart attacks, my son, who was inseparable from him, joined him on his bed so they could play together. Abe would throw his bathrobe over his head, transforming the bed into an imaginary vehicle, and the two of them would journey around the world. In the last year of his life, sensing his impending death, he continued to affirm life and his love of existence:

Proclaiming presences:
"I am. I was here."
I leave marks, signs, meanings.
A meaning.
I signify. I imply. I fly.
Decipher the foot-writing of a reading of the sky
the sea, the air, the sand, the land

In life Abe's presence was indeed always known and felt. He was curious about the mysteries of human nature, the meaning of art, and the path leading toward untraveled regions. He responded sensually and instinctually to the beauty of a painting or a Chinese stone rubbing, the graceful movements of a dancer, the hopping sandpiper in the sand, the sumptuous flavor of a delicate Chinese dumpling or an aged southern bourbon. I can still hear his booming voice reciting Whitman, whom he had studied and communed with since early youth:

O the joy of my spirit—it is uncaged—it darts like lightning!
It is not enough to have this globe or a certain time,
I will have thousands of globes and all time.

In Whitman Abe found a kindred soul who inspired him to explore the untried and to cross all boundaries. Abe's life took him from Chicago to Jerusalem, to New York, Manila, Mexico City, Prague, Moscow, Berlin, Warsaw, Peking, Canton, and finally Stevens Point, Wisconsin. His complex life was filled with motion, action, excitement, and everyday joys as well as hardship, political misjudgment, mistakes, and in the end painful disillusionments and regrets. Yet the magic of life overcame all. His passions led him to challenge the established conventions and to risk the unknown.

Most of all I remember his strong, dynamic voice: fast-flowing, full of texture and nuance, continually formulating and arranging words into combinations that shocked, probed, and often stimulated further thought. He was never at a loss to capture the wonder and force that made life worth living, even during its darkest moments:

I began to write
a poem about
death
after a bout with death
but the acts and awes
of living
grabbed me so
I never finished
my death poem.

Chapter 6
. . . .
Prague

My name is Tsoai-talee. I am, therefore,
Tsoai-talee; therefore I am. The storyteller
Pohd-lohk gave me the name Tsoai-talee.
He believed that a man's life proceeds
from his name, in the way that a river
proceeds from its source.
—N. Scott Momaday, *The Names*

I continued to repeat the name of the
country where our long journey ended: Czechoslovakia in English and
Československo in Czech. The dissimilarity between the two names,
each representing the same word, made it possible for me to imagine
they were two different countries. Pronouncing this new word, Československo, helped make my presence there real. This country had a
language and physical landscape different from what I was familiar with
in America. The narrow streets of downtown Prague were lined with
buildings that had been built centuries ago. My heightened senses registered the unusual smells of rye bread and crusty, long rolls sprinkled
with caraway seeds and coarse salt from bakeries; sizzling fatty sausages
with strong mustard from vending stands; whipped-cream-coated and
chocolate-covered cakes from pastry shops and the bitter scent of beer
mingled with overpowering whiffs of sauerkraut and simmered cabbage
from the pub kitchens. From my hotel window I heard the hollow sound
of shoes hitting against the cobblestones on the main square, Václavské
Náměstí. I studied the activity in the streets below me, noting the smallest details: manner of walking, gestures, expressions on people's faces,
dress, and the sounds of speech. These scenes were like photographs of
a distant, exotic place, but unlike in a museum or in a book there was
no accompanying text to decode the unknown.

I was a detached observer unrelated to the people around me. Pedestrians scrutinized my mother and me when we walked in the streets,
straining to hear the English words we exchanged with each other. The
stares made me wonder if something was wrong with the shape of my
nose or the arrangement of my clothing. Why else would they look at
me with such penetrating glances and speak to each other in their mysterious language? I wished they would smile. The little girls watched

me from a safe distance. I hoped that if my mother bought me one of the long salty rolls the other children were eating, the Prague pedestrians would not pay so much attention to me. Nonetheless, after months of confinement it was exciting to walk freely in the streets and to feel the rush of bodies around me. The winding, narrow streets and the ancient, ornate buildings made me feel I had been transported to ancient times. Hardly anything around me had a connection to the life I had known before.

My sister was still in the hospital, and my father was in a country whose name my mother refused to divulge. When I questioned her about my father's disappearance, she told me to be patient and that in due time he would join us. Not knowing when he might return made the days seem longer. Belle told me that when my father returned from his mission, he would bring us news about the location of our future home. Meanwhile, I felt like a captive, waiting for the adults to make the necessary arrangements for us to continue our disrupted lives. In New York my parents frequently went to meetings and rallies, leaving my sister and me with friends or neighbors. They had explained that their activities were important because they were fighting for freedom and justice. It was hard for me to imagine, but I tried. Now in Prague I dreamed my father was searching for a land of freedom, like the one they wanted America to become. After all, from storybooks I knew the world was a large place and there had to be a home for us somewhere.

There was plenty to distract me during those last December days of 1950 when my mother and I roamed around Prague. The new, unusual sights fascinated me. In the stores there were fragile hand-blown glass Christmas tree decorations, one more beautiful and colorful than the other. The newly nationalized state stores were filled with frustrated Christmas shoppers who had trouble finding what they wanted on the depleted shelves. Some customers shrugged their shoulders in despair as they hurried to the next shop, hoping to find presents for their families. On street corners peasant women in hand-embroidered multilayered starched skirts and large kerchiefs sold homemade goat's cheese shaped like a football and fresh eggs from worn suitcases. Prague residents indifferently rushed by these plump village women in their ornate folk costumes, but I stared at them as the people on the street stared at my mother and me when we spoke English. Grumpy shoppers, in no mood to smile, stood in long lines. They carried their unwrapped purchases in net shopping bags so I could see what they had bought. Small Christmas trees and the delicate glass ornaments added excitement and beauty to the damp chill in the air. Muddy-colored carp swam in large barrels on the downtown sidewalks. People gathered around the barrels deliberating about which one they wanted to bring home.

I was told by the English-speaking receptionist in our hotel that the festive Czech Christmas Eve meal consisted of carp, always bought live and killed by the head of the family. She explained that the carp spent the last few hours or days of its life in the family bathtub until it was time to kill and cook it. I asked how people managed to bathe if the carp was in the tub. She looked at me in surprise at such a silly question, reminding me that I misunderstood the way things were done in this country.

My sister, still recuperating from hepatitis, was released from the hospital in time for the holiday season. She did not look well. She spent most of her time in bed and could only eat special foods that were difficult to obtain in a city plagued with food shortages and postwar rationing. Most evenings she pushed away her plate of unfinished food containing the same mashed potatoes, peas, and, if lucky, a piece of boiled chicken. I tried to make her laugh by entertaining her with my invented stories. My efforts were not very successful. Unlike Laura, I was bursting with pent-up energy that had no outlet. For all of us it was the first New Year without my father, who loved holidays as much if not more than a child. When he was present, the room was filled with conversation, laughter, and song. He created a commotion over the most insignificant preparations. Without him it was difficult to believe it was a holiday.

Shortly before New Year's Eve, we heard an explosion outside our hotel window. We traced it to a bottle of milk we had been keeping cold on the wide windowsill. It froze, and the glass bottle shattered. This unexpected explosion signaled our welcome of the New Year in the lonely Prague hotel room. We hugged each other, crying and laughing at the same time. My mother wanted to cheer me up with the only holiday sweet she could find. They were small chocolate figurines of angels and Saint Nicholas wrapped in colorful tin foil. As Jews, we had never celebrated Christmas in New York. This chocolate Saint Nicholas was just a fat, little old man to me. These chocolates were not the same as the chocolate coins wrapped in golden foil we used to get for Hanukkah. But nothing then was the way it had been.

In America every December my mother had decorated our home

with metal Stars of David she hung on strings in the doorways and lit the menorah as we gathered at the table. The potato latkes she fried in the kitchen filled the house with an aroma of oil mixed with potatoes and onions that lingered for several days. Hannukkah in our home had always been celebrated with family friends who helped Belle grate potatoes and onions for the heaps of latkes she turned out. On the tables there were bowls of sour cream, applesauce, and generous amounts of chocolate "gelt." We played dreidel games and sang holiday Yiddish songs while the menorah lights flickered until they went out altogether. The Hebrew letters *nun, gimel, he,* and *shin* were engraved on the dreidel I left at home. These were the initials of the words that meant "a great miracle happened here." My father told us the story of the great miracle when the oil found in the temple burned for eight nights instead of one, and now the victory of the Maccabees was symbolized by lighting the eight candles on the menorah. The storytelling, the delicious latkes, and the warm candlelight of the menorah made the room feel cozy and festive. This year, however, there were no latkes, no menorah, no dreidel games, and no miracle to bring my father back to take us to a home of our own. I had to make do with the sweet taste of the chocolate Saint Nicholas and the angels my mother got in place of the chocolate gelt.

Late one night during our stay at the Zlatá Husa Hotel (the Golden Goose), I heard my mother's excited voice repeat rapidly into the telephone receiver, "Where are you? Yes, we will be there! Yes, yes, we will see you, my love, right away. What did you say the name of the hotel is?" After a three-month separation, my father announced his arrival in Prague. All we knew was the name of the hotel where he was waiting for us. We rushed into the street, too excited to know which direction to go in, screaming "Alcron, Alcron" into the faces of the weary pedestrians. We ran frantically to the left and then to the right along the street. Through gestures we understood that the strangers we approached were sending us down a narrow, winding street only two blocks away from our hotel. There we saw an elegant building with a sign proclaiming ALCRON.

My father welcomed us in a huge, elegant room with hugs and kisses and delicious Russian chocolates called *mishki* (little bears). Instantly they became my favorites. More significant, he was bringing us the much awaited information about our future. Not until now were my sister and I told what my mother knew all along, that Abe had been in Moscow all this time. Originally the plan was for our family to settle in Moscow. Abe told us that the Soviet comrades had changed their minds and decided that our family was going to live in Prague. My parents reassured me that in this country, in this very city, I would have a home, a school to attend, and friends of my own. I was running circles around the room kissing first my father and then my mother and sister. In a daze I listened to my father's stories about the incredible city he had just come from. If Prague looked like an ancient fairyland, Moscow sounded like paradise. My father described a majestic, gigantic city, full of life and activity, where the miraculous was about to become a reality.

My new home thus was to be Praha (Prague). The root of the word *Prague* in Czech is *Prah*, which means *threshold*. For all of us settling in Prague was like crossing the threshold into a strange world. This was the start of our new lives, driven off course by a deep and ultimately dangerous involvement in world politics. For my parents it was the beginning of their exile. For my older sister, whose American origins were already firmly established, it imposed an unwanted adjustment to a life and culture that deprived her of her own. For me, the youngest, it was an adventure because I was not old enough to understand the distinction between a homeland and an exile. Christmas Eve carp, chocolate Saint Nicholases, medieval streets, and the mysterious Slavic sounds of the Czech language were just a small sampling of the many experiences awaiting me. I was on the threshold of absorbing an identity that would no longer be American.

The burst of joy released by the safe family reunion did not last long. After Abe's return from Moscow, we moved into the Flora Hotel in Vinohrady, away from the center of Prague. We could not leave our hotel rooms until we had documents that would establish new and "legitimate" identities for us as Czechs. Our family name had to be changed to erase our previous existence or possibly to protect us from Western agents and to allow our full integration into Czech society. It took time for the communist authorities to create these new documents. For the time being, we had to stay secluded in our hotel room. It was excruciating torture for me to have to remain incognito in the dreary walls of the Flora Hotel. My sister and I were told repeatedly that our hiding in the hotel room would come to an end when we received papers with our new names. I could not grasp how a piece of paper could change who I was. I knew I was still the same person who had been walking the streets with my mother just a few days ago. All that mattered to me was that I could no longer run free in the streets. Life beyond these walls was shapeless, yet being trapped within them was suffocating. My only desire was to shed this secrecy and isolation.

We could not even go to the hotel restaurant in the Flora for fear that foreign journalists, residing in the hotel, might ask us questions we were forbidden to answer. We could not very well introduce ourselves with a Kafkaesque, "How nice to meet you, but my name is still unknown." Once again, as I had learned to do in Mexico, I lived in my dreams. My days were dominated by the anticipation of the event that would end this waiting. Because we could not be seen in the hotel restaurant, my mother had to prepare food on a hot plate in our room. Comrades who spoke broken English or no English at all brought food to our room in large bags. My mother, worn out and worried, did not complain. She took care of the practical daily chores with grace and fortitude as she did in all the crisis situations we encountered.

With curiosity I watched the children, dogs, and grown-ups move about on the street below our hotel window. I wanted to know more about their families and homes. I tried to reconstruct their lives from the way they walked or the size of the bags they were carrying. I watched mothers with net shopping bags and their small children go into the grocery store that was across the street from our hotel, imagining what they bought and what they would be having for dinner that day. If only I could have changed places with them or had a chance to feel a part of the ongoing flow of their lives. When would I ever understand what they were saying? What must it feel like to speak the way they did? Some of the sounds were comical, but all of them were a jumbled maze to my ears.

I longed to feel the sun, the wind, even the raindrops on my cheeks. As usual, I looked to Laura for answers. At times she was too sad to want to play with me or answer my stream of questions. Most of the time she was patient and attentive. Being four years older qualified her, in my eyes, to figure out the mysteries of the adult world. Abe and Belle, immersed in hushed, animated conversations with each other, were unable to ease the tedium of this isolation. At times, Czech men appeared in our room either to explain or to discuss things with our parents.

Today I cannot remember a single face, but I can recall the sound of their voices. Desperately I wished for something to happen. It no longer mattered what exactly I was waiting for. I knew only one thing—I did not want to remain in this room another month, week, or day. I lost all sense of time, and to this day I have no idea if we were at the Flora for a few weeks or a few months.

Finally, I sensed that a change was about to happen when the family gathered for an important conference. The news we were to be entrusted with was serious, as was evident from the expressions on my parents' faces and the restrained movements of their bodies. Taking time to light a cigarette, my father carefully explained our situation and the changes that were about to take place in our lives. Laura and I were introduced to the rules of our newly reinvented identities. We were to return to "normal" living in a new guise, like a butterfly emerging from its cocoon. But unlike a butterfly, for which this was a natural process, for us it meant a denial or at least a distortion of our earlier existence.

To escape from my confinement I would have to exit this room under a new name, Anna Čapková, a little Czech girl I had never been. I was told never again to say the name given to me at birth and to act as if this newly created name was the only one I had ever had. I was warned that telling anyone, even a close friend, that my name had been Chapman could endanger our lives. From now on Ann Chapman did not exist. My parents, who exercised self-control and who were practiced in keeping secrets as a result of their political activities, never again used that name in front of me. If my sister remembered our last name, she would not tell me. Their efforts worked, not immediately, but over time the name vanished from my memory. By the time I was twelve or thirteen years old I could no longer recall it. An instinctual fear of consequences, coupled with not hearing its sound, wiped it out of my memory. My parents always vehemently maintained that our safety depended on keeping that name secret, although they never said why.

What had once been a relatively carefree, childhood life became complicated for me by this dark, burdensome secret. I could not remove it from my life or escape it. I never had to think about what my name and American citizenship meant to me until I lost it. Now, instead of fearing the neighborhood bullies, I feared people would discover I was lying when I introduced myself as "Čapková." What if they made a connection between my name, my former nationality and background, and who I am pretending to be now? What would happen if I were to tell or be discovered? Would the terrible danger that justified this secret behavior do us harm?

I practiced my new name diligently, understanding that it would be the password out of this oppressive room. Slowly I repeated the strange, foreign word Čapková, Čapková, fearing I might forget it or not know how to pronounce it. I rehearsed, introducing myself, "Hello, my name is Anna Čapková," in a whisper, then daring to say it aloud. At first, each time I said my new name I was reminded of the untruth it was based on. The urge to tell the truth about my existence never left me. But now I did not want to think about these disturbing feelings. I was too anxious to see what would happen to us once released from this dreary hotel room. I had yet to discover what it would be like to live as Anna Čapková.

For my parents, our name change was part of a strategy in a political game whose rules they understood and accepted. For me, capable only of the simplicity of absolute truths, it was an entrance to the world of falsehood and intrigue. I walked out of that hotel room an eight-year-old Anna Čapková, who had to bear the unwanted responsibility of a former self I was forced to conceal without knowing why.

When I left the Flora and moved to Kobylisy, our new Prague neighborhood, I entered my invented existence. I never did return to those simpler days when I was just plain Ann Chapman. The dissimilarity between Chapman and Čapková made it possible to harbor the illusion that these might be two different people. By annihilating one name and taking another, I created a singular concept of myself, just as the word "Československo" superseded the English word "Czechoslovakia." The life I was to create for myself in this country using my new name slowly replaced what had been taken from me and it became the reality that defined me.

Chapter 7

. . . .

Czech

Language

Children trust in language. They are open to the power and beauty of language, and here they differ from their elders, most of whom have come to imagine that they have found words out, and so much of magic is lost upon them. Creation says to the child I Believe in this tree, for it has a name.

—N. Scott Momaday, *The Names*

Our new home stood on a peaceful street with large homes and flourishing gardens that my mother called *villas* (a word I had never heard before). I absorbed the silence more than the new neighborhood sounds. So finally a place belonged to us! Here, in the residential area called Kobylisy that was a considerable distance from the center of Prague our escape and hiding had ended. The privacy of the residents in these solid houses was guarded by stone walls and tall fences. The cement walls with wooden fences made me feel shut out from those who lived on my new street. The tall, locked gates and my inability to communicate made it impossible for me to penetrate the unknown.

The neighborhood was calm and orderly. A stranger to its established rules and patterns, I studied the behavior of my new neighbors. The chatter of the women and the children who played in the street made me feel like a deaf mute. The sounds they created were useless for me. There were no clues that would guide me toward comprehension. It frightened me to be an alien, enclosed in my foreignness. I watched the other children play street games, too shy to join them. I could not overcome the disturbing distance between me and them. In America our neighborhood was divided into "them" and "us" based on political beliefs, but now that division was between "them" and "me" because of the language barrier. I desperately wanted to fill the gap that separated me from those around me.

My new school was a couple of blocks from our house at the bottom of the hill. It had gray stone walls and resembled a towering fort. The sparkling clean classrooms had shiny wooden floors on which schoolchildren were forbidden to walk in street shoes. Everybody had to change into cloth slippers, *cvičky*, to keep the floors clean. On my first day of school the principal reprimanded me for not bringing my *cvičky* by pointing to my street shoes and shaking her head disapprovingly. Belle had no idea what I was talking about when I returned from school in tears trying to explain that unless she bought me a pair of *cvičky*, I couldn't go back to school. Belle threw up her hands at the insignificance of such a request. I got my sister to help me purchase them, well aware that it was not a negotiable point at school.

In these classrooms several generations of Kobylisy children had been prepared for their adult lives. For the Czech children the sudden appearance of an eight-year-old English-speaking girl in their classroom was a major event. I introduced myself as Anna Čapková. For the time being I had to rely on what I could see rather than on any meaningful verbal exchanges. Each student had a wooden desk with storage room for notebooks and books under the desktop, and each desk had an inkwell filled with dark blue ink. On the walls there were bulletin boards and pictures of smiling pioneers and portraits of Joseph Stalin and Klement Gottwald, the president of Czechoslovakia. The teacher wrote neat rows of Czech words on the board which the children copied. I waited to see what I should do. One of my new classmates slipped a wooden pen holder in my hand. I dipped the metal tip of the pen into the inkwell, and slowly I moved my hand toward the paper when to my shock three large ink spots appeared on the white page. It took practice before I learned to control the flow of ink and apply the right amount of pressure on the pen to form letters. After much discipline, determination, and a great deal of frustration, I could finally relate to the words these letters formed.

The reaction of my new classmates to my presence overwhelmed me. The news of my appearance spread fast. When we went to the playground for a break, the excited children examined me from head to toe, and, exchanging loud comments, they pointed their fingers at my clothes and freckles. I listened to their fast-flowing sentences. When I tried to get them to understand me, they laughed. Some of the kids were soft-spoken, others were loud and boisterous, and a few stood back silently as they watched the commotion my arrival created. The expressions on their faces told me things about them they could not explain in words. From their behavior I could sense their personality differences, although I could not pronounce their names.

On that first day, surrounded by my new pushing and shoving class-mates, I decided to make learning Czech my first priority. I took to the task with the appetite of a starved animal. From then on I devoted all my attention and energy to this new undertaking. I worked on it day and night, not sure where to begin. I knew that English was my past, but Czech had to become my present. English separated me from my classmates, but Czech would bring me closer to them. Instinctively, I knew that mastering this language was the only way to break out of my solitude. And I had been alone for such a long time. I had no idea how enormous this task was going to be, but I was ready to start.

I mimicked the sounds my classmates made when they read aloud from their reader, seeking approval from the stern teacher. At first, I practiced these Czech words by myself in my bedroom, too afraid to do so in class. I familiarized myself with their articulation and texture. I could feel the muscles in my cheeks stretch and pull as I tried to imitate the sounds I had to pronounce. I became frustrated by my slow progress.

Fortunately, a caring young teacher at the school, Kamilka Svobo-dová, noticed my frustration and invited me to her home to help me learn this language, which she loved passionately. After trying differ-ent approaches, I knew that learning Czech would require more than simple determination and energy. I had trouble figuring out how to ar-range words into meaningful sentences. Daily new words filled my head that had no relationship to what I had learned the day before. I went to Miss Svobodová's home hoping for a miracle.

I took the number eleven tram to the very end of the line, following the pictorial map Miss Svobodová made for me. In this countrylike set-ting on the outskirts of Prague there were rows of cherry orchards and small cozy-looking houses. My teacher lived with her mother in one of those houses. When I arrived, she took me to her room and we went to work at once. She fixed her lively eyes on me, commanding a response. I watched her curls swing to the determined deep breaths she allowed herself between the stream of Czech words she wanted me to repeat and use in sentences of my own. She sought a way to explain the rules and exceptions I did not know how to apply when forming sentences. We used our hands and a fair amount of pantomime to communicate because she did not know English. Her expressive face helped guide me to an understanding of what she meant, though I was not always sure I understood her correctly. She demanded that I follow her orders. I had no choice if I wanted to reach my desired goal.

On those Saturday afternoons we worked long hours on making order out of the chaos of thousands of disconnected words, grammatical endings, prefixes, and prepositions. The highly inflected Czech language and its grammar were completely unlike English. I never had to think about *how* English worked, I just used it. Now I could not even say something as simple as "Could you please give me that book" without knowing if the book was masculine, feminine, or neuter, nominative or accusative, if the verb was present or past, and if the manner of address was formal or informal. The effort of producing one simple, coherent sentence in Czech exhausted me. Whenever I thought I knew which ending to use, Kamilka made me use the word in a new context which instantly demanded a different inflection. Not until I understood the logic that governed the choice of case endings could I gain the independence to create sentences that made sense. Kamilka never let me rest. As soon as I mastered a concept, she immediately moved on to the next set of rules. I told my parents Czech children must be geniuses, for I could not imagine a language more complicated than theirs. I still believe it.

In mid-afternoon Kamilka's mother would quietly enter the room with a plate of freshly baked *koláčki* and a cup of *melta* chickory coffee. She smiled warmly and gave me an encouraging pat on the shoulder when she put our afternoon snack in front of us. There were times when Kamilka was unyielding; I was confused and mentally worn out. Words were floating around in my head like balloons filled with helium that could not be kept down or in their proper place. I broke out in beads of sweat, struggling to control and reproduce the stream of Czech words Kamilka wanted me to remember.

I was bursting with feelings, trapped in my speechless prison and struggling for expression. I dreamed of the day I would join the crowds of kids talking with each other in the playground, but so far those dreams were still in English. Each school day that I failed to follow what was going on around me made me struggle with renewed vigor.

One day, while studying with Kamilka, I kept confusing the newly learned words for north, south, east, and west. The more I mixed up one word with the other, the louder and more commanding Kamilka's voice became: "No, that is not it, that is the wrong word." Finally, I jumped up and in a fit of humiliation and rage ran out of the house. I ran down the streets until I could hardly catch my breath. Tears of anger and hopelessness poured down my cheeks. The next day in class, however, I realized that running away postponed the day I would be able to join the conversation of my chattering classmates. I returned to Kamilka's house to continue my battle with Czech until I no longer needed her help. One day I was shocked to realize that my thoughts were no longer just in English. Some of the new Czech words started to seep into my inner self: "Tomorrow in *škola já budu sedět* next to Eva." In time, the string of Czech words got longer and longer.

Meanwhile, I spent my evenings reading poems aloud from my second grade reader, gesticulating emphatically with my hands to the rhythm of words I could not understand. In Czech the accent always falls on the first syllable, which made the regular, monotone beat of the poetry soothing and predictable. Curious over the loud sounds coming from my bedroom, my father would leave his typewriter and wander in to see what he was missing. When he saw I was speaking Czech to myself, he quietly left the room. I was gradually moving into a new linguistic territory we could no longer share.

I read the thin elementary school magazine *Mateřídouška* (Mother's Soul) out loud from cover to cover. It was filled with short poems, stories, and proverbs with amusing, colorful pictures to engage the beginning reader. Initially I tried to imagine the meaning of the short stories. Eventually guesses became certainties. I played with the texture of the sounds so that the foreign became familiar. The pages of this magazine became my daily companion, as I wove in and out of the words piecing together first a meaning and finally a whole story. I listened, imitated, copied, wrote, struggled, and ultimately succeeded in mastering Czech. I celebrated my final victory by rereading the story until I knew it by heart. By breaking the complex language code, I had removed the last barrier to this exciting new world. I began to explore Czech books, the history and temperament of the Czech people, and, above all, to communicate with the people around me.

The more my Czech improved, the less I wished to use English. Of course, I had to speak English at home with my parents and their friends. But I stopped reading and writing in English. By age ten or eleven I stopped thinking and dreaming in English. English no longer related to my daily school life and new relationships. The stronger my Czech became, the more rapidly my English faded. Switching to English was an undesirable interference with how I expressed myself in my day to day life. Czech connected me with my classmates, my teachers, my schoolwork, and Czech literature, but at the same time it separated me from my parents, who had no desire to learn it and whose everyday life did not demand it of them.

One day I was sitting on my bed memorizing portions of Karel Hynek Mácha's poem "Máj" (May):

Čechové jsou národ dobrý,
A Ty Cechů věrný syn!

My mother came into the room saying, "Ann, I have to send you to the store for some fresh bread. What is it you're studying?" I immediately translated the lines of poetry for her:

The Czechs are a good nation,
And you are a loyal Czech son.

"Do you want to hear how beautiful the opening lines are in Czech?" I asked, eager to recite those beloved lines every Czech child knows by heart: "Byl pozdní večer—první máj" (It was a late evening—the first of May). But when I lifted my eyes from the page, she had already turned around·in the doorway, leaving only a circle of cigarette smoke where she had been standing just a minute ago. I recited the next line of the poem even more loudly: "Večerní máj—byl lásky čas" (On a May evening—it was time for love). The only audience left in the room, however, was myself.

It upset my parents that the more competent I became in Czech, the more resistant I was to using English. The weaker my English became, the more my confidence grew in my Czech. My sense of style was getting quite sophisticated with complex shades of meaning and colorful slang expressions. I took great pride in pronouncing the sound "ř," which was difficult even for some Czech children. It is a sound that distinguishes Czech from all other languages, and the Czechs are usually amazed when a foreigner masters it. My father, who loved the beauty of English, read me Walt Whitman's poetry, luxuriating in the sounds and richness of its vocabulary. He worked at his typewriter experimenting with varied combinations of English words ready to share his discoveries. He chose his words deliberately, relying on his intuition and profound knowledge of English. Words excited him; the English language defined him. I understood that excitement when I expressed myself in Czech.

My English vocabulary never developed beyond that of a nine-year-old. Czech was the language I read, wrote, talked, and imagined things in; it was the language I shaped abstract thoughts and complex feelings in. It was the language I used when I first fell in love and the language that defined my deepest observations and feelings. It was the language I thought in when I entered adulthood. English belonged to the child I had been when I left the United States. Czech expressed my new self from middle childhood to early adulthood.

I never touched the English books and newspapers in our home even though I was a voracious reader. I was accumulating a substantial library of my favorite Czech books. The older I got, the more challenging it was to find the right English words to explain what was going on in my Czech classroom. I lacked the English words to translate the slogans on the bulletin boards and the jargon that was used at pioneer meetings. My Czech school life became a private domain that I could not easily share with my non-Czech-speaking parents. Many new words were an exclusive part of the communist environment I lived in and had no equivalents in the experiences of my parents. The pioneer greetings that opened our meetings, "To the defense and construction of our nation, be prepared, always prepared," sounded strange when translated into English.

Occasionally, when I could not find the right word to explain to Abe and Belle what was going on in school, I lapsed into Czech. My parents objected vehemently. Czech grammar began to erode my intuitive feel for a correct English sentence. My use of the double negative in English, common in all Slavic languages, horrified my parents, who continually corrected me: "No, you can't say, 'today I nothing can't do.'" They tried to correct my errors, but I would stumble into the same construction a few sentences later. My mind automatically gravitated toward Czech.

Finally, my desperate parents instituted the "penalty box." Each Saturday I received a five-crown allowance for a movie and ice cream. Every time I made a mistake in English or used a Czech word instead of an

English one, I had to pay a fine to the penalty box. At the end of the month the loot from the penalty box was used to buy candies or ice cream for the entire family. Bit by bit, sentence by sentence, my entire allowance was consumed by the penalty box, reducing me to tears. My parents finally abolished the penalty box because my English was not improving and my morale was deteriorating. My parents did not know how to preserve my interest and skill in using English for they could not compete with the importance Czech held in my daily life.

I learned that language was not only words and grammar but also a re-flection of social and political attitudes. Words had the power to convey political values that changed as thinking and beliefs changed. For in-stance, a child never addressed an adult with the familiar pronoun *ty*. In-stead he had to use the formal *vy* as a sign of respect and social distance between the world of child and adult, a distinction that does not exist in English. In Czech social titles of the past like *pan* (Mr.) were replaced by the word *soudruh* (comrade), distinguishing the bourgeois past from the communist present. Many new experiences existed for me only in Czech, for I was unable to find the words to translate the full range of nuances associated with words that lived only in their Czech setting.

At night I listened attentively to my parents' English conversations in the other room. Hearing English but thinking in Czech, I tried to grasp the split between a singular object like a book and the two words in my mind that represented it: *book* in English and *kniha* in Czech. As a nine-year-old, I was mystified that a singular object, book, was expressed by vastly different words, each representing a different world. I struggled to understand this as my eyelids grew heavier and my sleepy mind pushed such puzzling thoughts further and further away from consciousness.

My lips silently molded the words, *kniha . . . kniha,* as the fleeting image of my favorite book passed before my eyes, slowly easing the ten-sion in my limbs with the soothing, rhythmic repetition of those sounds. When the shape of the book reappeared in my dream, I knowingly nodded to it, realizing that my parents insisted I call it by the name they were used to—*book*. Nevertheless, I felt reassurance from the fact that for me and my new friends it was, of course a *kniha*. It opened its pages to me when I called it by its real (Czech) name; it obeyed my command to appear or disappear from my dream whenever I beckoned it to respond to the word *kniha*.

The rule in our house remained firm, however: the language of communication was English. And so began and continued a complete separation between the English world of my parents and the Czech world of my new environment. As English faded from my mind and diminished in importance in my day-to-day life, so did the memories of my old life. All that lingered in my thoughts were fragmented images of an American food I used to like or the voice of a person I had once known. Most nights after we turned out the lights in our bedroom, Laura and I played a favorite game of pretending we were either Mrs. Dvořáková or Mrs. Nováková, both models of typical Czech mothers who lived on our street. We discussed the behavior of our pretend children and the dinner we were preparing for the family, which inevitably included *knedlíky* (dumplings), which my mother never prepared. We sent our children to the pub up the hill for a pitcher of beer, scolding them for sampling the golden beer through the thick foam. We complained bitterly about the lines in the stores where we had to shop. In this game of being Czech mommies, we practiced new words we heard spoken in our neighborhood. We imitated the voices of Mrs. Dvořáková and Mrs. Nováková. We felt important as we discussed the day in the life of our "household." Little did we realize that slowly these conversations began to supplant the English we used to speak together until one day the Czech took over completely as our mutual language of communication.

My sister and I switched back and forth from the Czech we used together in the bedroom to the English we used in response to my mother's questions in the kitchen. Moreover, we did it without losing a beat in the flow of words. The only other times I heard Czech creep into the house was when I was sick (which was often) and a Czech friend of my parents would come to stay with me while my parents were out. She would tell me stories and read my Czech books to me. My desire to use Czech as often as possible almost made me look forward to being sick.

There were other American families in exile in Prague, each with its own unique story. I do not remember the details of their particular circumstances, but I do remember that living a bilingual existence was not easy for most of the children. In one such American family, a little girl of about five or six, who was expected to speak English with her older sister and parents and Czech at school, rebelled. She was an unusually beautiful child, with long, wavy blond hair and bright blue, probing eyes. When we visited them, she usually stood reproachfully and defiantly in the doorway of the living room with her hands on her hips and a hard, immobile gaze in her eyes. She never spoke to anyone, never shared her thoughts or reactions in spoken language. She just stood there, unreachable, like a princess in an impregnable tower. Her speechlessness worried her parents. They could not provoke her to talk. They tried everything: love, anger, punishments, encouragement, medical tests, and psychological consultations. She had no discernible physical ailment to explain her silence, yet she skillfully outwitted all efforts to break through it. We learned that when the family returned to America in the late 1950s, the child started to speak perfect English. Her stubborn rebellion frightened me. Her silence said much more than words. I, on the other hand, was determined to acquire a Czech voice of my own. And that Czech voice had to express my feelings and thoughts exactly as I wanted it to. The Czech words I was now able to speak released me from the captivity in which the little silent princess remained secluded. Those Czech words I was able to produce were the keys to the tower unspoken words built around us.

Ann Chapman on the stoop of the family's last home in New York before their departure and disappearance

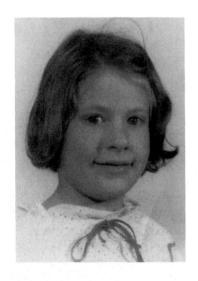

Ann's last American school
picture, ca. 1949

Abe and Belle in the early 1950s visiting Czech friends in the countryside
outside Prague

The house on Nad Rokoskou Street in Prague where the Čapek family lived
on the top floor

Abe and Belle after their return from China in the home of Czech friends in Prague

Anna Čapková, sixth from the left in the back row, a pioneer in 1953 or 1954 under Stalin's guidance

Anna's Koráb gymnasium (high school) in Prague

The Čapek family at a refreshment stand in Prague before leaving for China

In Peking during the campaign to kill the sparrows, Anna is in a tree holding a stick with a white flag to scare the sparrows into flying until they drop from exhaustion

Anna—in old and new China

Anna in Peking in 1959 in the Foreign Language Press compound
when furnaces to melt down steel were built everywhere

Abe, Belle, Anna, and Chinese translator on their trip through China in 1959

Elsie Epstein and Anna on their trip through southern China. Anna is trying to get away from the children who are following because she is such a curious sight.

Anna's graduation ball in Prague shortly after returning from Peking. Anna (second row, first on the left) is the only one in a store-bought nylon gown instead of a tailor-made one.

Anna visiting a machinery factory as a translator in Hronov, 1961

Anna translating a welcoming speech in 1961 at a collective farm in Dolný Kubín for the delegation from Ghana. The villagers and the local pioneers are present to welcome the foreigners.

Anna seated at a press conference between the Ghanian representatives under a welcoming sign, "We greet the delegation from Ghana"

Anna the translator in the Old Town Square in Prague in 1962, wearing the suit that was made for her to represent Czechoslovakia in Helsinki at the Youth Festival

Abe in the last year of his life, 1975–1976

Chapter 8

. . . .

Living on Nad Rokoskou

Tamina spent her childhood on Stalin Avenue, and when her husband came to take her away, he went to Vinohrady— that is, Vineyards Avenue. And all the time it was the same street; they just kept changing its name, trying to lobotomize it.
—Milan Kundera, *The Book of Laughter and Forgetting*

Czech words slipped off my tongue, impinging upon my solitude. Now I could satisfy my voracious appetite to integrate with my new surroundings. Once I could speak Czech, I felt more comfortable exploring my neighborhood and then the larger Prague streets. There was much for me to learn and discover. The young socialist state, in existence only since 1948, had layers of complex meanings hidden within the individual lives of people, not readily obvious on initial contact. When I moved to Nad Rokoskou Street in 1951, I lived strictly in the present, absorbing the communist reality but unaware of the subtle undercurrents that had turned people's lives around drastically since 1948. I was far more interested in my new physical surroundings than the history that had created it.

Our apartment in the Kobylisy villa was in a neighborhood that was once the home of successful professionals. Now these well-built homes had been taken over by the new government and subdivided into smaller apartments to house people the Communist Party wanted to reward. Presumably that explained why we were given our apartment there. Each neighborhood had a Národní Výbor (National Committee) at which all residents were registered and which controlled neighborhood affairs. In the social upheaval of converting the society from a democracy to a communist state the previous owners lost their homes to the newly privileged. The new and the old, the haves and the have-nots, the believers and the faithless, the angry losers and the newly established victors exchanged places. For me such changes were invisible on the surface. From without, the streets and houses still looked the same, but within all was changed. Our neighborhood reflected everyone's precarious status relative to the communist government.

The villa we lived in was surrounded by a strong wooden fence secured in a cement wall with barbed wire on top. A locked wooden gate shut out strangers and guarded the secrets of those who resided behind it. Our villa was a solid two-story house with shiny, dark green ivy clinging to its walls as high as our bedroom windows on the third, top floor. A small balcony off our kitchen overlooked the immaculately groomed garden with perfectly lined fruit trees and bushes planted at least a generation or two ago. Political regimes changed and peoples' lives were thrown into turmoil, but the ivy continued to grow on the walls and the garden remained as it had been in the past. [On *a recent trip to Prague, at least thirty years after I had lived in this house, I found the garden, the crawling ivy, the sturdy wall around the house all unchanged.*]

Our living quarters in the villa were located on the top floor of what had been a comfortable home for one upper-middle-class Czech family before the 1948 communist takeover. Now this villa housed three families, one on each floor. Our rooms were fully furnished. We moved into these quarters without possessions of our own. We slipped into the chairs and beds left behind by the previous occupants, claiming them as our own. We even used their dishes and linen. On the floor underneath us lived a family of four, the Shneibergs. We knew them by the sounds of their voices through the walls rather than through face-to-face encounters in the hallway. They made no effort to know us. It took time for the story behind the unfriendly glances directed at us by those already living in this house to unfold. This villa and the people in it had a history that started before I was born.

The ground floor servants' quarters were now occupied by the bitter and openly hostile spinster sister of the former owner of the house, Miss Zapletalová (literally Miss Tangle). Miss Zapletalová was not very tall, a bit dumpy, with rusty graying hair pulled tight around her head in a braid that framed her round, freckled face. Unruly strands of hair fell randomly around her forehead. The skin on her face was wrinkled, and her freckles stretched tightly around her small, clamped mouth, giving the impression of a hurt, misunderstood child turned old and bitter. Miss Zapletalová guarded this house and the possessions in her cluttered room like a warrior defending the family honor against enemy forces.

She forbade me to play in her neat little yard, forcing me to bounce my ball in the street. She spent hours working in the garden in the company of her dogs, maintaining every bush and plant in perfect order. She exercised her power as an adult to keep me out of her garden, her domain. She never ceased to show her resentment of our presence in "her" house. She inventoried the fruit on her trees and automatically assumed, since I was the youngest in the building, that I had helped myself when she found some of it missing. My mother defended my honor in the most incomprehensible mess of Czech sounds when Miss Zapletalová complained about the missing pieces of fruit. I wondered if the adults could detect from the shape of my stomach that I had indeed eaten it. Miss Zapletalová, unable to make sense of my mother's gibberish, with hunched back and a disapproving shrug of her shoulders, ultimately turned away from our door and quietly made her way back to her cramped room at the foot of the stairway.

In this room filled with family treasures Miss Zapletalová spent her days in the exclusive company of her two devoted, fat little dogs, to whom she talked throughout the day. I received her messages of hatred through her body language and the hostile glances she directed at me every time I walked by her. I automatically assumed she was a nasty old maid who hated children. I tried to tiptoe into the building to avoid facing her, though most of the time it was impossible to enter without being noticed. She usually stood in the entrance with her hands threateningly placed on her hips following me closely with her cold, beady eyes.

My mother skillfully ignored Miss Zapletalová's hostile glances with the flair of someone experienced in handling the "class enemy." One cloudy morning I watched out of our kitchen window as a tearful Miss Zapletalová buried one of her two beloved dogs. She had already lost her brother, who lived in the West (as I was informed years later), the family house, which had been taken over by the communists, her middle-class social status, and now even her loyal dog was no longer alive. She was left with the distasteful reality of having to live under this new socialist regime that made her angry and bitter. And to make matters even worse, she had to endure a communist American family residing as Czechs in the upstairs rooms of her former home without her consent.

In the hallway of our building there was a large, old-fashioned mangle for pressing sheets and tablecloths with an enormous metal handle. I had never seen anything like it in a modern home. It looked like a medieval torture device. The laundry room was on the ground floor, where clothes were washed in a huge vat in water heated with red-hot coals. The clothes were scrubbed on a washboard and then carried, wet and heavy, to the attic three flights up to be hung on clotheslines. In the winter I loved to go up to the unheated attic to hide behind the stiffly frozen sheets and shirts, imagining creatures thawing and coming to life.

The cellar was divided into partitions large enough to store an entire winter's supply of potatoes and coal. Every fall my mother had to order enough potatoes to feed our family because in the winter potatoes were unavailable in the stores. Amazed, I watched the husky men deliver enormous sacks of heavy potatoes just for our family. I tried to calculate how many potatoes I would eat in one year. If it is possible for a family of four to consume such huge quantities of potatoes in one winter, how many potatoes did the entire city of Prague need? The figure was beyond my mathematical skills. By spring, the potatoes grew big white eyes, and their bodies shriveled as they lost both youth and flavor. By March our monotonous dinners made me long for the arrival of the spring harvest.

In the entranceway to our apartment there was an elegant, rose-colored marble mantelpiece. Large glass doors led to the living room, off of which there was one bedroom for my parents and one for my sister and me. The kitchen at the end of the hall had two stoves: a gas stove and a coal stove with an oven large enough to roast a suckling pig and a large cast-iron cooking surface. My mother had her share of culinary disasters before she tamed the coal stove, which she grew to love and use masterfully.

During long winter nights, when the electrical power went out, a frequent event in the 1950s, our family huddled by candlelight at the kitchen table. I did my homework, deciphering black print on the page which moved in and out of focus according to the whim of the candle flame as it created playful shadows on the page. The heat from the coal stove warmed the kitchen but left the rest of the house freezing. I never minded the electrical blackouts: it was cozy hovering around the warm kitchen table with the rest of my family. My mother regularly heated large pots of water on the coal stove for our sponge baths. The supply of hot water was cut off for days and then reappeared without warning or explanation.

In place of refrigeration or cabinet shelves, there was a walk-in pantry for groceries as well as our annual supply of canned fruits and vegetables. Next to the pantry there was a tiny closet-sized room large enough for a bed for a servant or cook. We used this space for storage. A stately black grand piano none of us could play stood under the large living room picture window from which you could see sturdy houses and patch gardens across the street. The bedroom I shared with my sister had gaudy white furniture. The intricate patterns carved into the wood were highlighted with a golden finish that accentuated the curves in the designs. The furniture was quite the opposite of my parents' simple, modern taste. The furniture had short, bulging legs, just like the legs of Miss Zapletalová's aging dogs. At night when I looked around the dark room, I could see moonbeams touch the golden curves of the furniture, creating a glow that illuminated the shapes and contours floating through the room. These objects were a reminder of the lives of the former inhabitants who left these rooms in too much haste to take their personal possessions. Especially at night, I felt the invisible presence of our predecessors in the indentations of the stuffed chairs on which we sat and in their pictures that still hung on the walls. I did not know who was sleeping in the bed that used to be mine and who got my toys and books that remained in New York, as I did not know why I had to be the one to sleep in this bed now.

When my parents decided I was old enough to be trusted with confidential information, they told me the villa in which we now lived had been owned by a Czech pilot who had been trained by the British Royal Air Force. He had lived in this house on Nad Rokoskou Street until the communist takeover. [*The communists, who gained power after 1948, mistrusted foreign-trained military personnel. The RAF-trained Czech pilots who remained in their native land did so at the risk of being politically persecuted. A brief notice in the October 5, 1950, New York Times records the defections of Czech pilots trained in Britain:*

London: 8 Czechs Escape in Plane
3 former R.A.F. Pilots in group that landed in Britain.
8 Czechs who fled Prague in a stolen plane landed in Britain on Saturday. The story of their escape was told tonight by the spokesman for the party, which is now staying in the Free Czech National House in London.
*   The plane, a Dakota of Czech airlines, was piloted by Capt. Jan Kaucký . . . a wartime R.A.F. pilot. After taking off from Prague on*

Living on Nad Rokoskou . . . 69

a test flight without the customary police escort he flew to a rendez-
vous with the 7 others. Ninety seconds after landing in a field he
took off with the group. After a 10 min. flight over Russian territory
he headed for Frankfort and hence to England.]

These pilots defected just a few months before our arrival in Prague. It is not improbable that our Rokoska villa belonged to one of the three pilots who escaped in October 1950 or some other pilots who fled the country illegally at about that time. Our family replaced one of these families that fled from the communists for a better life in the West. These defections, which our neighbors had to know about, helped explain why our presence in the Kobylisy house evoked such hostile reactions. For these people, whose property was confiscated by the communist government, we were indeed the enemy who profited from their loses. We represented everything they hated. In Czechoslovakia in the 1950s personal relationships were never perceived outside of the political realities that controlled lives, not unlike my parents' friendships, which were inseparably connected to their political beliefs. The irony was that there were many in this communist state who neither loved nor wanted communists like my parents in their community.

I gradually discovered that my friends would say things in private that they would deny at school or never mention once the teacher entered the classroom. For instance, Nataša, the daughter of a doctor who had to give up his private practice, openly scorned the communist slogans we had to repeat at school, but in the classroom she repeated them with a rigid, stony look on her face, along with the rest of the class. She never joined the pioneer organization, which, in those years, was a daring gesture of defiance. In school there was strong pressure to become a pioneer. Being a pioneer was the first step in becoming a communist youth. These political organizations were the training ground for the future supporters and builders of the communist state. Most families felt their children had to join the pioneer organization to secure their personal futures and careers in the new society. Who in our class was a pioneer out of conviction and who out of expediency? Each family had to decide how much it was willing to sacrifice to establish its public relationship to the state and at the same time preserve its principles and self-respect. Some were indeed convinced communists, and others mouthed communist doctrine because it was advantageous to do so. A few dissented. Considering the family I came from, I went along enthusiastically and could not wait to become a pioneer.

From the very beginning I was seduced by the charm and power of Prague. In Czech *Praha* is a feminine noun, and I always thought of her as a beautiful mother. The more I explored, the more I loved her. Centrally located in the heart of Europe, Prague was linked with the history and culture of other European nations. The architecture of Prague's ancient buildings kept alive the memory of past kingdoms. The modern skyscrapers and wide avenues I associated with New York bore no resemblance to these narrow, winding streets. New York had a short history and people of many nationalities; Prague had centuries-old traditions and a homogeneous people with a strong national identity. In Manhattan I had encountered diversity. I heard different languages and tasted unusual foods such as kumquats, halva, goat's cheese, and mangoes. In Prague, aside from the dark-skinned Gypsies, who spoke their own language and who kept to themselves, everyone spoke Czech. As far as I could tell, only native foods were available, chiefly dumplings, meat and gravy, and soups. When I had these foods in my friends' homes, they were always prepared the same way.

Prague's history was preserved in the castles, statues, bridges, churches, and pubs that created the unique magic of this city. Hradčany, the famous castle site that dominates the Prague skyline, was the residence of Czech rulers since 973. The section of the old city, Malá Strana (Little Town), was founded in 1257. Every building, every square had a story to tell. Plaques informed me that Beethoven stayed in this tavern or that Mozart composed *Don Giovanni* at Bertramka, a short distance from the center of the city. Statues and signs with commemorative wreaths preserved the names of those who had been shot on this very street corner or by this particular building while defending the country during World War II. Bullet holes were visible on the walls of buildings, and repairs of destroyed structures were still in progress. In this city the past lived on, but the interpretation of past events differed from government to government.

During the 1950s, statues of Stalin and other communist heroes such as Pavlík Morozov were being constructed throughout the city. These were the symbols that established the new mythology. Stalin's gigantic statue, the largest in the Eastern bloc, dominated the ancient skyline of

Prague. It consisted of a giant stone figure with his right hand tucked into his jacket and of lesser stone figures representing soldiers, workers, and farmers. The statue embodied the concept of the collective—one for all and all for one—the motto we were instructed to live by. Today all that remains of Stalin's statue is the stone foundation, which is used to store apples and potatoes. When I traveled on the tram, I watched old ladies cross themselves quickly when they passed old churches, but when we passed Stalin's overbearing statue on Letenská Pláň, most of them averted their eyes.

The battle between Prague's past and present was reflected in the naming and renaming of its streets and squares. Old people often refused to use the new street names, thereby passively rejecting the political changes. The battle of the names was a subtle battle of wills. When I asked directions, I was often told to go to Victory Square, now named the Square of the October Revolution. The former Masaryk Train Station was now Prague Central, and Wilson Station was reduced to the Main Train Station. The former Belcredy Square was now the Defenders of Peace Square, and so it went throughout the city. The past, which the communists wanted to abolish when it suited them or to reinvent if they had to, lived on, however, in people's memories. Fortunately, I loved the streets of Prague so much that I did not mind getting lost or going in circles looking for what no longer existed under the former name.

Downtown buildings were decorated with oversized signs carrying slogans such as THE SOVIET UNION FOR ETERNITY or THE PROLETARIANS OF THE WORLD UNITE. Likewise, ideological messages covered the city billboards pronouncing that KARL MARX AND FRIEDRICH ENGELS ARE THE LIVING TEACHERS OF COMMUNISM, or OUR DEAREST COMRADE LENIN IS NOT DEAD, HE LIVES FOREVER IN OUR HEARTS! The billboards did not advertise products or material goods; they promoted socialist ideals. Striving for material gains was denounced as bourgeois thinking, and in its place we were taught to adopt the Marxist ideals of equality and the unity of the working class. Yet during those days of repression and scarcity, finding an unexpected piece of sausage, a roll of toilet paper, or a bar of soap or sharing a political joke with a trusted friend brought a brief but cherished moment of happiness. The suppression of human initiative in the public arena and the crushing of any expression of individuality were counteracted by coded language and secret personal deals. The ideological slogans that covered the walls of Prague and advertised the Communist Party's philosophy did not eliminate opposition or doubts and the need to question. Human ingenuity survived, finding an outlet in a politically risqué joke or in negotiating a clever, perhaps even shady arrangement outside the bureaucratic structure. That was how things got fixed or products purchased that one could not get on the open market.

One joke that circulated around town in the 1950s went something like this. Soviet dignitaries were promised a spectacular feast. They were to be served delicate elephant ears with chopped onions. In time for the dinner preparations a truck arrived delivering the elephant, but the feast was a flop. Why? There were no onions available in Prague to prepare the dish. My mother always said that if you wanted to get something done in Prague and the initial response was "No," it was preferable to being told "Yes." If you were told flatly "No," at least you had something to work with. You could pay somebody off and probably get what you wanted done. But if they said "Yes" right off and then did nothing, there was no maneuverability within which to change things.

The Czechs had always taken pride in maintaining their national identity through clever reasoning rather than force. Three and a half centuries of Austro-Hungarian domination had taught the Czech people patience and shrewdness in resisting the attempts to Germanize them. The Czech language and national spirit survived Austro-Hungarian rule just as the good soldier Švejk in Jaroslav Hašek's classic novel survived his military experiences in the Austrian army by cleverly feigning stupidity. In times of crisis the Czechs reverted to Švejk's tactics, pretending not to comprehend what was asked of them. In this way they protected themselves until the danger passed. In 1968, when Russian tanks rolled into Czechoslovakia, the villagers, instead of resisting with guns, which would have led to a pointless bloodbath, ripped out or reversed road signs to confuse the Russians heading toward Prague. This Czech form of resistance based on strategy rather than force taught me a valuable lesson: a big nation has power, a small nation must have wit.

Unlike the ruling Communist Party, the Czech people had a remarkably humorous outlook on the absurdities and contradictions of life. The Czechs knew that man was not capable of living in paradise. Miloš Forman in his 1994 memoir, *Turnaround*, tells the following old Czech joke: "A husband comes home unexpectedly. The wife barely manages to hide her lover in her bedroom closet. For two hours, the lover sits there among the best perfumes, the most exquisite fragrances, the rose oils and orchid scents and passion musks, the jasmine soaps and baby powders and the talcs and ointments. The wife finally manages to shoo the husband out of the house again, and the lover rushes out of the closet screaming, 'Quick! Get me a piece of shit!' "

When I started to attend elementary school in 1951, I was surprised that classes were also held on Saturdays. In America Saturday and Sunday were family days, but here only Sunday belonged to the family. It puzzled me at first why some children left school on Saturday by lunchtime. Was I expected to stay or leave? I waited to see what was going to happen. The remaining children gathered in one of the classrooms and instead of a teacher, a soft-spoken, mild-mannered habited nun distributed pictures of saints. She wanted the children to color them in. She talked about the lives of the saints and the angels depicted on the pictures and their religious meaning. The children repeated the prayers the nun recited. I watched in silence.

How would my parents react to the colored angels I was to bring home that day? In our nonreligious home, there were no angels or saints; instead, the religion in our home was the Marxist party line. Marxist theoreticians and the political leaders who were carrying out the social changes my parents fervently believed in were their chosen saints. I was exposed to a dialectical Marxist interpretation of human nature rather than the mystical-spiritual one the nun was talking about in class. Instead of heavenly angels and the struggle between good and evil in the hearts of earthly creatures, my parents talked about class struggle and the need to rid the world of class oppression. Their earthly saints were Marx, Engels, Lenin, and Stalin.

When the nun recessed the class, she asked me to write down on a piece of paper what my religious background was. I did not know if I should put down American, Jewish, or nothing at all. Finally I decided to write *židovka* — Jewish. I placed the folded paper on her desk. Before I got back to my desk, I heard giggles coming from the front of the class. A group of children had peeked at the paper while the nun was out of the room. Feeling their stares directed at me, I turned around. I wondered if I had written the wrong answer. When the nun returned, she quieted the children. Slowly she unfolded the paper I had left on her desk. She smiled at me. In a very soft voice she said, "I don't think you need to stay in this class, go and use your Saturday afternoons for play."

A year or so later, when the government forbade the teaching of religion in or out of school, all the other children also gained their Saturday afternoons for play. No saints or angels could help change that reality. The communists dismissed religion as another poisonous invention of the former ruling classes. From now on, paradise was to be found here on earth, and instead of religious instruction we had civics classes in which we were taught the communist values that we were to live and think by.

My favorite teacher in elementary school was a short, stout, soft-spoken woman, Marie Kotková. Her face was compassionate and wise. She could command obedience with a mere glance; she dealt with unacceptable behavior with a gentle word and a disarming squeeze of the hand. In 1953, when I was in fifth grade, her father, to whom she was devoted, died. Our entire class went to his funeral, which was held in an austere crematorium. The closed casket, surrounded by flowers, rested before heavy metal doors on a podium along with a lectern and microphone. The ceremony started with eulogies. For his family and friends this man's death was a great loss; for me it was the first awareness of life's finality. So many people were fond of him and admired the life he had lived that I wished I had known him. His middle-aged daughter, our teacher, sat in the front row with tears streaming down her cheeks as the words of her father's friends and colleagues warmed the cold room.

After the speeches ended, the ornate metal doors opened and the casket slowly moved into the darkness on metal tracks. For a loyal communist, as this man was, there were no religious ceremonies. There was only the finality of life marked simply by the respect of friends and the love of family. The heavy metal doors closed, making a screeching sound. Everybody sat in silent contemplation. While her father's favorite music was played, I imagined the burning flames that were consuming the casket, turning his body to ashes. For days after the funeral, the image of those heavy metal doors opening to claim the casket bothered me. I knew the body was not going to return, but I had no framework, religious or otherwise, to deal with the thought that this creative man's life had been reduced to ashes. Death was frightening when it was just a dark void. Life had a shape, a taste, a feel, a meaning, while death was just the silent darkness on the other side of those metal doors. Life, unlike death, was something concrete; death meant nothingness; it implied a movement from light to darkness, from action to inaction. A secular burial such as this did nothing to lessen my confusion, my fear of the unknown.

I knew no prayers or words to help me overcome the anxieties that took hold of me. I had to look for answers elsewhere. The communist ideology that we learned in school told us that the solution to man's unanswered questions was in the ability to sacrifice for the future, for creating the perfect socialist man and society. This was our model, and it made the truth seem simple and within reach. Living on Nad Rokoskou Street and learning more about the personal histories of my neighbors, however, provided my first awareness that the myths of socialism that I was taught in school and at pioneer meetings were far from reality and that life was not so simple or easily explained.

In the early 1950s my parents went through a difficult period getting employment and learning how to manage in their new setting. My mother used her English editorial skills to help support the family. Rudolph Slánský, the minister of foreign affairs, promised my father a job suitable to his American communist background and experience. Unexpectedly, though, Slánský was arrested in November 1951 and became the central victim in the famous 1952 political show trial. The Slánský trials were set up to distract the public from communist mismanagement of the economy, visible to everyone, and to establish even greater control over the country's inner life. International communism used the trial (and similar ones in other satellite countries) as a propaganda spectacle to mask Stalin's move to consolidate control over Eastern Europe. Insecurity and fear became even more pervasive throughout Czechoslovakia as the force of absolute power was felt in the Slánský proceedings.

The atmosphere was charged with uncertainty as some of the party officials (most of them Jewish) who had been arrested with Slánský pleaded guilty to crimes they had not committed. On November 20, 1952, the front-page headlines in the Czech communist press announced "THE TRIAL FOR THE ANTI-STATE CONSPIRACY OF RUDOLF SLÁNSKÝ." On November 21, 1952, a *New York Times* headline read, "4 PURGED CZECH REDS GO ON TRIAL; SLÁNSKÝ PLEADS GUILTY

TO TREASON." The *New York Times* reported that the doors of Bratislava houses and apartments occupied by Jews bore chalked inscriptions reading, "Down with capitalist Jews!," "Jews live here!," or simply "Jew."

There were reports of suicides among Jews in Czechoslovakia as the highly publicized Slánský treason trial neared its end. A Jewish housekeeper at the Israeli legation killed herself after being questioned by Czech police. Several high Jewish officials also committed suicide. Who would be next? Who could be trusted? Who would survive to tell the truth? Yesterday these men held high political offices; today they were traitors whose lives were endangered.

Prague was not a chosen place of exile for my parents; the choices that controlled their lives were governed by the international communist movement and its directing forces in Moscow. The Slánský trial meant that my parents exchanged the tensions of the McCarthy witchhunts for the anxieties of the political trials staged by the Czech Communist Party. As a result of the political purge of the foreign minister, Slánský, my father had no permanent employment for several years and perhaps even narrowly escaped the loss of his own personal freedom. He earned a living writing articles for the communist press. We managed with his honorariums and Belle's editorial jobs. By the mid-1950s, after Stalin's death and a slight liberalization in Czechoslovakia, Abe received a position at the Czech Academy of Sciences, lecturing and writing about American literature.

Some of the wives and children of the victims of the Slánský trials were frequent visitors in our home. The wives of these prisoners were forbidden to hold jobs as punishment for the alleged deeds of their husbands. Those who were bilingual survived by translating under friends' names. I knew from snippets of conversations that serious and terrible things were happening to them. My parents did not discuss these political problems with me directly, but I came to realize that their relations with the shunned wives of the men executed at the Slánský trials were dangerous to their personal safety. This might well be one of the first instances when human compassion was in conflict with their unquestioning loyalty to the party.

[*In later years the falseness of the charges against Slánský and the thirteen others tried (eleven were sentenced to death in 1952) proved an embarrassment to the party leadership. In 1963, the year we left Prague,*

Slánský was posthumously absolved of all criminal charges of treason and espionage. His party membership was restored in 1968, but it was too late to undo the damage that led to eleven executions.]

I was too busy with my own adjustments, however, to pay much attention to the Slánský trial. I had enough mysteries right in my own bedroom to preoccupy me. One day when we were rearranging our bedroom, my sister and I accidentally discovered a secret vault. Directly above my sister's bed there was a opening in the wall that was hidden by a framed painting. Under the painting we could see the faint outline of a square door that had been painted over. We used hairpins and keys to enlarge the cracks between the wall and the carved square door until we could open it to see the thick metal walls of a safe. We could see the intricate mechanism of the lock, but we could not open it without knowing the combination or having the necessary tools.

Night after night, fascinated by our discovery, we invented stories about this mysterious safe. We fantasized about the presence of enormous sums of money, beautiful jewels, documents, and maps leading to forbidden territories and, above all, a clue to the lives of those who had abandoned all this for a life elsewhere. We dreamed about what we would do if we had the money that might be in the safe. Repeatedly we failed to hit the combination that would open the safe. Not knowing the contents of the vault fueled our resourcefulness. What we could not see, we could imagine. Over the years our fantasies grew in magnitude and complexity. Many years later, when we were absent from the apartment, the Czech authorities opened the safe, and they discovered enough money (which they confiscated) to buy several houses and cars. And to think that all these years my sister slept with her head against this gigantic pile of money!

I remember well the day in 1953 when people were in the streets throwing handfuls of money into the air. I was shocked. I immediately ran home yelling from the doorway, "You will not believe what is happening outside, money is flying in the air, filling the garbage cans, and nobody is picking it up!" My mother explained that a monetary reform had just devalued the previous currency. The money we bought bread with yesterday was today toy money. The recent political and economic changes would have made the money stashed away in our bedroom no more valuable than play money in a Monopoly game.

Destinies were changed and lives were so altered by communism that those who owned nothing suddenly had something to gain from the new system, while those who owned property or had businesses lost everything unless they got out of the country with some of their assets. Now the former privileged class was at a disadvantage. It was eminently clear from Miss Zapletalová's behavior toward us that we were unwanted intruders placed here by powerful political forces she detested. If I had understood this political conflict better when I was a child living at Nad Rokoskou, the cold and hateful Miss Zapletalová would not have been the resident witch in my imaginary games. Instead, during those years I was haunted by the mean, ever-present, angry Miss Zapletalová who guarded the house filled with her brother's possessions. These possessions she held on to were her only evidence of an existence her family once led. Guarding the villa from enemies like us was her only hope that her brother might return someday. Our presence was proof of the new and loathsome life she now had to live. She would not talk or explain herself; she just stared at us with hard, cold, unforgiving eyes, a daily reminder of her resistance to the social and political changes she hoped would someday be reversed.

Chapter 9

. . . .

Kobylisy,

My New

Neighborhood

Even my drama is coming to an end.
I haven't written the ending for it.
I don't know what it will be.
That is no longer part of the drama.
That is life. And life has no spectators.
The curtain is lifting.
People, I loved you. Be vigilant!
—Julius Fučík, *Notes from the Gallows*, June 9,
1943, written in the Gestapo prison at Pankrác

Our neighborhood was full of wonders:
hidden narrow streets behind cobblestone staircases, houses camou-
flaged by shrubbery, giant chestnut trees in bloom, groomed gardens
glimpsed through the wooden slats of a gate. Each season held new
surprises. Once I discovered the best spots for hide and seek and knew
the rhymes for street games such as THE BLOODY KNEE IS COMING, I
became part of the "gang." I practiced bicycle riding in the school playground under the supervision of my classmates; I slid down the snow-
packed hill behind our house smashing our next door neighbor's sled
by hitting a tree, and I climbed fruit trees helping myself to the apples
and pears. We adjusted our street games to an unexpected snowfall, the
appearance of the first juicy cherries, or a new crop of chestnuts. I was
once again a tomboy on the hilly street called Nad Rokoskou.

Faces and distinct body movements of neighborhood regulars were
now part of the scenery, not just strangers I studied from a distance. On
the other side of the street, eight houses down from our villa, lived a
family of three: a thin, blind father who always wore dark glasses, his
emaciated wife, who led him by the arm on their daily walks, and their
self-effacing, kind daughter Mařenka. Across the street in the house
above ours lived the Marek family whose daughter Naďa (one of five
children) taught me how to climb trees which the two of us used as
our neighborhood watch towers. Eva's family situation was different;
her mother was separated and she had a lover living with her, while her
first husband still lived in the same building because the wait for new
housing arrangements took years. Eva's descriptions of the arguments in
her household were our soap opera series with characters whose faces

we recognized. We did not miss growing up without television. We had enough drama right in our neighborhood. On my way to school I met up with Blanka, who lived halfway down my street and whose anorexic body and sunken, pale cheeks reminded me of the tubercular heroines of novels I read; any day I expected her to be taken to a sanitorium in the Tatra Mountains.

In my neighborhood each street, home, and family whose history I got to know provided a missing link to my deepening understanding of the recent past. Memories people shared with me changed my outlook on those early years after my arrival that were a drastic political transition from one social structure to another. Through my friends and the family history they were a part of, my initial impressions were replaced by a deeper understanding of how complex the communist changes had been for each individual. When I visited my friends I saw photographs of family events and books with writings (Franz Kafka, Karel Poláček, Karel Čapek, for example) that were now censored, denied, repressed, or destroyed. Despite the state's efforts to obliterate both the reality and the memory of a bourgeois class structure, a photograph of a grandfather's days in the now banned Sokol (an athletic patriotic middle-class organization) was preserved in the family album alongside the baby picture of mother's baptism. Today children had to join the pioneers, and church celebrations were replaced by civic ceremonies. And then there were the secrets, like the safe in our bedroom, the family past Miss Zapletalová would not discuss, and the impenetrable silence of people like Tonička.

Belle hired Tonička for heavy cleaning jobs she could not manage on her own. Tonička washed the windows and floors, and she did the laundry in the basement washroom. She was a large-boned, big-hipped woman who moved with slow, deliberate grace. She scrubbed the kitchen floor on her knees, pressing hard on the rough brushes and leaving a trail of soap bubbles flying through the air. She scrubbed the heavy wet sheets on the washboard until the skin on her fingers shriveled. She carried full baskets of wet clothes up to the attic with the perseverance and strength of a mountain climber. At lunchtime, she slowly and meticulously sucked every shred of meat off the bones of a smoked mackerel, her favorite. Her big eyes were fixed on a far-off point on the kitchen wall while she ate.

It was her silence that made the deepest impression on me. Tonička hardly ever talked; I cannot even remember her voice. She was in her mid-fifties. I knew that she had lived through difficult years, but I never knew what she thought about those experiences. She had spent her entire life cleaning houses, many of whose owners had left after communism. I wish I had talked with her about what she had lived through, and I wish she had asked me some questions. Instead, she battled the clumps of dust and splashed soap suds around in the laundry room maintaining her silence. I watched Tonička maneuver her big, wrinkled hands, and I followed her blank eyes, but I never found out what she thought about our presence in this house or the disappearance of the original owners, whom she must have known much longer and better than she did us.

It was not easy to know which children wanted to be friends with me because they liked me or thought I was a rare curiosity, even a potentially useful contact. One of my classmates was Nataša, the prim and proper blond who wore austere, metal-framed glasses and whose square face was dominated by a jutting jaw. Nataša was always better dressed, better prepared for class, and indeed better than most of her classmates, whom she regarded with a disdainful gaze. Even her posture was as straight as a ruler. Nataša, the star student, intimidating in her aloofness, was one of the few in our class who refused to become a pioneer because her parents forbade her to join.

Her family lived down the hill from us. They had been accustomed to a life of comfort from the days when her father enjoyed a thriving private medical practice. He still held a respectable status in the community, a vestige from the old days. But now, like everyone else, he had to work for the state at a clinic. The mention of his name usually brought knowing looks. In the neighborhood they still referred to him as *Pan doctor* (Mr. doctor). The address *Pan* (Mr.) was discouraged in public in favor of the politically approved adult address *soudruh* (comrade). In private conversations, however, the term *Pan* (Mr.) was still used. I always used *soudruh*, as I was expected to and believed I should. The status symbols of the past, however, still had a powerful hold on people's thinking. No magic wand, not even a firmly controlled communist society, could change ingrained thinking or force people not to acknowledge social distinctions that were still within living memory.

When Nataša's family discovered that there was a child in their daughter's class who had arrived from America with a Czech name, they included me on the exclusive list of guests for her birthday party. Nataša was going to be eleven years old. There was a lot of talk on the playground about who was invited and who was not. To be among the invited was an honor I did not fully appreciate. The summer birthday party was held in a large fenced-in garden invisible from the street. Nataša's father skillfully questioned me about my background, and I proudly informed him that my parents were loyal communists and builders of socialism. He immediately lost interest in me. Those credentials did not make me a welcomed guest in their home. After I had been permanently scratched from the list of suitable associates for their daughter, Nataša avoided me.

A bouncy, bushy-haired girl with a devilish twinkle in her eyes, Saša, named by her parents after a heroine in a Russian novel, became my closest friend. She first gained my trust and affection on a wintry day when she offered me three *medvědí tlapičky*, which she brought to school especially for me. These were special Christmas cookies in the shape of a bear's paw, after which they are named, a delicious combination of butter, flour, crushed nuts, and spices. The cookies were not supposed to be eaten until Christmas Eve as a way of heightening the holiday excitement, but Saša sneaked into her mother's hidden supply to bring some of them to me. Those cookies helped seal a long-lasting friendship between us. Saša was fun, a daring and a passionate spirit.

Now I had a fearless companion to venture into the streets with in search of excitement and action. I loved the walnut- and chestnut-lined streets by the Vltava (Moldau) River as it twisted its way up to the lower end of our neighborhood from downtown Prague. There we collected fallen chestnuts out of which we made little animal figurines, and we snacked on fresh walnuts extracted from prickly green shells that left dark stains on our hands. As a ten-year-old, I was forbidden to wander as far as the river Vltava, but with Saša by my side the temptation to play along the bank of the river was irresistible.

On a cold January day, the two of us went gliding along the icy edge of the river. Unexpectedly, the ice gave way under our feet and we were dragged into icy water mixed with sewage. The weight of our wet winter clothes pulled us down. Frantically moving our arms and legs, we sank further into the freezing, filthy water. We shouted for help, trying to get the attention of the people on the distant bridge to whom we were no larger than floating ducks. We paddled our feet and rotated our arms wildly until we were lucky enough to pull ourselves out of the water. A stranger who lived near the river found us filthy, wet, shivering, and scared. She took us into her home, where she wrapped us in blankets, scolded us, made us hot tea, and called our mothers.

Despite Belle's scoldings, I continued to defy her restrictions on my wanderings, assuming that her inability to speak Czech would generally act in my favor. I continued to return home in filthy clothes from my neighborhood prowls, bursting with stories about my most recent adventure. I became an expert scavenger for treasures in the hidden nooks around our house. I knew the maze of back secret passageways to the playground and my friends' homes that got me there in a matter of minutes. Saša taught me about the flowers and wild berries that grew in the neighborhood gardens. My finds were strange surprises for Belle. Some days I brought home sweet-smelling white lavender flowers, *levandule*, that had to be dried before they could be used to give the laundry a perfumed scent; other days I brought back firm red rose hips *šípky* and *lípový květ* for tea or even a dislodged cobblestone from the sidewalk.

Saša's working-class parents were long-standing communists who enthusiastically welcomed the new government. Saša and her lively mother, who was an avid reader, introduced me to Soviet novels. I read quickly so I could keep up with her. We had heated discussions about novels, life in general, and the difference between boys and girls. I loved going to their simple home, where I sampled ordinary Czech food and listened to stories about life "in the olden days." Saša's parents believed it was wonderful the communists had gained power. According to Saša's mother, the past was terrible, the present was good, but the future was going to be glorious. They were a hardworking family, happy to include me in their intimate circle in the cozy kitchen where we most frequently gathered.

On Saturday afternoons Saša and I would curl up on the kitchen couch to listen to radio broadcasts of dramatized readings from Soviet fiction or Czech socialist realist novels. We snacked on home-baked goodies, nodding our heads to the rhythm of the actor's voice. Radio was our link to the outside world. We heard the same messages daily, whether in school, on the radio, or in the newspapers: Love our brother, the Soviet Union, for together we will march toward a glorious future once we shed the remnants of the bourgeois past. The following poem is typical of what we recited in elementary school or heard on the radio broadcasts for youngsters:

Greetings to you, beloved Comrade Stalin!
You and Lenin have thrown open to us
Boundless sunny expanses,
And filled us with hope and joy . . .
Following in the footsteps of Lenin,
And learning our lessons from your works,
We have built a mighty power
That makes us rejoice, and puts fear into
Our enemies' hearts.

Lenin was not only a hero in Saša's home but in mine as well. Both families, one Czech and one American, arrived at their shared beliefs from completely different backgrounds. I took this irony for granted when I spent time with Saša's family.

Sometimes on my way home from school I would stop at Vlasta's home. She was usually there by herself because both her parents worked. The two of us shared childhood secrets and planned our futures together. Vlasta lived in an apartment in an old building that had windows facing an indoor courtyard where women gathered to hang clothes, bang the dust out of carpets with a *rákoska* (a special carpet beater), and catch up on the latest neighborhood gossip. Vlasta's apartment was filled wall to wall with furniture. It was more like a warehouse than a home. There were bureaus on top of tables for lack of floor space, and carpets were in a heap on top of the closet because there was no room for them on the cluttered floors. Beds were squeezed in between bookcases, stacked chairs, and ornate, dark end tables. I could not understand why anybody would want to live like this. Vlasta explained that they used to have a much larger home, but after 1948 they were moved into these tight quarters. The family salvaged as much as they could of their possessions, piling them into this tiny apartment. They continued to hope that they would return to their former home someday. Meanwhile, they lived maneuvering between the bulky pieces of furniture.

After school I had to go to the *Družba* (Russian for "friendship"), an after-school day care center for children of working parents. I attended the *Družba* when I was in the fifth grade at the *Základní škola* (elementary school) at the bottom of Nad Rokoskou Street. It was housed in a confiscated home (everybody in the neighborhood called it by the name of its original owners, the Neumann house) in a serene country setting. Here at the *Družba* I tasted my first Czech food and spent my afternoons playing, doing my homework, and improving my conversational Czech. There was no way I could fall back on English here. It was at the *Družba* that I came to love my new Czech name.

My friends never called me "Anna," which is rather formal in Czech. Instead, they introduced me to the rich variety of Czech diminutives for "Anna." The diminutive used varied from speaker to speaker, depending on the degree of intimacy in the relationship. I loved the endless possibilities of my Czech name. Most of the time I would be called Anička, Andulka, Andulička, Anča, or Anka, depending on the speaker's mood or feelings toward me. These nuances opened up new and thrilling possibilities for tailoring one's words to reflect the emotions one felt. Czech was marvelous in this respect. It had a playful range of choices that made Ann, the name my family used at home, sound dull and ordinary. I did not become Anna until I was closer to adulthood. Most names had diminutive, endearing versions which were a means of separating the childhood years from the adult ones and formal relationships from intimate ones. I grew to love this expressive quality of the Czech language.

It was in Prague that I fell in love with bread. Our food supplies were constricted by the severe shortages, which made dinner planning simple: you prepared dinner from what you could get and what you could get was always unpredictable. The scarce food supplies made shopping a nightmare for my mother. Belle's high standards for feeding the family a nutritious, well-balanced diet (one of those American habits Czechs could never understand), combined with the lack of refrigeration, forced her to spend frustrating hours searching for ingredients or sending my sister and me on extensive search missions. We ate whatever she made. There was, however, never a shortage of delicious bread and crusty rolls that we got fresh from the neighborhood bakery. Breakfast and after-school snacks were always thick slabs of *vejražka*, rye bread with butter (if available) or jam. Bread was my main food and fortunately the one I loved the most. On my way home from daily trips to the bakery I could not resist the enticing aroma of the fresh bread in my net shopping bag. I never brought home a perfect loaf, for once I started to take little and then larger nibbles from its heel it was hard to stop. My parents could not convince me to wait till I got home to slice the bread. In the homes of my friends Saturday mornings were devoted to baking, but not in our home. I loved the yeasty baked goods my friends' mothers made. I begged my mother to learn how to make a sweet yeast bread, and she was willing to try. I got a recipe from a girlfriend's mother and carefully translated it into English, struggling to convert from grams to ounces, which my mother was more accustomed to using. My mother, resolutely tying her apron around her waist, warmed the milk to dissolve the fresh cake of yeast. Fully concentrating on what she was doing, she dropped cigarette ashes on the kitchen table. This project had to work. I could not wait for the flour, milk, eggs, butter, and yeast to turn into bread, spreading a yeasty aroma throughout the house.

Belle poured the liquid mixture into a bowl before she added the flour. My sister and I watched. We waited to see the dough become elastic as the recipe described. By now Belle's hands were buried in the gummy dough that stuck to the sides of the bowl. My sister and I came to her rescue, plunging our hands into the resistant mess. Now there were six hands instead of two pulling at the unmanageable heap of dough. That Saturday morning there was no aroma of home-baked bread in our house. Instead, there was a huge clump of gooey dough on the bottom of the garbage pail. The attempt at bread baking in our home was declared a disaster. I had to rely on my friends' generous handouts.

An encounter with a rusty-maned horse hitched to an old man's scrap cart parked by the curb of our house made it clear that my mother would never behave like a Czech mother. I had never seen a live horse so close before. His head was buried in a canvas food bag filled with hay. When I inched close enough to see what he was eating, he picked his head up and grabbed my shoulder in his mouth, pressing his teeth into my skin.

I ran home in tears. The teeth marks the horse left in my shoulder horrified my mother, who was used to cars and subway trains and not horse-driven carts. She was neither amused nor pleased with my curiosity about horses, and she whisked me onto a tram for an examination at the local hospital. At the hospital she unveiled my shoulder in the middle of the lobby to display the indentations the horse's teeth left there. Screaming in English and gesticulating furiously, she demanded immediate attention. Entertained by this foreign invasion, the hospital staff gathered around us. I only wished the horse had been kind enough to have completely consumed me, sparing me this embarrassment. I knew this was just one of many public encounters during which my mother would attract unwanted attention. I thought it would have been much easier to bear if only she could have done her shouting in Czech. At the hospital I envied the other children and their mothers who waited for their turn without a fuss.

From then on I went shopping, to the neighborhood library, and the local movie house by myself. My parents were indifferent to the reactions of others, but I was not. I was devastated by stares they attracted when they spoke loudly in English. The sounds of English made heads turn when we walked in the streets or traveled on the tram. I did not want to be identified as a foreigner; I wanted to be the unnoticed native riding the tram, handing the conductor the exact change, absorbed in an appropriate Czech book, quietly getting off at the right station. Usually I selected something to read on the tram that was approved reading at school such as Julius Fučík's, *Notes from the Gallows,* the work of a communist journalist who had been executed by the Nazis and had become a national hero. Adult passengers surely had to approve of a young girl who was no different from the other pioneers riding the tram.

My mother, a woman of many remarkable talents, had no natural aptitude for or interest in languages. Both my parents knew a few isolated Czech words, which they invariably mispronounced and abused grammatically. Belle's unwillingness to learn Czech was an expression of resentment over her forced exile in a country she had no connection to. For thirteen years she managed to combat drastic food shortages, get clothes made by a Czech-speaking seamstress (decent ready-to-wear clothing was not readily available), and to keep our house functioning through her energy and wit. She did all this without ever learning how to speak Czech.

When I was about thirteen, I begged my mother to let me teach her Czech. I spent an entire week preparing charts to make her functional in my language, in my world. I wrote out the masculine, feminine, and neuter nouns and their seven declensions in singular and plural, separating the roots from the endings with multicolored pencils. I used all my ingenuity to convince her that the entire meaning of a sentence depends on the grammatical relationships between the words. My mother listened to me carefully. She glanced at the charts covering the table and, overwhelmed by the enormity of the task, concluded that the roots were enough for her. "But Belle," I exclaimed, fearing the situation was hopeless, "nobody will understand what you want to say." She replied, "If they try hard enough they will figure out what I am saying." Discouraged, I gathered my neat, now useless charts. My sister tried to remedy the damage. "Then at least, Belle, promise not to go to any more school conferences. The teachers make fun of us because you can't speak Czech." And so it remained throughout my childhood: my school life was in one language, my home life in another, and the gap between these worlds got deeper and deeper over the years.

My growing love of Czech and my increased skill at using it was a sensitive, even painful barrier between my parents and me. Abe knew the importance of language as well as the Czechs did; both were fiercely in love with their own language and literature. Abe was devastated when he found me reading Theodore Dreiser's *American Tragedy* in Czech translation. When he saw the Czech words on the pages of Dreiser's novel he shook his head in disapproval. His eyes pleaded with me, though he said nothing. "Abe, it is a great novel. It is so powerful in Czech, I love it," I said with a glimmer of hope that I might soften his sadness. Reading in Czech was one thing, but reading English and American literature in Czech was a tragic violation of his culture, which he wanted to share with me. It was a personal betrayal.

My mother's inability to conduct a conversation with the shopkeepers made me the chief shopper. Because we had no refrigeration, I made daily trips for groceries. Besides, it was a fun way to know what was going on in the neighborhood and to get a treat for myself if I had some spare change. I caught up on the local gossip while I stood on long lines waiting for deliveries. There were no self-service stores in Kobylisy. At the little corner grocery store on the top of the hill you had to ask the shopkeeper for the merchandise. On my way to the grocery store I would rehearse what I was told to buy, trying not to forget the quantities my mother wanted: 25 dkg (grams) of cheese, or 50 dkg of butter. I did not want to come home with the wrong purchases or, worst of all, say things incorrectly while the other shoppers listened.

For several years there were no sanitary napkins in the stores. We had to make them at home out of gauze and cotton. By the late 1950s coarse sanitary napkins were on the market that irritated one's thighs. The first time Belle told me to purchase sanitary napkins I had to use the new word, *vložky* (inserts) when it was my turn to ask for groceries.

I froze, mortified that I had to say something so private in such a public way. I panicked. I could not remember the word I had repeated so many times as I walked to the store. I ran out of the store in tears and came home empty-handed.

As soon as I could read well enough in Czech I became a weekly visitor at the small one-room Kobylisy library. I read with a passion. My library card entitled me to two books at a time. I did a pretty good job of reading my way through the books on the shelves, looking for my favorite ones that brought me into the daily lives of people. The library was filled with Soviet and Czech socialist realist novels, Czech classics, and carefully screened selections of contemporary literature. I did not know how many books were not on those shelves. I was content to read what was there. Once I started a novel, I never wanted it to end. The fictional characters became friends who stayed with me for a long time. Novels that moved through the generations pleased me the most, for they had a completeness that life lacked. When I finished an epic-length novel, I mourned the loss of my companions for several days. The immediate cure for my grief was to start reading a new novel, the fattest one I could find on the shelf. Through literature I entered the dreams of young men and women who joined the struggle to build a communist Soviet Union. I was with them in spirit, impatient to be old enough to accomplish equally heroic deeds.

I read my thick library books in the neighborhood clinic where I spent hours waiting for my turn. Overcrowded clinics and overworked doctors who had no time or motivation to provide individualized care were a direct by-product of socialized medical care. Patients and doctors alike were too taxed by the system to bother with pleasantries. I depended on the clinic for my medical needs. By the time I was twelve, my hands were covered with persistent eczema. The doctor prescribed a series of medications and salves that failed to cure it. Finally, my mother, who believed there must be a solution to just about every problem, decided to go to the doctor with me to deal with the matter in her own way. After a long wait in the company of depressing and predominantly elderly patients, we entered the doctor's office.

The doctor was a rotund, middle-aged man with wire-framed glasses halfway down his nose and a tired, listless face. He looked up indifferently when we entered the room, unprepared for my mother's insistence on getting results. She pointed to the irritated, cracked skin on my hands, shaking her head in disapproval. A strange form of communication began between them. First, Belle started to use her meager supply of Czech words, which did not work, and then she slipped into English while the doctor addressed her in German, which she could decode from her knowledge of Yiddish. She demanded a more effective treatment; the doctor refused to accept any responsibility for my inability to heal.

I could almost feel the eczema spread over my entire body while I silently observed this battle of wills. My mother continued to voice her dissatisfaction with the doctor, demanding the impossible. When the doctor had enough, considering we had overstayed our few allotted minutes, he shouted, "What do you want, a WunderMast?!!" (Wonder salve). "Yes," my mother answered. "That is exactly what I want." I went to the doctor by myself from that point on, but he was never able to cure the eczema that caused me such agony and pain throughout my youth. The eczema was a curse I had to live with. The severity of the outbreaks was usually a barometer of my internal stress. My skin separated my internal world from the external one, but it could not conceal the conflicts raging within.

After I got tired of the familiar back alley streets of Kobylisy, the walk to the playground in front of our school, the local grocery store up the hill, the bakery, drugstore, local library, and neighborhood milk store, where I bought fresh milk early in the morning in a tin milk can *bandaska*, I ventured into nearby neighborhoods. The district that bordered with Kobylisy was called Libeň. The Koráb gymnasium that I would transfer to after elementary school was in Libeň. This opened up a whole new world to me. Libeň was larger than Kobylisy. It had a hospital, a restaurant, and a large movie house. When I took the tram for eight stations down the winding hill from Kobylisy, I got to the small square on which there was the Dukla movie house, a larger selection of stores than I was used to, and a variety of pubs. I bought books at the Libeň bookstore where the books were not on display; you had to ask for what you wanted and everybody heard what you were getting. On Saturday afternoons I went to the Dukla with my friends, not only excited about the upcoming entertainment (mostly Soviet films with Czech subtitles) but also for the chance to see the Gypsies who hung around the movie house alley. The Gypsies fascinated me. They were loud, colorful, and free-spirited, and they kept to themselves.

The Gypsies gathered in large groups, shouting and joking in their native Romany. Their black, unkempt hair and dark complexion immediately distinguished them from the Czechs. The women wore long, colorful skirts and oversized shawls draped over their shoulders. Young women rested their latest baby on their pregnant bellies. The Gypsy men flashed flirtatious glances at the women, who responded with teasing laughter. The Gypsy men and women were much more playful and physical among themselves than the reserved Czechs. Even the high-pitched sounds of their language had a rough sensual quality Czech lacked.

There were no Gypsy children in my classes. I often heard comments from my neighbors about the efforts the government made to move the Gypsies into apartment houses, which, according to the local Czech women, they ruined by peeing on the floors and treating their living quarters like outdoor campsites. The communist government made a conscious effort to reeducate the Gypsies and assimilate them into the Czech culture. In the 1950s there was a popular film we discussed in school about a small Gypsy boy who resisted learning Czech when brought to class, preferring his own Romany language. He continued to come to classes late and to dress sloppily. He was portrayed as a wild animal who bit the Czech teacher when she tried to tame him. By the end of the film, the boy made a miraculous adaptation and allowed the Czechs to civilize him. Although there were no Gypsy children in my school, I did see many of them and their parents (who would not work nine-to-five jobs) roaming the streets of Libeň while we Czechs attended school and were taught how to live by civilized rules.

In my own surroundings I saw the openly proud and defiant Gypsies and the neat, clean Czech kids in the classroom next to me: two entirely separate worlds. What I envied most about the exotic Gypsy girls I secretly admired was their sense of belonging to their own social group. They were not welcome in the Czech culture, but they had no desire to be a part of it. Unlike the Gypsies, I was working very hard to become part of the Czech culture, though deep down I knew I was an outsider. Czechoslovakia had become my home, and the Czech culture was the one and only culture I could belong to. Yet the otherness of my parents' language, their unconventional circle of international friends, their secretive party connections, and my American past had never let me forget that I was not a genuine Czech with roots and a history of my own but merely a temporarily converted one. I realized I had something in common with the Gypsies, the only difference being that I belonged to no group with which I could share my unique cultural predicament.

Chapter 10
· · · · · · · · · · · ·
Koráb

My home, obviously, is also the country
I live in, the language I speak, and the
intellectual and spiritual climate of my
country expressed in the language spoken
there. The Czech language, the Czech
way of perceiving the world, Czech historical experience, the Czech modes of
courage and cowardice, Czech humor—
all of these are inseparable from that
circle of my home. My home is therefore
my Czechness, my nationality, and I see
no reason at all why I shouldn't embrace
it, since it is an essential part of me, for
instance, my masculinity, another part of
my home.

—"On Home," a speech given by Václav Havel,
October 1991

I left the confines of my immediate
neighborhood when I became a sixth-grade student at the Koráb gymnasium in Libeň. My walk to the gymnasium took a good half hour instead of the fifteen minutes to get to my old elementary school. When I
wandered through the long gymnasium hallways that had large wooden
doors leading to classrooms, offices, laboratories, and art rooms, I was
overwhelmed. The change in schools was like a move from a village to
a city. Everything was larger and more complicated. We studied a new
variety of subjects, and we no longer spent the entire school year with
the same home room teacher. I left behind my elementary school teachers, Miss Svobodová and Mrs. Kotková, who witnessed my first attempts
to adapt to the Czech language and way of life. I entered Koráb gymnasium with my identity as Anna Čapková already established. I spoke
and behaved like the other children so that my new teachers, comrades
Tichý, Dostrašilová, Laštovková, and Krupka (who taught Czech, Russian, math, biology, history, and geography) did not know about the
duality of my background.

On my way back and forth from school I devised counting games as I skipped between the square cobblestone patterns on the sidewalks. The Prague streets were paved with small bluish-gray, white, and soft pink cobblestones arranged in symmetrical patterns. I skipped between them from square to square counting how many squares it was to Vlasta's house, to the library, or to the school building. Cobblestones connected me to all the places I needed to reach.

In the morning on my way to school I met my classmates Eva, Jarka, Jitka, Saša, Karel, Toník, and Václav. We piled out of our houses balancing our bookbags and increasing in numbers as we got closer to the school building. We climbed the steps and used the remaining minutes before the start of the school day to share the latest gossip or to plan our after-school games. Once we were seated at our desks, we put our private concerns aside until we were again on the other side of the school door.

The school day was long and consisted of classes in six subjects. When the teacher entered the classroom at the beginning of the lesson, the entire class stood up as a sign of respect. We were kept busy memorizing, repeating, copying, writing, reading, and listening. When classes were over, we gathered in cliques in the school yard or nearby streets and evaluated the day's events. If I had enough change, I stopped at the neighborhood store for some Turkish candy or chocolates called *Italská směs*, an "Italian mix" that my mother never suspected I was eating.

All schoolchildren had to attend political rallies and participate in the annual May Day march. These rallies displayed the strength and power of the party. When foreign dignitaries visited Prague, we left our schoolroom to welcome the visitors. The schoolchildren from all the Prague districts lined the streets along the parade route. During the long wait for the procession to arrive, we played tag and the more aggressive boys pulled the girls' braids or tried to get the attention of their favorite girl by clowning around. Then the dignitaries would whizz by, and we would cheer, sing songs, and wave flags. The greater part of our enthusiasm came from the thrill of being out of class for the day. Our joy had little relationship to the party's desire to convey to visiting foreigners the impression of a happy communist collective of students and workers (also let off for the occasion). Visiting Western communists who wanted to believe in the authenticity of communism were often taken in by these staged demonstrations of loyalty. Czech schoolchildren were forced to comply with demands they did not have to approve of personally.

Participation in the annual May Day parade was the high point of this "voluntary" demonstration of gratitude to the communist state. Yet, despite the hypocrisy of these situations, for a child they were also an exciting release from the ordinary, which helped feed certain idealistic fantasies. On the eve of my first May Day parade I was too excited to fall asleep. I had seen film strips of previous May Day parades during the weekly newsreel at the local movie house. My imagination was stirred by the sea of people seemingly united by one idea. I dreamed about marching in my pioneer outfit down Václavské Náměstí (Prague's main street) shouting slogans with thousands of other people and waving to the party leaders on the grandstand.

My pioneer troop gathered at the crack of dawn to start the long march from our school to Václavské Náměstí. We had a large banner identifying our troop number and the name of our school. Touched by the natural excitement generated by a special holiday, we proudly carried flags and posters with imprints of heroes of labor and models of communist youth. The significance of the individual heroes was lost in the general enthusiasm to enjoy the day and indulge in the fantasy it created. On that day Anna Čapková, the eager eleven-year-old pioneer, joined the happy socialist family she had seen in the newsreel and became a part of history's march to a glorious future.

As I prepared to leave the house for my first May Day parade, dressed in a crisp white blouse and flowing pioneer scarf tied around my neck, my mother pinned our Rokoska address to the inside of my skirt just in case I became lost in the downtown mobs. She kissed me on the cheek and waved to her little pioneer dashing out the door at the first sign of the sun's rays. On the march downtown schoolchildren joined hands with factory workers, doctors, nurses, journalists, store clerks, Charles University faculty, actors, and artists under banners proclaiming unity and equality. The songs we sang and the slogans we chanted could be heard throughout the city. I blended with the hundreds of bodies around me. Feeling a part of this large mass intoxicated me with a sense of the power and the ability to conquer anything.

That evening I returned home barely able to move but too filled with wonderful impressions to give in to my exhaustion. The bond I felt with the thousands marching in Prague that day made me forget my thirst, hunger, and other bodily needs. I felt, on that glorious day, a sense of belonging that far transcended the narrow political scope of the occasion. Not until I collapsed in bed that night did I realize I had huge blisters on my feet.

When I became a teenager, May Day acquired other associations. During one parade, I watched a marching soldier curl his arm around a young girl's waist as she dug her chin into the lapels of his military uniform. Their eyes were filled with desire and, though they were physically present, it was obvious that they were in a world of their own. By fourteen I too became excited when we marched alongside young military recruits. Soldiers in coarse khaki uniforms winked playfully whenever they passed alongside us. I liked the rough feel of their uniforms as their arms brushed against me and I caught the scent of their perspiration. I absorbed the energy of their voices and marching bodies. During my teenage years May Day festivities ended as my friends and I danced and flirted with the soldiers on the square until late into the night. Eventually the political significance of May Day was submerged beneath the personal meanings I attached to it. For me, its original meaning as a rite of spring assumed more and more importance as my loyalty to socialist ideals and a communist future faded along with other childhood illusions.

Communist education at Koráb was based on memorizing one interpretation of events without analyzing it. Conformity and regimentation of thought made debate impossible. The importance of our close ties to the Soviet Union was reinforced in all the material we were taught in school. The Russian language, the language of our big brother, was compulsary and taught from the fourth grade on. Like most Czechs, I did not learn much Russian in these classes because resentment against Russian domination was expressed by a minimum exertion to learn the language of the occupier. Previously, schools had offered a choice of language, either German, English, or French. Now everybody had to take Russian. Our Czech teachers spoke Russian with a heavy accent and were often unenthusiastic themselves. Most of our Russian classes were uninspired and dull. We were also taught large doses of Russian history and geography and had to read selections of Soviet socialist realist literature in Czech translation.

Moral examples of how to become model socialist citizens were taken directly from the lives of Vladimir Ilich Lenin, Joseph Stalin, and other prominent communist leaders. We learned that our president, Klement Gottwald, had as a youth such an avid devotion to literature and such a passion for learning that he read under a street lamp, too poor to afford a candle. Lenin's childhood was upheld as our ultimate model. We read that as a child Lenin broke a vase in the family living room. At first he denied doing it, but afterward he realized it was wrong to lie and admitted the truth. The teacher instructed us: if you behave like Lenin and always tell the truth, you will be living the "right" life of a good pioneer and a worthy citizen. I wanted to be as strong and honest as Lenin, but I could not reach his level of perfection. I could not get myself to admit I had eaten the last chocolate that disappeared from the kitchen or that I had spent time at my girlfriend's house instead of doing my homework.

Was it perhaps the demand for perfect moral behavior expected of me as a pioneer that tempted me to steal from Miss Zapletalová's fruit trees? Or was it her contempt for me and my family that made me get back at her? As a private individual I asserted my freedom to disobey and rebel without assuming that I was deviating from the model the socialist society taught me to follow. As a (nearly) perfect pioneer I did everything that was demanded of me. I was a tireless collector of scrap paper and metal, and I helped make banners for pioneer activities. The model of a perfect Lenin made me feel guilty that I lacked the will to control my selfish urges but did not teach me how to tame the irrational and willful impulses that refused to fit into formulas of communist perfection. The appearance of perfection in my thoughts and actions was made possible only by the minor social deviations I permitted myself. Slowly, yet uncritically, I was becoming aware of the distance between illusion and reality, truth and hypocrisy, ideals and imperfections.

Weekly pioneer meetings were held at our local school, and the most accomplished pioneers were chosen to participate, along with others from the entire city of Prague, in workshops and study groups at the Dům Pionýru (the Pioneer House). The Dům Pionýru was the elite Pioneer House in Prague. I was selected as an exemplary pioneer to take part in a theater workshop there. We were asked to act out a scene, pretending that we were participating in an annual May Day parade. The young communist leader conducting the workshop lined us up in the middle of the spacious room. He encouraged us to show our enthusiasm for the marchers and to recreate the excitement of the parade.

Instead, we stood in the middle of the large room, a row of model pioneers, and did not utter a sound. The leader prodded: "Well, go ahead, don't just stand there, use your hands, smile, say something, shout, sing. Show your feelings! Can't you show the crowd's love for our leaders? Don't you remember the slogans?" After he spoke, there was complete silence in the room. Expressionless, we stared into the distance.

I lost the ability to move my limbs. My body felt like lead and would not respond to the demands of the youth leader. Paralyzed, our stiff bodies welded into a single mass, made powerless by the irrepressible force of an inner honesty. We could not pretend or cover up our disdain for the pretense demanded of us. Our session that day ended without the theatrics expected of young communists. Yet the scene was not devoid of drama. We left the room slowly and sheepishly, avoiding each other's eyes and embarrassed to acknowledge what the collective silence had revealed.

Loyalty to communism penetrated our school curriculum, which emphasized adoration of the Soviet Union. In grade school we recited the following poem:

> Where it rises in the morning,
> there is the East where Czechoslovakia's
> good friends, the Russians, live.
> Where the sun goes down, that is the West.
> There, behind a big sea, is America
> where a few rich people have everything and
> workers and peasants live in misery.

The message of this poem was not much different from what Abe and Belle had told me about America. They encouraged me to believe that now I lived in a country that was going to be fair to all, not just to a few. A socialist society was the kind of world they envisaged for America and hoped that Czechoslovakia would become. Dark images of America's evil had a powerful hold on me. In my early teens I did not doubt that the Soviet Union had the power to lead mankind to a more radiant future. In contrast to many of my friends, who were far more interested in America and the forbidden West, I was fascinated with all things Soviet and the beauty of the Russian language. Yet it was becoming clear to all of us that the political future of the Czechs was in the hands of the Soviet Union and that admiration for the West or its ideals could have serious repercussions for our careers and social standing.

The Soviet Union, however, could not totally eclipse the strong Czech identity in the educational system. We were also taught that the Czechs had an important history of their own. The legend of how the Czechs came to live in Bohemia validated their unique history and preserved a sense of national continuity. The legend that begins with the words "A long, long time ago . . ." says that when Čech, the chieftain of roaming shephards in search of a permanent settlement, brought his people to mountain Říp (a volcanic hill near Prague shaped like a bell surrounded by flat fields) he said, "This is a country overflowing with milk, butter and honey, this is where we shall stay." Čech, in his long robe and with his white beard, saw far into the future and had a vision of well-being for his people. It was reassuring for Czechs to have a long history that started before the birth of Christ, connecting them to a land of beauty and bounty, carefully chosen by ancestors with the good of future generations in mind. In turn, this meant that the Czechs also had a responsibility to the past, to care for the beautiful land they had inherited.

The special history of the Czechs and their central geographical location connected them more strongly to Western European culture than to Eastern Europe or Russia. In our class there was a portrait of Comenius (Jan Komenský), the seventeenth-century reformer who believed in the humanistic goals of education. In class, we read excerpts from his satire about worldly pretense, The Labyrinth of the World, a work that opened up for me an imaginative and wonderful universe. The books of Comenius and other Czech writers kept the European humanistic tradition as part of our curriculum and competed with the more one-dimensional, simplistic vision of life conveyed by Soviet propagandistic literature.

On one wall of our class I looked at Comenius, whose attitude toward learning was that "nature cannot be forced, but must be led willingly. All senses must be called into play by the lesson, and the later lessons should be the natural development of the earlier ones." On the other wall there was Vladimir Ilich Lenin, whose motto was simply "to study, to study, to study." Comenius's notion that children learn when their interest is aroused and his belief that the teacher should appeal to the ear and the eye was not completely overlooked by our teachers. In their hearts, Lenin was not on an equal footing with Comenius, despite his equal place on the wall.

Though a small nation, the Czechs had pride in their spiritual heritage and its power to prevail, in the end, over sheer physical force. For generations of Czechs the legacy of Jan Hus, the fourteenth-century religious dissident, ready to die at the stake rather than give up his vision of the truth, remained an important symbol. The Old Town Square, Staroměstské Náměstí, in central Prague is dominated by Hus's statue. During oppressive times the Czechs always looked up to Hus for courage and strength. At the base of the statue is the inscription: SEEK THE TRUTH, LISTEN TO THE TRUTH, TEACH THE TRUTH, LOVE THE TRUTH, ABIDE BY THE TRUTH AND DEFEND THE TRUTH UNTO DEATH. When I was a young pioneer, the simple truth of the message made little impression on me; by the time I was a university student, however, I knew the search for the truth was far from simple and to abide by the truth an extremely complex undertaking.

Hus's slogan that truth prevails, *Pravda zvítězí*, inspired Czechs to find ways of resisting oppression despite the disadvantage of being a small and vulnerable nation. This inspiration was proudly passed on to each new generation. One of the most important forms this resistance took was the struggle to perserve the Czech language. During the three hundred years of Austro-Hungarian rule, German was forced upon the population, and efforts were made to restrict the use of Czech. The survival of Czech, however, is testimony to the perseverance of the people to their unique identity. In school we were reminded of the importance of the Prague National Theater, Národní Divadlo, a monument of the sacrifices Czechs made to have a stage on which they could keep their language alive when German was imposed on them. When the theater burned in the 1880s it was rebuilt out of the money collected from the Czech people, rich and poor, nationwide. Above the stage curtain are the words NÁROD SOBĚ (From the nation to itself). The writers of prose and poetry who continued to use Czech maintained the nation's identity and hope for a revival of national independence. In school, we were taught the importance of Czech music, literature, art, and architecture as ways of preserving identity and affirming a sense of nationhood.

In 1984, when I returned to Prague after a twenty-one-year absence, I visited Vyšehrad, the cemetery where the most important Czech artists, composers, writers, and historic figures are buried (Antonín Dvořák,

Bedřich Smetana, Božena Němcová, Karel Čapek, and many others). While strolling in the cemetery I met a retired high school history teacher who told me he came there every day for an afternoon walk. He insisted on showing me the graves of people whose histories he knew in great detail but about whom he could not teach as an instructor in communist school systems. He maintained his sanity by studying and preserving the past in his mind while he waited for "truth to prevail" sometime in the future. History taught him that remembering and knowing strengthened the spirit for a better day; history also taught him that nothing lasts forever.

Although in the 1950s many important figures in Czech history were purged from our textbooks for political reasons (Thomas Masaryk, the founder of modern Czechoslovakia, is one example), classic authors were taught. Along with my classmates, I memorized patriotic nineteenth- and twentieth-century poems by Karel Jaromír Erben, Jaroslav Vrchlický, Jan Kollár, and Karel Hynek Mácha. Many of these poems, such as the excerpt from Mácha's "Máj" (May) below, celebrated the beauty and glory of the Czech land and became outlets for feelings that in more public forums were subordinated to a forced love of communism and the Soviet Union.

> Věrný syn jsi Čechů kmene
> Věrný bratr bratřím svým;
> Jazyk Český je i Tobě
> Otců drahým dědictvím.
> České hory- České doly-
> České luhy- Český háj-
> Šírá vlasť- ta Česká země
> Nejmilejšíť Tobě ráj.

> You are a loyal son to your Czech roots
> A loyal brother to your brothers;
> The Czech language is a precious
> Heritage to you and your fathers.
> The Czech mountains and Czech valleys—
> The Czech fields and green woods
> This vast homeland—This Czech land
> Is your beloved Paradise.

I recited these lines, I felt those feelings. I read Alois Jirásek, Božena Němcová, and Jan Neruda. I loved what the Czechs loved in themselves: their determination, their deep and meaningful roots, and their remarkable ability to survive against all odds. The opening lines of Božena Němcová's novel *Babička* (Grandmother), written when the Czechs were still under Austria-Hungary were passed on from generation to generation as a way of perpetuating loyalty to roots and love of one's own:

Dávno, dávno již tomu, co jsem se dívala do té milé mírné tváře, co jsem zulíbala to bledé líce, plné vrásků, nahlížela do modrého oka, v němž se jevilo tolik dobroty a lásky: dávno tomu, co mně posledně žehnaly staré její ruce.

It has been a long, long time since I looked into that dear, gentle face, since I kissed those pale cheeks full of wrinkles and since I have gazed into those blue eyes in which there was so much goodness and love: it has been a long time since her old hands last blessed me.

Even today when I say those words I feel the comforting warmth of the familiar that brings me back to my childhood. Němcová's fictional grandmother replaced the American grandmother who was beyond my reach. On the pages of Němcová's book I could revisit and relive those close family relationships I missed and which otherwise lived on in my imagination.

In school we were also introduced to the two most important Czech composers, Smetana and Dvořák. Their works were performed at special morning concerts that became for the Prague schoolchildren exciting class field trips. Explanations of these musical pieces were given to us so we would know the circumstances under which they had been composed and the patriotic themes they expressed. This is where I heard Smetana's *Má Vlast* (My country), his six symphonic poems celebrating national traditions and the Czech landscape through evocative musical motifs. In seventh grade we were gathered in the auditorium of our Koráb school to listen to portions of Dvořák's *New World Symphony* performed by musicians from the prestigious state orchestra. Our music teacher prefaced the performance by telling us that Dvořák composed this symphony in America, where he longed for his beloved homeland and the beautiful rolling Czech countryside.

Listening closely to Dvořák's mournful melodies, I responded to the deep longing expressed in the music. I focused my eyes on the window near my seat in an attempt to hide the unexpected tears that began to roll down my cheeks. But I could not stop them. Dvořák brought out a deep personal sorrow. My mind wandered back to the America I had left and that inspired Dvořák's feelings of sadness and longing. I cried for something I did not understand, a country I was no longer connected to, a longing that lived in me but whose roots had vanished. I could only remember a small corner of a playground, a portion of a street, a vague house, part of the way to a corner drugstore, and the faint outline of my grandmother's face. In Prague, however, I knew every pattern in the cobblestones on my street and the streets leading to the grocery at the top of Rokoska hill, the local library, and my school. The warm tears and uncontrollable sobs drained me. They expressed a sadness that no words could capture. Only the music could bring out the intense emotions and confusion within me. For native Czechs art, music, literature, and poetry provided a haven for intense feelings of national pride and patriotism that were complicated by the realities of foreign domination. I empathized with and shared these feelings but, unexpectedly, found they also stirred up other emotions within me. Dvořák's music brought out the dualities that battled within me. Once again I was reminded of the pain of not belonging and not knowing where my homeland was.

Chapter 11

Becoming a Pioneer: The Soviet Union, Our Model

Pioneer greeting:

K Budování a obraně vlasti buď připraven!
Always be ready to defend and build our nation!

Pioneer reply:

Vždy připraven!
Always ready!

In school we compared all societies and our national accomplishments against the model of the first socialist state, the Soviet Union. It was a force larger than life that permeated our lives and actions. Czech pioneers followed the model of the Soviet pioneer organization. Pioneers were expected to build socialism and were taught to scorn and eradicate the values from the bourgeois past. The pioneer motto to live for the needs of the collective rather than for the will of the individual was the opposite of what the previous generation did or believed. But contrary to the hopes of the communist leaders, not all "bourgeois" customs disappeared quickly or completely.

In the "old days" adolescent girls and boys made their debut into society at a gala ball which concluded formal dance classes that prepared them for the event. At these dance classes mothers were on the lookout for an advantageous partner for their child's future. Not my mother! Though the formal dance classes were still in vogue in the 1950s and 1960s (an entrenched custom Prague families were not willing to give up), the guidelines for a suitable social match were not as clear-cut as they had been in the past. If it was a status symbol in the past to accumulate property and riches, now a working-class background and a communist political affiliation was the ticket to success for college acceptances, choice jobs, and politically powerful positions. Any public expression of "capitalist" values was not advisable. In private it was a different matter.

My mother, the radical nonconformist, refused to accept the traditional values of middle-class Czechs. My sister's decision to attend these formal dance lessons caused a major clash of values; my sister wanted to be with her peers, while my parents wanted her to live by their communist values. For a revolutionary like my mother, the formal etiquette taught at these lessons was not the social training she had in mind for her daughter. These customs were unsuitable for the new era she believed in. There was a major upheaval in our family when Laura announced she was going to participate in the *taneční hodiny* (dance lessons) at the Lucerna dance hall.

My sister and her friends were consumed with preparations for the upcoming dance classes, which were about to start now that they had turned sixteen. "What will you wear? Do you think he will dance with me? My mother and I went for a fitting of my gown the other day. I will be like a princess in it!" I overheard the excited sixteen-year-olds discussing the dances in our bedroom. At these dance classes, held in downtown Prague ballrooms that signified the wealth and glory of a previous era, teenagers were taught to dance the fox-trot and the tango and use proper social manners. One did indeed learn to dance, but one also learned the social register. In the "old" Czechoslovakia these dance classes fulfilled a necessary social function. They still did under socialism. The young ladies were chaperoned by their mothers, who sat on the balcony to observe their daughters (with a sharp eye) and their dancing partners. The dance classes culminated in a gala ball at which the young ladies wore floor-length gowns and dainty gloves and the young men dressed in suits. Your partner for the night might become your partner for life if you were lucky.

My mother's undisguised mockery of the ballroom scene turned what in most homes was an exciting experience into a miserable tension for my sister. Belle, utterly bored with her passive role as a chaperone, behaved inappropriately in regard to the formal decorum that was expected of her. Each week my sister pleaded with my mother to conceal her distaste for the role she was expected to play as her daughter's chaperone and for the dance classes in general. The "bourgeois" manners perpetuated at these *taneční hodiny* were precisely the customs Abe and Belle wanted to eliminate. Their own social life was informal. The communists in Czechoslovakia aimed at destroying the middle-class institutions, but the values of the "bourgeois" world now under attack had been ingrained for generations. Ours was the first generation under communist rule, and no doubt it was unrealistic to eliminate all the customs of the past at once. My radical parents made it virtually impossible for us to be like most of the families around us. It was the Soviet model that worked for them, not the social conventions of the dying Czech bourgeois class, even if in this society it was only allowed to live on the creaky boards of the dance floor.

My father loved all things Russian: the language, the music, the character of the Russian people. While we cooked, did the dishes, or did schoolwork, Russian tunes and news reports from the radio about farm and factory production in the Soviet Union were a daily presence. My father paced back and forth, swaying his arms to the Russian melodies without interrupting the rhythm of his work. The Russian music energized him, judging by the fast movements of his feet and the animated expression on his face. Occasionally he would wander into the kitchen to see what smelled so good on the stove. Smiling and waving his pen in the air, he would hum the Russian tunes. "Isn't that beautiful? I can feel the big Russian soul in those melodies! And the magnificent sound of the Russian language!" he would say with deep feeling.

Abe got tickets for the entire family whenever Russian choral or dance groups came to Prague, particularly for the Moiseyevs, who were the best. They performed dances from different ethnic republics. The smiling performers made it seem as if their homeland, where these dances originated, was a land of eternal happiness. Brisk foot movements ballooned the male dancers' pants, and the colorful ribbons in the girls' hair twirled gracefully around their heads. The radiant dancers looked like the smiling Soviet pioneers on the posters in our school. They were messengers from the Soviet Union—the happy paradise. I could not wait to see Moscow and the large landscapes of the Soviet republics we studied about in our geography classes.

In our classroom the framed photograph of Stalin hung alongside that of the Czech president. Quotations from Stalin's writings cropped up everywhere—on theater programs, exhibit walls, in shop windows, and on the pages of our textbooks. Stalin's and Lenin's messages followed us in all our endeavors and studies. They were upheld as our visionaries and spiritual-political guides. We were instructed to be directed by the teachings of Marx, Engels, Lenin, and Stalin so that we would become useful to society.

The hallways and classroom bulletin boards in all Prague schools were covered with oversized banners and poster boards with slogans like this:

> March forward with boundless love for the Soviet Union, the protector of our freedom, independence and socialist development!

> Limitless love for the great Stalin who leads all the working people of the world toward the victory of communism! ·

> Love for the working class and the Communist Party, the foremost fighter for a joyful and happy tomorrow!

> Rejection of all remnants of bourgeois thinking and behavior!

> Love your glorious communist leaders!

I absorbed these slogans and eventually grew immune to them. Stalin's favorite slogan defining the communist years was "We are living better, we are living more joyfully." It was a far cry from the reality I saw when I stood on line at the neighborhood grocery store with grim-faced, tired people waiting for a delivery of eggs. When, or if, the eggs arrived, each customer got four, regardless of the size of the family. Occasionally one would hear an agitated customer on the line grumble, "Yea, we sure are living better and more joyfully!" getting the others to chime in. Serious food shortages and impersonal medical service at overcrowded clinics made it hard to believe there was any connection between the slogans and the reality we were living.

On March 5, 1953, when the leader of the communist international family, Joseph Stalin, died, life in Czechoslovakia came to a standstill. Some Praguites wore black bands on the sleeves of their overcoats as they did when a close family member died. The communist world was shocked and grief-stricken. Buildings were covered in black flags, schools conducted ceremonies, radio stations devoted all their programming to the funeral arrangements and commemorations of his life. People cried openly in the streets. The magnitude of the nation's mourning made me fear that our emperor had died and the sun would never shine again.

I mourned that our caring grandfather of communism had left us orphaned. Stalin's death was discussed in class. Because of the great loss the communist family had suffered, I believed the state needed my energies. I wanted my hands and able body to be of use to help support the nation in its time of sorrow. The Czech president, Klement Gottwald, joined the other communist heads of state in Moscow for Stalin's funeral. Nine days later, on March 14, Gottwald himself died. Because of the closeness between the Soviet Union and Czechoslovakia I reasoned that Gottwald had died of a broken heart, unable to continue without Father Stalin. The official explanation for Gottwald's death was pneumonia, caught at Stalin's funeral in the subzero Moscow temperatures. (I learned later that he died of alcoholism.) For me the two deaths were mythically linked, confirming that the fate of small Czechoslovakia was interconnected with that of our giant brother, the Soviet Union. It was about this time that I became a pioneer.

I do not remember becoming a pioneer, I merely remember being one. Pioneers were distinguished as special in their white shirts and red scarves. The intent of our pioneer leaders was that we would first learn and then follow the political doctrines and values we were taught. I took my obligations seriously and was proud to be a pioneer! I did whatever pioneers were expected to do to help strengthen the weak economy of the country. Diligently I collected scrap paper and discarded objects for the *sběr*, a central recycling depository. In theory I embraced the concept that the individual should submerge himself for the good of the collective, but in reality I found a way of maneuvering between the slogans and my personal desires. I tried to deny myself candy, which I loved, and to do without certain comforts to train myself to survive under harsh conditions. I worked on making myself as tough and brave as the partisans I admired so I could be useful to the nation in crisis. When we had no hot water for long stretches of time, or when my mother could not find meat for our dinner, I felt I was being a good pioneer if I did not complain.

When I rode the tram I always got up to give my seat to an older person, not only because it was expected of me but because the red pioneer kerchief around my neck mandated that I demonstrate selflessness and respect. During my years as a pioneer I was searching for my own set of beliefs. Vulnerable and naive, I succumbed to the comforting simplicity of the propaganda. Being a pioneer made me feel my efforts and contributions were important. I was a pioneer with heroic dreams, but at the same time I was a youth with a will of my own which I did not know how to assert under the pressure of performing for the good of the collective. Obeying orders and following doctrines delayed the development of my aspirations and individual responses. In each situation I knew what reaction was expected of me without asking myself if I genuinely felt that way or not.

As students we worked in factories and went on *brigády* to work in the fields to help production and to become closer to working-class people. On these field trips we were expected to function as a harmonious collective. The weekly newsreels shown in the neighborhood movie house before the feature film informed us of the production results of building communism in the factories and fields. Soviet films praised Stakhanovite workers who worked double, even triple shifts to fulfill and overfulfill the five-year plan at the industrial plants and on the collective farms. Today's heroes were the steelworkers, the brick layers, and the farmers who spent more hours at the hot furnaces and laid more bricks per hour and milked more cows than previously was believed possible. Workers became eligible for sainthood in the task of building communism and surpassing the planned production quotas. These Stakhanovite workers, whose oversized photographs decorated the bulletin boards of Prague, were upheld as examples. If we were productive pioneers today, tomorrow we could be the Stakhanovites.

Czech films reinforced communist doctrine and portrayed the attitude we were expected to demonstrate toward the collective. The political message in these movies influenced me, as did the socialist novels I read. On one Saturday afternoon in our Kobylisy theater the following films were shown: *Katka*, about a naive country girl who was reeducated through factory work and who became a socialist worker, which showed us that everybody can change and become a contributing socialist; *Grinder Karhan's Shift* (which encouraged the shockworker's movement), about a worker who inspires other workers to overfulfill the plan through the example of his own dedication to hard work; and *The Rocks and the People*, based on the motto "To work in the socialist manner and to live in the socialist manner."

There were also inspirational films like *Warning*, which described the struggle against traitors and foreign agents in the Stalin Works, a huge synthetic gasoline plant in northern Bohemia. This theme kept the fear of the lurking danger of the enemy raw. We had to be vigilant! For variety we could watch *The Church Warden and the Hen*, a story of a farm wife who was persuaded to join the collective farm despite the saboteur efforts of a church warden, or *New Fighters Shall Rise,* a filmed version of Zápotocký's novel about the beginning of socialism in Bohemia. With choices like these, my Saturday afternoons reinforced my pioneer calling. These dull films did not fill the movie houses, but I was there almost every Saturday.

Meeting older members of the community taught me firsthand about the past. I was especially fond of the white-haired elderly woman, Hana, who lived in a tiny apartment with mementos of her devoted life as a communist. Her stories showed me how difficult life was for those who were born into poverty. These stories were about real people who faced hardships I could not even imagine surviving. She fought in the resistance movement with her family and lost both her husband and son. She fought for better rights for workers and selflessly risked her personal safety for her beliefs. She was grateful to the party for the education it gave her after the war. She was proud of the communist victories and accomplishments. Learning about what Hana lived through made me think about the responsibility our generation had toward those who died in battle. We owed our peace to their courageous deeds, and I in turn owed them my dedication to furthering social improvement, if not perfection.

Once a week I took the tram to visit and to help Hana with her shopping and household chores. After the work was done we had tea and cookies. We talked about her past and my present life and future plans. She told me stories about the days of her youth when the world was very different. In her youth she worked as a servant for a wealthy family. Her husband worked long shifts in the mines. Despite their hard work, they lived poorly and were not treated with respect. Joining the Communist Party gave them hope that they could change their lot. She owed everything to the party. Then the war came and everybody's life changed. I loved the warm, deep lines on her wrinkled face and her penetrating eyes. Her stories taught me about people, places, ways of doing things that were new to me. She had lived a full life, and she was fearless.

She fed my voracious appetite to understand what people's lives were like and why life was the way it was. She suggested books I should read, which we discussed the following week during tea time. Our visits were the highlight of my week. Hana was easy to talk with, always interested in my thoughts and feelings, which I freely shared with her. The photograph of her murdered husband and son was within my sight as we talked and sipped tea. The knowledge of their lost lives made me try even harder to act like a worthy pioneer.

Hana's fighting spirit resembled the one I saw in action at home: when facing inequality, evil, and injustice, one resisted, organized, and fought back. That is what my parents did in America and what Hana did in Czechoslovakia. As a novice pioneer, I could also work toward building a better future. This was not like playing with dolls. I had graduated from the playground to the battlefield. I no longer needed play. Life could be far more exciting than anything I could try to imagine! And most important, I had a role to play in this drama. I was told that every insignificant good deed today made a difference. I attended pioneer meetings that opened with the slogan commanding us to "always be ready to defend and build our nation" to which I replied with my fellow pioneers: "Always ready." I was ready for combat!

I repeated the slogans, making them my own. The selfless heroes in the socialist novels instructed me to believe that evil can be fought with personal sacrifice. I knew from my readings that the Russian people withstood insurmountable hardships and were capable of untried feats. The mythic stories about the past and present of Soviet Russia shaped my own future goals. For example, in a popular Soviet novel by Nikolai Ostrovsky, *How the Steel Was Tempered*, the hero, Pavel Korchagin, who was one of the most promoted socialist idols for our generation, stands in the cemetery where his comrades who died during the war were buried. These are the thoughts about the meaning of life that run through his mind and which I wanted to live by:

> Man's most precious possession is life itself. It is given to him
> but once, and he must live it so as not to feel agonizing regret for
> years wasted in aimlessness, so as never to know burning shame
> of an ignoble, petty past, and so that when he is dying, he should
> be able to say: "All my life and all my strength have been devoted
> to the finest cause in the world—the struggle for the liberation of
> mankind." And one should make haste to use every moment of
> life, for after all an illness or accident may suddenly cut it short.

In addition to reading and discussing Ostrovsky's novel, our class saw a dramatization of it at the Youth Theater. I can still picture the scene in which Korchagin, squatting by a small woodstove in a barren room, dressed in a shabby jacket with a long scarf wrapped around his neck, talked passionately about his dedication to the cause. His words made my lungs expand and my heart beat faster. His superhuman message rushed through my veins: man had a higher calling that elevated him beyond his petty self. Life had an intoxicating significance. Korchagin, the perfect hero, denied himself the pleasure of a personal life to make the communist ideal a possibility. If Korchagin could do it, why couldn't I? Didn't Abe and Belle intend to do the same?

Korchagin was not the only hero who lived in my fantasies. I admired Zoya Kosmodeyanskaya, the young *komsomol* (Soviet Communist Youth League) girl who went into an occupied village as a partisan scout, fell into the hands of the Nazis, and was tortured and hanged. Her last words, her short, courageous life, and her tragic death showed me how to value life and hate the enemy. Could I possibly be as brave as she was? Gorky's character of the mother in his socialist realist novel *Mother*, who lost her sons, glorifies the same courage and strength as Korchagin and Kosmodeyanskaya did:

> Our children are treading the path of truth and reason, bring-
> ing love to the hearts of men, showing them a new heaven and
> lighting up the earth with a new fire—the unquenchable fire
> of the spirit. From its flames a new life is springing, born of our
> children's love for all mankind. Who can extinguish this love?
> Who? What force can destroy it? What force oppose it? The earth
> has given it birth, and life itself longs for its victory. Life itself!

I could only sketch this idyllic future in unclear contours, but I was ready to be led to it. A mere pioneer today, I could be a hero tomorrow. In this society ordinary people could be elevated through dedicated work and faith. And as an active member of the collective I would do wonderful things for mankind, turning ordinariness into the extraordinary and making our world a paradise. My life on Nad Rokoskou Street, at the Koráb school, and in the Kobylisy neighborhood stretched in my dreams to all corners of the nation and the world. These dreams lifted me beyond the physical confines of my own life. I dreamed of scientific discoveries that would make peach trees blossom in the hostile Siberian climate and of machines that would liberate man from the tedium of repetitive tasks. The future had infinite possibilities and I was going to find my place in that remarkable future when the time was right. The hype was working on me; I was hooked!

At school, I was asked to give a speech about the origins of the May Day holiday in America. I worked on my speech with my father, who supplied the facts. I translated his words into Czech, but the opening and closing lines were my own, written from my heart. This was my first public speech in Czech. The entire school gathered in the auditorium. With trepidation I awaited my turn in the long program of songs, poems, speeches, and short skits. Finally my turn came.

I told my schoolmates about the international holiday of the working people, established in 1889 by the Paris Congress of the Second International to commemorate the strike of the Chicago workers. My father was born in Chicago, I told my classmates. I had visited Chicago, and I was proud to tell them about the struggle for justice that took place there. The workers organized a strike for May 1, 1886, demanding an eight-hour workday, and they held a demonstration that ended in a bloody confrontation with the police. And now I was a pioneer in Prague joining them in their celebration of a holiday that united the working classes all over the world! We were members of a large international family though we spoke different languages and came from different cultures. Together we aimed for the same goal—justice and peace for all.

I read these words as loudly and firmly as I could. I can no longer hear the sound of the applause that followed, but I can still see those neat Czech words I wrote with my blue fountain pen on small pieces of notepaper. I had become one of them, speaking and thinking like a Czech and a pioneer. And along with adopting the language, I acquired a new manner of expression, a new way of thinking in which the new socialist man, the communist future, and the bourgeois past were part of my vocabulary and perceptions. The communist perfect man was a fantasy creation like the world of kings and princes, whose deeds I did not question, that led to believing in saints like Stalin and Pavlík Morozov. I had entered an adult fairy land thinking it was real.

As a pioneer I repeated the slogan "Place the interests of society above those of the family" without challenging its meaning. This message was conveyed through the much publicized story of fourteen-year-old Pavlík Morozov. He denounced his father for hoarding grain when farmers were being collectivized and was brutally murdered in the woods by angry villagers, some of whom were his own relatives. He became a Soviet hero and in Prague pioneer homes and schools were named after him. We were encouraged to emulate Morozov's heroism, to think like him, and above all to act like him. To be like Pavlík Morozov meant you were loyal to the state, rather than to your own family. Stalin made a saint out of Pavlík Morozov for denouncing his father to the Soviet authorities as a class enemy.

Nonetheless, I observed the irreconcilable contradictions between family values and state doctrine in Nataša's and Vlasta's families. But who was I to believe? My parents, their parents, the state, or my own judgment? Children were recruited to denounce their parents and relatives if their parents' behavior or thinking was suspect or a threat to the security of the party. The state continually fueled the notion that there was a dangerous anticommunist enemy within our society. It was our duty to help destroy this evil force. What sounds absurdly unreal today was more than real at the time. The communist motto stated that for the protection of the state no sacrifice was too much to ask, even when the loyalty of children was put to the test, though it could mean pitting children against their parents.

Family loyalty was sadly exploited and twisted during the Slánský trials. Heda Margolius Kovaly, the wife of one of the fourteen accused in the Slánský trials, describes in her 1989 book *Under a Cruel Star* how the accused, subject to brutal psychological torture and threats to their families, though innocent, did not deny the accusations made against them:

> Day after day, the newspapers carried detailed testimony from the accused, who not only made no attempt to defend themselves, confessing to all crimes as charged, but even kept introducing new accusations against themselves, heaping one on top of another.
>
> *Is this all or is there more you did to betray your country? Did you sell your people to the enemy in other ways?*
>
> *There is more. In my limitless hatred for the popular democratic order, I also committed the crime of. . . .*

In a letter of denunciation, Lisa London, the wife of one of the three men sentenced to life imprisonment in the Slánský trials, publicly stated, "I lived with a traitor." In a letter to the editor of a leading newspaper Ludvík Frejka's (one of the accused and executed men in the Slánský trials) sixteen-year-old son Tomáš stated, "I demand that my father receive the highest penalty, the death sentence. . . . And it is my wish that this letter be read to him." The father went to his death knowing his son publicly denounced him. A decade later, the son witnessed a review of the false criminal charges against Slánský and the thirteen other accused men. His murdered father was innocent.

In 1952 young Tomáš did not know the charges were false and the accusations fabricated. He believed his truth was the real truth, and for that he has no doubt paid a high price. In his letter published in all newspapers, Tomáš declares his Morozov-like faith in the communist future I myself was striving toward when sixteen: "I pledge that wherever I shall work, I shall always carry on as a loyal Communist. I know that my hate for all of our enemies, and especially for those enemies who wanted to destroy our ever richer and ever more joyous life, and most of all my hate for my father, will always give me strength in my struggle for the Communist future of our people." I shudder to think what price I would have been willing to pay for my faith in the communist future. I am lucky that when I was as young as Tomáš Frejda I was not challenged or used the way he was. For the communists fiercely holding on to power, nothing was sacred, not even the preservation of the family.

These tense political times were not particularly unhappy years for me. I responded to the grand performance the government staged unaware of the backstage intrigue. The parades impressed me, the sense of unity assumed under the slogan "All men for one and one for all" was real to me. There was only one official, absolute *truth*, one interpretation, one way of understanding things. The past was dismissed as "capitalist," "feudal," "bourgeois," all of which were discredited, invalidated, and attacked. It is one of the many tragedies of the communist era that the coverage of the Slánský trials in *Rudé Právo* (the leading communist newspaper) or the halo created around Morozov's death was based on falsehoods. But how could Americans know who was telling the truth when Ethel Rosenberg's brother David Greenglass testified against his sister at the Rosenberg trials in America? How do we judge a situation when crucial information is concealed or distorted? Was I, this made-up person, Anna Čapková, a truth or a lie? During the years

1953 to 1956 I believed what I was told, what I read in the press and in books selected for me, and what I saw at rallies and demonstrations.

In my home there was a lot of talk about the Rosenbergs' trial. My mother was particularly concerned about the Rosenberg children and how they would survive in America. Often there were visitors in our home from abroad who brought my parents news from America. My mother, on a rare occasion, would admit: "There was one thing I would not let the party do; I would never consent to the breaking up of our family." We never, of course, even discussed what other options there might have been. No wonder Belle could project into the magnitude of the Rosenberg family tragedy. Once I overheard my mother say to one of their comrades, "Do you think it is safe for the Rosenberg boys to stay in America? Maybe they should come to Czechoslovakia. We could adopt them. It might be easier for them to grow up here, away from the anticommunist hostility that is raging in the States." That evening I asked my mother if it was true that I would have two new brothers. "No," she sighed, "the idea was rejected by the comrades." I was not surprised at the possibility of another upheaval in our family

In 1953 Stalin died. In 1953 the Rosenbergs were executed. In 1953 I became a pioneer. I was eleven years old, and I believed in the future.

Chapter 12

. . . .

The Communist
Family in Exile

My son is already twenty-six years old and he doesn't want to get married. He says he is a socialist and he is too busy. Socialism is socialism, but getting married is important too.
—Bintel Brief, in the *Forward*

It takes so little, so infinitely little, for a person to cross the border beyond which everything loses meaning: love, convictions, faith, history. Human life—and herein lies its secret—takes place in the immediate proximity of that border, even in direct contact with it; it is not miles away, but a fraction of an inch.
—Milan Kundera, *The Unbearable Lightness of Being*

I was not only a child in the family I was born into; I was simultaneously brought up by the communist family my parents belonged to. The primary lesson my parents taught me during my preschool years was that conflict was unavoidable and that confronting issues and taking a firm stand were part of life. I always knew I was loved, though there were larger, more important concerns than my grades and bruised knees.

In the United States my parents' friends made themselves at home, helping out with the cooking without interrupting the flow of dialogue. During meals, the conversation switched back and forth from in-depth political arguments to discussions of family and personal relationships. I did not know how serious the situation was when they anxiously questioned each other: "Has he left town?" or "Will the party help his wife and children?" I never suspected these phantom dangers would ever apply to us or me.

Like my parents, their communist friends believed in a political vision. Joseph Starobin, a former communist and journalist, explains that vision that set things in action for the communists in the preface to his book *American Communism in Crisis, 1943–1957.* While communists worked to make this international vision a reality, it controlled every aspect of their lives:

> This book has to do with the political experience of several hundred thousand Americans who gave the attempt to build a revolutionary community in a nonrevolutionary situation their best years, their immense energies, and highest hopes. . . . It was a community that went beyond national boundaries and differences of race and creed: it was driven by the certainty that man's sojourn on earth could be happier if only his social relations were transformed from competition to cooperation. These Americans were sure that a universal strategy for creating a new society had been found in the experience of Russia and China. . . . Here were a group of men and women who believed they had found the assumptions and allegiances that would enable them to "make history."

My parents were part of the revolutionary community that Starobin accurately portrays as makers of history. As members of this communist international family, Abe and Belle journeyed in search of that vision of a new society as far as Russia, Czechoslovakia, and China.

In a 1994 letter I received from a former editor of the *Daily Worker*, A. B. Magil, who spent the years 1950–52 as a correspondent in Mexico, he recalls how he learned not only where but who my father was when he came across the name A. Čapek: "I was in Mexico as correspondent for the *Daily Worker* and Telepress, a news agency whose headquarters was in Prague. I began receiving mail from Telepress signed A. Čapek. I assumed this was a Czech journalist, but learned on my return to New York that A. Čapek was Abe Chapman." In the higher party ranks secretive missions and mysterious names were an unchallenged reality. Party members knew only what the party wanted them to know. This mode of functioning led to both amusing and painful surprises.

Gil Green, a member of the Communist Party's National Board indicted in 1948, spent many years underground. He wrote in his book *Cold War Fugitive* that "the Party compelled by circumstances had to work in a twilight zone of semi-legality." The fear of persecution forced party members to be fiercely loyal and dependent on each other for their very survival and safety. Active communists like Abe and Belle trusted party leaders far more than their own family members in an atmosphere Gil Green describes as unsafe: "At the same time, it [the party] would have to learn to survive in semi-darkness, doing its best—to protect workers and professionals from wholesale firings, and Party leaders from all being put behind prison bars." In that "semi-darkness" which we lived in, my parents' communist friends played a major role in my life, no less significant than a grandparent, aunt, or uncle.

When we lived in the Eastern bloc in the 1950s and 1960s, communist governments welcomed the "disappeared" American fellow communists, glad to use either their scientific knowledge or English language skills. In exchange for jobs, homes, and political loyalty to the Soviet Union and the respective communist country they were living in, these communist governments provided a home for a small group of communist and left-wing Americans and their families. These American expatriates shared a common ideology rather than a cultural tie to their newly adopted homeland. And these were the people who became my substitute and only extended family.

Spending time with my parents' comrades gave me contact with people from all parts of the world. I was exposed to different languages, unusual accents, fascinating stories, music, and foods from the African continent, Europe, and Asia. I never knew who would turn up for dinner or how long they would stay in Prague. Curious about the countries our visitors came from, I asked questions and imagined the lives and families they had left behind.

I checked out books from my local library about Africa and Asia because I was interested in learning more about these faraway places, which became closer to me through their stories and presence in our home. These comrades described the loved ones they had not seen or heard from for long periods of time, their travels in other countries, and in some cases the difficulty of their escape and hiding. It was their communist involvements that connected them to my parents. These friendships based on political beliefs automatically shut out those who did not share Abe and Belle's communist values. The communists had no tolerance for the world they had rejected. In her 1977 book, *The Autobiography of an American Communist*, Peggy Dennis, the wife of the general secretary of the American Communist Party, wrote: "We had no truly personal friends—internalized political considerations domi-nated relationships." I believe the same rules worked in our home.

My mother made sure she gave special attention to visitors in our Prague home who needed a hug or an extra portion of their favorite food. Comrades who missed the children they were separated from lav-ished attention on me, bringing me gifts from their travels. I in turn told them stories about my daily life and took them on elaborate tours of my neighborhood, showed them the pictures I made in school and trea-sures I found growing on the neighborhood trees and bushes. Proudly I described my pioneer activities and sang the new Czech songs I had just learned. An insight into my thoroughly Czech life, in our other-wise American home, was a curiosity for the steady flow of visitors. Some comrades stayed in Prague for months, others disappeared in a few weeks never to be seen again. I never knew who would be leaving or staying. Some were regulars who visited a few times a year over many years. There was a short Englishman and a tall, thin Scotsman, both of whom loved to drink and tell stories in their hard-to-understand ac-cents. They never forgot to bring me a large bar of English chocolate or a piece of clothing from the West. Some of the visitors brought me chewing gum, a rare treat. I saved the gum in a glass from day to day until it disintegrated.

For these dedicated comrades the pursuit of the political struggle was far more important than personal happiness. While these loyal commu-nists were dodging persecution or making communist contacts in other countries under secretive conditions, reunions and lives with lovers, mates, children, and parents were on hold. For many of them their family lives were disrupted or destroyed. There were discussions in our kitchen about lovers, betrayals, separations, and other personal sacrifices their tumultuous lifestyles demanded of them. My parents provided warm support, food, drink, and engaging conversation for the wander-ing communists who found themselves in Prague. When visiting with them Abe and Belle caught up on news of political events elsewhere, debated ideological party tactics, and had uninhibited discussions of their complicated personal and sexual relationships. It was not uncom-mon for their comrades to be free spirits living by unconventional rules, either maneuvering between a married partner and lover or maintain-ing a lesbian or homosexual relationship. In progressive circles, asserting one's individuality and living a radical lifestyle was an accepted norm. In this atmosphere of strong closeness and absolute trust they could tell their most revealing secrets. Conversation was usually intense, intimate, and almost always passionate. In the banter with their closest comrades there was the same openness and brutal directness in their sexual confessions as in their political discourse. Visits with my parents' Czech friends were far more formal and inhibited.

Frequently my parents' visitors waited until I went to bed to discuss secretive or serious matters. At a certain point in the evening the restless grown-ups would prod me, "Annie, it is way past your bedtime, you have to go to school tomorrow." I took it as a signal that they were anxious to switch the conversation from casual topics to the ones I was shielded from. I forced myself to stay awake so I could catch their words, a passionate cry, a clink of a glass. I could smell the heavy cigarette smoke seep through the crack under the door. The disconnected, fragmented sentences did not satisfy my desire to make sense out of the situations they analyzed late into the night. I could hear, "You know that they had to leave their son in the Soviet Union," after which their voices would trail off into a whisper, or "She hasn't seen her husband for four years," until someone else started to inform them that "the jail sentence is" or "the parents and the children are separated until," and I would lose the rest of the sentence when they lowered their worried voices.

Words like *conviction, indictment, prosecutors, amnesty,* and *deportation* frightened me. They seemed to hold much more meaning than the dictionary provided. I did not want to know what those words meant. Occasionally unexpected laughter would garble the unfinished sentences. I sensed danger, pursuits, escapes, and arrangements for secret meetings. Tense, I anticipated that something was about to happen. I was afraid to close my eyes for fear of losing a chance to decipher the tangle of words that made my limbs cramp up and my mind fill with nightmarish visions. Had the world always been such a frightening enigma?

These communists became the heroes of my childhood dreams just as the characters in the Soviet novels did. Having direct relationships with them in my home made their charm and wit much more effective. In response to their stories, I set goals for myself that bordered on the phantasmagoric. I thought about how I could become part of their all-important mission. It was not clear if these people had regular jobs to earn a living. They traveled through the socialist world on papers and money that were part of those mysterious night talks I strained to decode. They came and went according to unpredictable timetables.

Overhearing their serious conversations taught me about the power of language both to confirm and to convey the ideological bond between like-minded people. There was also much laughter, joking, crying, singing, and hugging. Reunions with American comrades were rare occasions when Abe and Belle would allow themselves to bring up memories they concealed from my sister and me. They both maintained a deep emotional tie and connection to friends, family, events, and places in America. They would ask questions about friends who were living either in the United States or in other countries: "What happened to . . . , is he safe, did he go to prison or lose his job? Is he really living in Poland or East Germany?" They wanted the latest assessment of the political changes in the United States to know when, or if, it would be possible for them to return. Exile was a heavy burden for both of them.

My father, more likely than my mother, would lapse into reminiscences of his favorite Lebanese restaurant in New York or particular landmarks he missed more intensely as the years of exile accumulated. He longed for the exotic flavors and variety of foods unavailable and unknown in Czechoslovakia. Culturally, linguistically, and politically their loyalties were to America and the comrades they had left behind. Czechoslovakia was where they lived and worked, but America was what created them, had meaning for them, and kept them going. Our existence in this medieval city was merely a detour, an enforced separation from the life they had never wanted to leave for a culture they never felt at home in.

My father loved to sing the progressive American songs of his youth which expressed an absolute faith in conquering the world. Singing these old union songs with their comrades allowed them to rekindle the strong feelings that sent them marching in the streets to protest poor living conditions and exploitation. In their youth Abe and Belle joined a united, strong, and hopeful progressive force. They knew what they wanted to fight for and the kind of world they hoped to create. Now, in our Prague living room, the old songs were a sentimental, if at times painful, reminder of the changes in their lives. Singing "Solidarity Forever" or "We Got to All Get Together" brought them into a close, warm circle with other comrades who had to leave America:

When the union's inspiration through the workers' blood shall run,
There can be no power greater anywhere beneath the sun;
Yet what force on earth is weaker than the feeble strength of one,
For the union makes us strong.

Chorus: Solidarity Forever
    For the union makes us strong.

With smiles on their faces they sang on:

There's a farmer in the country and a worker in the town;
They've got to get together 'fore the sun goes down.
We got to all get together, We got to all get together.
All you hardworking people surely got to organize.

My father's melodic voice could be heard above all the other voices. Resurrecting the past with American comrades in exile softened their predicament for the few hours they were together.

Many of my parents' communist friends were fascinating, charismatic characters. It was fun to spend time with them. I was an expert at organizing guided tours around a city I knew well and loved passionately. I took my parents' friends down my favorite winding streets and to spectacular gardens hidden behind stone walls. "Look," I would say when we stood on the riverbank, "here is the Prague castle, this is where the Czech kings lived for centuries." Without fail, the city charmed them and I got a chance to teach them little Czech history lessons.

I was particularly close to Ken, a friend of my parents who teased me about being exactly twice my age; I was thirteen and he was twenty-six. Ken spent weekends at our house, where he had long, polemical debates with my father about Marxism and communism in general. Ken's calm voice contrasted with my father's dominating and excitable one. He helped my mother stir and chop in the kitchen and in the mornings he got up early to make me hot chocolate and to talk with me. Ken was the brother I had always wished for. His warmth, humor, love of ideas, interest in new experiences and food, and his remarkable talent to fix anything in the house made him a natural addition to our family circle.

Ken was one of the frequent partners in the late night poker games my mother made legendary. He tried hard to defeat my mother's shrewd maneuvers, ultimately declaring her the unbeatable queen of poker. But after two years Ken left Prague for good. I lost a brother whom I did not see again until we returned to the United States. When we were reunited with him in New York City seven years later, he asked Belle: "Well, were you bluffing that night in Prague or not?" Belle smiled flirtatiously, but she would not talk. For years I missed the fun we had with Ken, and now he was married and had a family of his own. The cycle of forming and losing close relationships was a way of life in these expatriate communist circles. Over the years I lost as many relationships as I had formed, moving back and forth from country to country crossing paths with some or just missing a chance to see people we had once grown attached to.

Louise, a black American exiled communist, was close to our family. She was different from the rest of my parents' friends because she listened more than she talked. Soft-spoken, shy, and extremely gentle, she nonetheless had a strong presence. Her dark, expressive eyes were at times sad. She contracted tuberculosis during her stay in Prague, and when she was sent to a sanatorium in the Slovak Tatra Mountains we visited her there. On those visits we brought her the sounds of English she missed hearing in the isolated Slovak mountains and the latest stories about life in Prague. Louise never returned to Prague, nor did she return to the United States. She died at the sanatorium, never seeing her family again.

Of all the people who came to our Prague home Irving Potash was my favorite. Irving had a soft voice and gentle eyes. When he told a story or a joke there was a witty spark in his eyes and voice as he patiently developed the story, stalling the punch line for as long as possible without losing the attention of his listener. Whenever he visited, I spent as much time with him as possible. Irving was always keenly interested in everything I was doing. I opened up to his natural ease. On long walks around my neighborhood I showed him secret places even my parents did not know about. Calmly he talked with me about things that would interest me, revealing nothing about his own complicated life. I had hoped my friends might take him for a visiting grandfather when they saw us walk down the street near our house.

Frequently Irving disappeared for long periods of time. He would reappear at unexpected and irregular times, bringing exotic gifts or delicacies from other countries. My parents would not allow me to ask him where he traveled and what the purpose of his trip had been. He was surrounded by an aura of secrecy. Sometimes a box of special foods would be delivered to our house with cans of Russian fish *shproty,* packages of Polish smoked meat, and Bulgarian canned fruits and jams. Belle would shake her head, trying to speculate if Irving had sent us these things from Poland, Romania, Bulgaria, or the Soviet Union. Meanwhile, I wished Irving had arrived with the box, or better yet in place of it. When Irving would reappear, as mysteriously as he had disappeared, he joined us at our dinner table with wonderful new stories. Once again it felt as if he had been with us just yesterday. As happy as I was to see him, I knew that within days or weeks he would vanish again. I feared one day I might lose him altogether as I had lost Ken.

Irving held an important party position: he was a leader of the International Fur and Leather Workers Union, and he served on the Politburo of the American Communist Party. He was born in Kiev in the Ukraine in 1902, and his family immigrated to the United States in 1911. At the age of seventeen he joined the Communist Party. In 1948 he was arrested and held for deportation. He became one of eleven party leaders indicted for violating the Smith Act. Convicted, he served his term only to be rearrested. In March 1955, Potash agreed to voluntary deportation to Poland in exchange for which the government dropped its case against him. I was thirteen when Irving appeared in my life.

Irving depicted prison life with such humor I forgot he was describing life behind prison walls. He told stories about the rats that would get into the prison bakery where he was assigned to work and the elaborate schemes the prisoners devised to outsmart them. These schemes kept them occupied for days. They were delighted when they scored a victory. At least in my presence Irving did not dwell on the loneliness or the problems of prison life. He described the interesting characters he met and the things they did to get through the day rather than the deprivations they suffered. Irving became friends with a convicted bank robber, Jim Leather, who worked in the prison butcher shop. Under Irving's patient and thoughtful guidance, Jim started to read and take classes at which he excelled. Irving introduced him to the distinctions between different social systems, which ultimately changed Jim's outlook on life. Irving did not waste his time in prison. He also changed my image of prison as a lifeless dungeon to one in which life does not stop happening. I learned from Irving's stories that even behind bars prisoners work, grow, form friendships, and experience new sensations.

Irving desperately missed his family in New York City. Spending so many years of his life separated from them was painful. Irving talked lovingly about his wife and daughter, remembering family events in great detail as if his words could bring them back. He devoted his time exclusively to his party work and to the personal relationships he had with comrades all around the world, but his personal life was solitary. Irving wanted to continue his party commitments without giving up his family life in the United States. Unfortunately, he could not do so.

One night, after a particularly long disappearance, Irving returned to Prague with a thick, bushy mustache that changed his appearance and concealed some of the kind facial features I loved. While Abe and Irving were absorbed in a discussion, I went into the kitchen to ask Belle why Irving had grown this unattractive mustache. My mother continued to busy herself with the dinner preparations, but I could see a slight smile in the corner of her mouth. After deliberating for a few minutes, she encouraged me to tell Irving that I did not like his mustache. I protested that it would be unkind because he must have grown it because he liked it, or didn't he? Slowly I made my way to Irving's chair, deliberating whether I should say anything to him. I sat on the edge of his armchair and looked into his eyes. I got up my courage to say, "Irving, I like you better without this mustache." His face broke out in a wide smile, and he readily agreed with me. "I also prefer my face without a mustache," and he gave me a reassuring hug and a big, tickly kiss. The adults looked at each other with one of those meaningful glances that meant they knew something about his unruly mustache they were not telling me.

Once again Irving disappeared. A couple of weeks after his departure, my mother was sitting on the edge of her bed with her face drawn into a tight knot. Had somebody died? Was there an unexpected revolution? When I asked what happened, tears poured down her cheeks. Between sobs, she told me that news had arrived that Irving had just been arrested in New York City. News had a way of materializing from invisible sources.

When he returned illegally to America, he was arrested, convicted, and sent to the Atlanta penitentiary. He was released in August 1958 after which he continued to work for the party as its labor secretary. His marriage did not survive the long, stressful separations. I seem to remember my mother saying that his wife left him after giving up hope they could ever lead a "normal" life together. The government continued to harass him, calling him before Congress on several occasions, attempting to force him to register as an enemy agent.

Now I knew why Irving had a mustache! He had been preparing for his illegal reentry, and the plan failed. Abe and Belle knew that evening was Irving's last stay with us. Belle said he reentered the country to be with his family, but instead he was in the same city, but secluded from them, behind prison walls. John J. Abt in his 1993 book *Advocate and Activist: Memoirs of an American Communist Lawyer* describes Irving's return and arrest:

> He left the United States a little more than a year before, but decided that he could no longer live apart from his wife, children, and grandchildren. . . . It turned out that he had come back via Windsor, the Canadian border town across from Detroit, entering the US during the Christmas season when there was a good deal of back-and-forth traffic. The next morning the top item on the radio news was that deported leader Irving Potash had gone to dinner the evening before and, by the strangest coincidence, the FBI agent in charge of his case chose the same restaurant in which to dine, spotted him, and arrested Irving on the spot.

I did see Irving one more time when I returned to the United States. In 1963, when we arrived in New York City, we spent a few weeks in a Manhattan hotel. Irving was living a few blocks away, at the Chelsea Hotel. Aside from Ken, he was the only person from our exile I wanted to see when we returned. He came to our hotel room dressed in a formal suit, as he had always dressed in Prague, and a fedora hat that looked becoming on him. He greeted me with a wide, delighted smile at the sight of the young woman I had become and a loving hug. His mustache was gone. Our visit was a pantomime act. Instead of having a conversation, we had to write notes on a pad of paper because Irving assumed the room was bugged. The concealment, the danger of being together, or just being noticed in Irving's company prevented us from ever seeing him again. Besides, my parents no longer wanted any involvement with the party, and Irving never left the party. After a lifetime commitment, the party was the only "home" he had left. Friendship, as always, was subordinate to politics. I was unhappy to be yet one more person who would no longer have contact with Irving at a time when he seemed so alone. Even now, when I think of him, I smile and feel sad at the same time. Russians call that feeling "bittersweet." Remembering the tragic breaks in family relationships saddens me, for the price of the personal sacrifice was unfairly high and long term and in some cases permanent. Irving died in 1976, the same year my father died.

New people came into our lives for indefinite periods of time, replacing those who disappeared. The relationships were intense but fleeting. During our years of exile, there was no correspondence between my relatives and our family. We could not exchange photographs or family news. Their family life went on without us. Our family life continued incognito. My parents hardly ever talked about their families with me because it was too painful and complicated, and the future was beyond our control. The four of us, though surrounded by people, were at times quite alone in the world.

It was November, the month when Americans celebrate Thanksgiving. My mother had been in the kitchen for hours preparing a festive meal. None of my Czech friends had ever heard of this holiday. My sister and I were helping my mother fix the meal for my parents' deported, exiled, or in-transit comrades. The wonderful aroma of food filled the house while my sister and I were busy cutting out handmade pictures of Indians and Pilgrims and corn on the cob to pin onto the living room curtains to decorate the room.

The ingredients for this special meal were not available in the Czech grocery stores. Most of the traditional dishes had to be made out of substitutes. Instead of a turkey we had a chicken, in place of cranberry sauce we had *rybíz* (red currants), and for sweet potatoes we made do with squash and turnips. After the meal my mother disappeared in the kitchen, warning us that the biggest surprise was yet to come. She returned with the most unexpected trophy: a fluffy lemon meringue pie with glistening light brown peaks. To get pumpkin for a pumpkin pie was, of course, out of the question, but she was able to find the lemons to make this American specialty. Belle was thrilled to watch our excited reactions.

The foremost rule of survival in a foreign country, according to my mother, was flexibility. In the land of dumplings, pork, and sauerkraut, one had to be imaginative about reproducing the foods the native American Indians cultivated. Just as the food on the table consisted of substitutes, so too the people seated at the table were substitutes for grandparents, uncles, aunts, and cousins. These dislocated individuals, separated from family and country, joined our family circle year after year, though the faces of the participants changed. The communist family was mobile and unattached. At our table they found the family warmth they missed. I knew more about the personal affairs of my parents' comrades than I did of the births, marriages, or deaths in my own extended family. Now those people who used to spend time with us are gone, scattered all over the world. I do not know what happened to them, except when I find a new book written about the past or an obituary of someone who used to be part of our communist "family" circle.

Years after our return to the United States my mother would sigh, saying, "And do you know that Daphne is living in England now," or "Janet left China but her daughter stayed," when the need to remember and feel connected to the past they had created and lost would well up in her. She would cheer herself up saying, "Those were some wild times we had," and I suspected she was not sure it had all happened.

There was no substitute for the exhilaration the communists felt in attempting to put their revolutionary dream into action. In history the years of communist idealism and faith were a matter of a few decades, a mere flash of time, but for their personal lives their commitments to the cause had a profound effect on that period of time when their children were growing up, when their parents were aging, when they themselves were going through the most productive and energetic years of their lives. Good intentions were in the long run no guarantee that the political action their lives were centered around would succeed. The popular progressive song "Banks of Marble," which I heard in my home quite often, captured their overiding hope of radical change:

> I've traveled around this country, from shore to shining shore;
> It really made me wonder, the things I heard and saw.
> But the banks are made of marble, with a guard at every door,
> and the vaults are stuffed with silver that the farmer (seaman, miner) sweated for.
>
> I saw the seaman standing, idly by the shore,
> I heard the bosses saying, "Got no work for you no more."

I saw the weary miner scrubbing coal dust from his back,
I heard his children crying, "Got no coal to heat the shack."

I've seen my brothers working throughout this mighty land,
I prayed we'd get together, and together make a stand.
Then we'd own those banks of marble, with a guard at every door,
And we'd share those vaults of silver that the workers sweated for!

The communists made it seem simple: the world was divided between the evil rich who robbed the poor of equality and opportunities and the good communists who followed the teachings of Marx and Lenin to establish a utopia. Secrets, hiding, and lies were not part of that dream, yet they became a reality in the new communist societies expatriates had to live in. At home I felt this atmosphere of secrecy through hushed sentences and by the presence of strangers who visited at unpredictable times and for varying lengths. This secrecy was connected to Abe and Belle's American past.

Periodically my father had private meetings with Russians from whom he received gifts. A few times I went with him to meet those large-framed, friendly looking Russian men. I never asked my father what they talked about. It was just part of the unexplained things that happened. Why did they bring him gifts, and what did they expect in return? I had no idea. A few years before our return to the United States my father brought home a bolt of blue fabric. It was sturdy material, perhaps even Russia's best; my mother put it away for a special occasion. In preparation for our return to the United States on the SS *France*, my mother and I each had a new wardrobe made out of this dark blue fabric the Russians had given my father. (When I got off the boat in 1963 in New York City I was wearing a navy blue dress made out of Russian material, made by a Czech seamstress, setting me immediately apart from those around me.)

In the early 1960s, shortly before our return to the United States, our family spent an evening with Henry Winston, a national organization secretary of the CPUSA. What happened that evening made a deep impression on me. Winston was a black party organizer who during World War II helped enlist more than fifteen thousand communists into the armed forces and who continued to play a prominent role in the leadership of the CP. In 1949 he was sentenced to jail for five years under the Smith Act, as Irving Potash was, but by the decision of the party he went "underground." He "came out" in 1956, but he had to serve the original penalties, which kept him in prison until 1961. According to Starobin, "Henry Winston was a self-tutored, former bootblack from Hattiesburg, Mississippi, a Negro whose winning personality and intelligence made him one of the Party's most attractive young cadres for many years. Winston took the post of organizational secretary in mid-1946 and was to figure prominently in the underground of the fifties."

Winston came to visit us on his way to Moscow after he was released from prison in 1961. The Soviet government provided medical care for top-level American communist functionaries at their best hospitals. My parents, overjoyed to see Winston, told me he was a wonderful man who had done much for the communist cause. They had been informed that he had suffered some serious medical problems in prison. My mother spent the entire day preparing her best dishes. My father paced back and forth smoking one cigarette after another, too excited to read or write.

As it started to get dark, I heard voices in the hall. Three men came into the apartment—one extremely tall, heavy-set black man in a suit that could barely cover his large body and two Russian men. Winston stepped into the apartment inching his way forward, his immobile eyes focused somewhere above our heads. He did not look around the apartment, and he waited until my father embraced him before he addressed him. My father introduced me. He asked me to step up to him to shake his hand. His large hand grasped mine, and once I looked directly into his eyes I realized he was unable to see our family, our home, our excited faces. He had lost his eyesight in prison as a result of a brain tumor that prison officials refused to treat until too late to save his sight. At Winston's insistence, a private physician removed the tumor, but complications from the operation and attending care led to loss of eyesight. His Russian escorts gently maneuvered Winston's large body toward a chair. We settled into an evening of food, drink, and conversation. After dinner my father played some old jazz records. My mother, visibly shaken to see the drastic physical change in a man she had remembered as active and dynamic, suggested I ask Winston to dance to the seductive jazz tunes.

When a Bessie Smith song came on, I took his hand and guided him to dance in the center of the room. He took me in his arms, moving forward awkwardly, but as he lost himself in the beat of the familiar tunes he started to sway to the music with confidence and grace. After a while I forgot he was blind and let him guide me. An unexpected smile softened the stiff expression on his face. After more than a decade of seclusion, in and out of prison, this tall, big-framed black man, once a charismatic organizer of a growing movement, was subdued, beaten down. He was no longer the powerful individual who had been in control in the past; he was in need of help and guidance. A metaphor for the movement?

Starobin says in the preface to *American Communism in Crisis:* "Here were a group of men and women who believed they had found the assumptions and allegiances that would enable them [the communists] 'to make history.' Yet because they could never bring themselves to re-examine these assumptions and allegiances, they became history's victims." Winston's change was physically obvious; my parents' change was hidden deep inside. But the hurt and sadness were shared. A few months later, my father had a near fatal heart attack at his desk in our Prague apartment. The three of us were the only family he had to help him through his recovery.

Chapter 13
. . . .
And Life
Continues,
1956–1957

History is time. History is people. History is place. History is not only then; it is also now. The powerful write history; the powerless suffer it. History hurts.
— Joe Schlesinger, *Time Zones*

It was a gloomy fall day, but our home was filled with excitement and anticipation. Abe paced through the apartment leaving a trail of cigarette smoke in his path. His dark suit made him look distinguished. The rhythmic strides of his long steps marked the passing minutes. Belle was in the bedroom putting on the new black taffeta gown a seamstress had made for this important evening at the Hradčany castle. Laura and I were making sure the soft pleats of her full skirt folded in the most becoming manner around her narrow hips. I could not take my eyes off my mother's transformation into a court lady. Each movement of her body made the stiff, shiny taffeta rustle. I was more excited than my parents about their invitation to the castle to dine with government officials, foreign journalists, and selected dignitaries. The Prague castle had always been the center of power, towering over the entire city. But tonight was special because my parents were going to enter the castle chambers that I had admired from a distance.

The year was 1956. Both my parents, now settled in jobs, had firmly established their social status in the political community. My mother worked at an international organization that had its headquarters in Prague. She used her knowledge of English to edit and proofread. My father was employed at the Czech Academy of Sciences where he did research and gave lectures on American literature. He continued to do freelance writing on tight deadlines. Belle disliked wearing a formal gown and the social formalities such an evening required, but she complied because it was necessary. Abe was more distracted than excited about spending an evening in the company of top government officials.

Later that night they described the beauty of the sparkling chandeliers, ornate rooms with shiny parquet floors, elegant banquet dishes, and dinner guests. But they were far more concerned about rumors they heard that night about trouble in Hungary than about the exquisite castle rooms or the fancy food that was served. Unconfirmed reports had leaked out of a rebellion and shootings in the streets of Budapest that were a display of defiance against the presence of Soviet forces in Hungary. Under the elegant gowns and suits were naked fears and uncertainties, ready to erupt anytime, anyplace.

While they were getting out of their formal clothes, my mother and father discussed the talk they heard from some journalists about a Hungarian film that had recently played in Prague until it was banned because of its mildly daring theme. The film's title was $2 \times 2 = 5$. The title itself was an act of defiance, for to imply that the answer to the rational mathematical equation of $2 \times 2 = 4$ could possibly be 5 was a sign of irrational thinking too dangerous for comfort in a communist society. Rebellious thinking was only one step away from rebellious action. The Hungarian film had been a preview of the deep dissatisfaction and restlessness in the Budapest intellectual circles that led to the recent outburst. The desire of the Hungarians to free themselves from Soviet rule and from rational dogmas was creating irrational chaos and violence on the Budapest streets. Nobody knew if the danger would spread or be squelched. Everybody wondered what this meant for communism not only in Hungary but in Czechoslovakia and the other Eastern bloc countries.

The established order in the socialist countries was no stronger than a thin layer of ice under which there were dangerously turbulent waters. My mother slowly slipped out of her gown, drawing on her cigarette. She puffed out words along with circles of smoke that rose above her head. "I would like to know what is real about these reports concerning the events in Budapest," she said. Without official reports to confirm the news, all was mere speculation. In place of facts, fear took over. The stability of our future was at stake. What could happen to us in Prague, only three hundred miles from Budapest? All communist countries were intertwined politically and economically, completely dependent on the Soviet Union for all major decisions and internal security. Was this why my father paced through the apartment absorbed in his thoughts while we helped our mother make herself beautiful for the castle reception?

The Western press reported (though in Prague we had no access to this information in 1956) that the events in Budapest that autumn began with a symbolic public expression of sympathy for Polish victims, which then became a protest against persistent food shortages and low wages in Hungary. At the time that was the only objective. But dissent once expressed proved to have a life of its own. Ultimately the tensions came to a head. A Hungarian university professor and author, Endre Marton, analyzed the events that led to the 1956 Budapest uprising in the *New York Times*: "When Stalin died, the 'God' fell, and there was nobody to replace him. There was 'liberalization' in Hungary and in other countries in the Communist orbit. There was loosening of control. But you know, when a dictatorship loosens control, sooner or later it loses control. And that's what happened with Hungary. The communist system collapsed." The Czech communist press had no reports about the Hungarian uprising. Such knowledge was potentially dangerous, for it could trigger unrest in the other communist bloc countries. After Stalin's death the Hungarian regime began to liberalize, which created a conflict between the former Stalinist premier Matyas Rakosi and the current premier Imre Nagy, who had instituted those liberal reforms. Communist intellectuals started to demand reforms. On October 23, 1956, violence erupted when police fired at students protesting among other things the presence of Soviet troops on Hungarian territory. Fighting broke out all over Hungary, and for a few days the revolutionaries won control of many key institutions.

On November 4 the Soviets attacked, and thousands were killed, imprisoned, or fled the country. The attempted revolution failed. The article "Russians Crush Hungarian Rebels" in the November 5 *New York Times* reported that "Hungary's brave hopes for independence lay crushed by the nailed fist of Soviet power." And in the Czech newspapers there appeared not a single word. There were no reports of protests, deaths, uprisings. But there were plenty of rumors circulating around town. According to the leading communist paper, *Rudé Právo* (a paper my father contributed to), life continued in Czechoslovakia as it had been programmed to run. Newspaper reports informed us that our nation was preoccupied with rebuilding and improving the socialist economy. The second five-year plan had set high goals for individual industrial plants and collective farms. Czechoslovakia was intent on building what Hungary was trying to destroy and change. Meanwhile, *Rudé Právo* obliterated the reality of the Hungarian situation. The assumption was that if the event was concealed, it really was not happening. The real was unreal and the unreal was made to be real. And the truth?

The absence of hard facts created panic buying in Prague. Panic shopping was an automatic impulse, a basic survival instinct against unconfirmed rumors. In the stores empty shelves were an indication that people's confidence in a secure future was at an all-time low. People exchanged reports of sighting trainloads of Czech crops heading for the Hungarian border. These reports made shoppers grab whatever food was left as fast as they could find it. I did as the others did; I stood in line for whatever was left, regardless of whether we needed it. Hoarding was at least a guarantee that we would have food if a social upheaval occurred. When I rode the trams or stood in food lines I tried to figure out from snippets of conversations what was going on. "Really, did tanks take over the city . . . how many were shot . . . how many sent to prison?" Their mouths clamped shut if a stranger walked by.

The rumors about Hungary brought the uneasy feeling that a drastic change was occurring in the communist world, yet everything stayed the same in our city, in my school, on my street, and in my life. People perhaps walked a little faster, smiled a bit less, asked more questions, provided fewer responses. It was clear that the great love between the Soviet Union and the other communist countries was not as simple as I had assumed. I felt confused. Without sufficient information I wasn't ready to mistrust the Russians or to doubt their good intentions. It would have taken much more than unconfirmed rumors to shake my faith. Eventually I pushed these troubling thoughts away. I still firmly believed in the communist brotherhood. I reasoned that in Hungary the people were wild and that their Gypsy blood made them dissatisfied and restless. In Czechoslovakia, after all, we were cultured, civilized, and, above all, united. I decided what happened there could not happen here.

Pressing demands in my teenage life took precedence over rumors of political chaos in Hungary. At that moment I was busy rehearsing for the major gymnastic event that was about to take place in Prague — the Spartakiáda, a major display of physical fitness and athletic feats in which all schoolchildren participated. The Spartakiáda took place in a huge outdoor sports stadium, and the patterns we worked on were formed by hundreds of human bodies working together. I was one of those contributing bodies, a tiny speck in a giant petal of a multicolored flower. The formation of the flower was a collective effort in which our unified bodies made the pattern come together. I was convinced my little speck in the flower was essential to the pattern's execution.

Physical fitness and team cooperation were valued in a socialist state. Every day after school, we spent long hours rehearsing our formations in preparation for the Spartakiáda. We each had a special skirt that had a different color on each side, and at the crucial moment during the maneuvers we would briskly turn the skirt to the other side to change the color of the flower. The timing had to be perfect for the color change to surprise and thrill the spectators.

At first I was honored to be a part of this historic event, but after hours of tedious lineups, long waits to enter and exit the stadium, and repetitive maneuvers in the heat and dust I was eager to have the event performed, finished, done. After months of rehearsals, the day for the Spartakiáda arrived. We had lined up for the last time, ready to perform. Anticipation was high. The coaches snapped us into our rehearsed formations, telling us the crowds were eager to see what we could do. Banners were flying, music was playing, slogans and posters decorated the stadium. Cheering crowds filled the stadium. I was swept up in the craziness around me. We waited in the aisles ready to march out to the playing bands. The time had come for us to create our giant flower that filled one corner of the enormous stadium and required hundreds of strong pioneer bodies. And I was one of them!

While we waited our turn to enter the stadium in the direct sun I fell to the ground in a faint. I was taken by ambulance to a hospital, where I received treatment for heat stroke. Instead of filling my spot in the giant flower, I was delivered to my parents, who did not expect me home so soon. Long months of practice and the final excitement of anticipating the chance to perform were never realized for me because I could not tolerate the powerful sun. As a pioneer I was ashamed of my body's failure to withstand the heat. As a young girl I was most disappointed to miss the climactic moment and the response of the cheering crowds. But as a sun-stricken victim I was glad to be in bed. The Spartakiáda went on without me; apparently the collective managed without my contribution. That was a shocking, incredible realization for me.

I did not react to my mother the same way at home as when we went to public places. As I got older her negative reactions to the way Czechs did things made me uncomfortable. She disapproved of the way Czech mothers behaved, upholding her American ways. She had strong opinions about food: she shared the American preoccupation with nutrition and health and was horrified at what the Czechs ate and how they fed their children. She was convinced that the steady diet of starch, fats, and sugar in the form of dumplings, thick sauces, fatty meats, and rich cream cakes, which my Czech friends thrived on, was harmful to me. As difficult as it was to get the ingredients she wanted for our family dinners, she made an enormous effort to find the last vegetable or lean piece of meat.

When Czech mothers wanted to treat their children to something special they went to the closest *cukrárna* (sweet shop) and piled as many slices of rich butter and cream cakes on a plate as they could, which they watched their child devour with pleasure. The mere sight of the cakes sent my mother into a frenzy of despair. How could they let their children eat such unhealthy stuff before dinner, she lamented. She ignored my pleading glances at my favorite cake, *rakvička* (little coffin), which was made out of fragile dough shaped like a coffin with a thick mound of whipped cream on top. When the cake melted in my mouth it was far from the kiss of death my mother thought it was—it was heaven.

In disciplinary matters my mother never acted the way Czech mothers did. Though the Czechs let their children eat rich cakes, if they walked through a puddle and got their clothes dirty, their mothers would give them a quick smack, which Belle thought unfair. Most children were raised to fear the iron discipline of their fathers; my mother had no use for this approach. She took charge of domestic affairs herself; in fact, there were times when Abe had to be put in his place if his exuberance got out of hand. As soon as I was old enough I tried to go places with my friends instead of with Belle. But at home, I loved spending time with her and what she did and said never made me upset; on the contrary, I admired her.

When I went shopping, I treated myself to one of those forbidden cakes. It was always in these little things that the essential differences showed up between my parents and me. More and more I gravitated toward Czech ways, the way my friends and their families did things, fully aware of what was expected of me in my own home and of how different those expectations were. I learned to conceal my little deviations from my parents. I remembered the contrast between my grandparents' kosher home and my parents' nonkosher, nonreligious one as evidence of how much my parents differed from their own parents. Intuitively I maneuvered between the stable, traditional world around me and the nonconformist one in my home.

Living for so many years in a country that celebrated Christmas and Easter as the most important nonstate holidays, my sister and I pressured our parents to celebrate these holidays with us. For as long as they could, my parents resisted having a Christmas tree in our Prague home. One year Laura and I purchased a Christmas tree by ourselves. It was not hard to get Abe excited about decorating it. Belle stayed in the kitchen, unwilling to participate. But once the tree was up and the record with the traditional Ryba Christmas mass was playing, she joined us with a drink in her hand and a festive meal she had prepared. From that year on, we started a new tradition in our home. It was a unique version of the holiday, not quite the same as in the Czech homes but one that made sense in our family. But Belle remained firm on Easter. There would be no Easter eggs in our home.

When Belle could get strong, flavorful garlic, she and Abe would gather at the table to share a ritual that chased Laura and me out of the kitchen or out of the house. It was the making and eating of Belle's Mexican garlic soup. First, she fried a pan full of garlic cloves until the aroma filled the house; then she fried slices of stale bread over which she poured hot broth. In the center of the bowl she placed a raw egg, which changed consistency in the hot broth. Abe and Belle would bury their faces in the warm garlic fumes and dig their spoons into the hot soup, breaking the egg yolk. Consuming this concoction brought contented sounds from both of them.

My sister hated the smell of the brewing garlic soup. The garlic smell reminded her of the days on the Mexican farm, her illness, the farm kitchen smells; she wanted to forget our days and nights of confinement. My mother thought Laura was too delicate to tolerate the smell of garlic. Past memories were easily resurrected by a particular smell, sound, or word. There were four people in our family; there were four different associations and perceptions of the past and four ways of dealing with them in the present. And that remains true even now.

Whenever it was possible, our family did things together on weekends. I went to many art exhibits with my parents, something we all enjoyed. There were two paintings in particular that made a lasting impression on me. Over a long period of time I examined those paintings, taking in every line, every expression on the faces of the figures, every shade of color. I was deeply moved and disturbed.

The first was Vincent Van Gogh's *The Potato Eaters*. It is a painting of a family, four adults and one child. The child's back is turned toward the viewer, forcing us to concentrate on the faces of the adults: one man and three women, two generations. They are sitting at a kitchen table in a simple farm room under a drab light. On the wall there is a picture and a clock. Members of this family have been brought together to share their meal, a plate of potatoes and a kettle of tea. Van Gogh captured the tenderness and resignation of this poor farm family. The man in the painting seems more crushed than the women. His eyes are directed into the distance, whereas the women's warm, compassionate gazes are turned toward the other family members. In a way, the painting, with its gnarled, hardworking peasant hands, celebrates the strength of the human spirit that survives despite life's hardships. Potatoes are their only reward for their hard work. But they have each other and the warmth they share. I kept returning to the *Potato Eaters*, magnetized by the hands that expressed so much emotion. Van Gogh's painting validated my abstract sympathies with the "suffering" masses.

The other painting that had a powerful effect on me was Picasso's *Guernica*, painted in 1937. This enormous mural engulfed me. In front of it I was small and powerless. The figures of the warrior, the dying horse, and the bellowing bull conveyed unspeakable brutality. I was paralyzed, devastated, horrified. I wanted to pull the outstretched hands out of their doom. I wanted to turn away from the dislocated eyes and the cries I could hear coming from the open mouths. Life was a distorted tangle of trapped humans and animals, suffering, unable to help themselves. None of the socialist realist paintings I had seen in the other rooms had so much intensity and power.

In my youth I was deeply affected by the power of a painting, the written word in a book, a piece of music, a fleeting image. My desire to imagine what a heroine in a novel looked like or the landscape books described had no limits, for growing up without television I had the freedom to explore and create my own images. Things I noticed during the day, the behavior of people or the changing seasons or the sounds and smells on the city streets, became the fabric of my inner visual world. The rich world of my imagination gave life a special meaning. It was something I could not share with others; it was my very own private treasure.

By 1957 the days of my childhood were already long gone. I was inching my way into the adult world. In the very back of our living room cupboard in which I stored some of my old toys there was a small rubber baby doll friends of my parents had brought me from America. She was naked, though I kept her tightly wrapped in a baby blanket. Whenever my mother asked me, "Ann, how come you never play with your baby doll?" I feared she would discover what I had done to her. I had pulled out her two arms: perhaps I had played too roughly with her, or perhaps I was curious about her anatomy, or perhaps the dismemberment was a way of indicating that I loved the doll that had been left in my bedroom in New York City much more. All I know is that I felt an overwhelming guilt that I had done something terrible to her that I wanted to hide. Years beyond the doll playing period, I was still aware of the presence of this doll with her two dislodged arms lying beside her. I will never know if my mother had ever seen what happened to the doll's arms or if she thought it best to pretend she did not know.

In the fall of 1957 there was talk in our home about the four of us visiting Moscow, the city my father had visited in 1950 and which he wanted us to see and learn about. Moscow—a city I had heard, read, and thought about a great deal—had more appeal to me than Paris or New York. I was anxious to see for myself if it was the way I had imagined it.

In Russian literature Moscow is depicted as the vital political, intellectual, and business center of the country. In Chekhov's play *Three Sisters* Irina exclaims: "Oh, I want to go to Moscow, to Moscow, to Moscow!" It was an unfulfilled hope that she dreamed about her entire life. I was lucky enough to go there for the Christmas season of 1957. I was going to celebrate New Year's Eve in Moscow. I was beside myself with excitement. My father was already arranging the necessary papers for our trip. At supper time he kept the excitement at a feverish pitch by describing Moscow's largeness, beauty, and uniqueness. Once our dates were confirmed Abe joyfully announced: "What a terrific people, what a beautiful language and culture they have, and in a few weeks, a few days, the four of us will be boarding a train that will take us there."

In preparation for the trip I bought a small diary with a tiny golden lock in which I planned to record my observations. I was fifteen years old and I was on my way to Moscow, the city that meant so much to so many people who passed through our house, the symbol of the revolution worldwide. What could be more exciting? We were packed and ready to go. I wrote on the first page of my new diary in big letters, THE DIARY OF MY TRIP TO MOSCOW IN THE YEAR 1957/58.

Chapter 14

. . . .

"Oh, I Want to Go to Moscow, to Moscow, to Moscow"

Moscow is enormous, the driver told us that if all the streets would be put in a line it would be 1400 km. Today after the New Year it was happy on the streets with groups of people with accordions or guitars walking on the street singing.

We tried to find the Chinese restaurant in Moscow. On the corner we asked a policeman. First he showed us which way to go, but then he reconsidered and he walked us over there. When he found out we were from Prague he told us he had been there. He hoped we would enjoy our stay and he wished us a Happy New Year.
—Anna Čapková, "Diary"

'Tis the final conflict,
Let each stand in his place;
The International Soviet shall be the human race.
—The chorus of "The International"

Our family spent two weeks in Moscow because of a slender book my father wrote, *Newspapers in the U.S.A.*, put out by the Czech publishing house Orbis in Prague in 1956. It was translated from English by K. F. Zieris; it cost 5 crowns and 76 hellers, which was almost as much as my weekly allowance, and the printing was seventeen hundred copies. It was a thoroughly propagandistic Marxist description of the American newspaper industry. The book shows, however, that despite the monopoly of the syndicates there was also a progressive press with an opposition viewpoint and that America had publications for black readers and foreign-language readers. Though the author had an exclusively communist interpretation, it was clear that one found in the American press divergent views that did not exist in Czechoslovakia. Shortly after its publication in Czech, the book was translated into Russian. My father received his payment in rubles, which he could not convert to crowns. He decided, with the encouragement of his Russian contacts, to bring the family to Moscow to show them the capital city of the USSR. The plan was to stay in the best hotel, go to the most expensive restaurants, and attend theaters, concerts, and museums so that we could spend the entire honorarium for his book. And that is exactly what we did. I had a wonderful, magical time.

In the course of our extensive family travels many things got lost or had to be left behind. It is a quirk of fate that the little diary I kept of my trip to Moscow is still with me. In 1986, when my teenaged son and husband planned a trip to Moscow, I decided to translate the Czech diary notes I had written when I was fifteen years old into English. I thought they might prepare my son for his trip and even evoke images of what Moscow looked like to me. Instead, when rereading them I realized what a big difference there was between the environment my son Daniel grew up in and the one I had been raised in. I went to Moscow observing things both as a Czech, comparing everything to the life I knew in Prague, and a believer in communism, while he read my diary as an American and an observer with an independent mind relatively free of political biases. The gap between our experiences was far deeper than a mere generational difference. He had had an entirely different preparation for life.

When I visited Moscow, I found the grandness, the friendliness, and the splendor my father prepared us for because I believed it had to be there. According to my diary, we boarded the train on December 21, 1957, and that very night I started to record my impressions with a description of the interior of our compartment on the silver-colored Russian train. We were given a boisterous send-off by our friends who followed us to the train station after a dinner at the restaurant for journalists a couple of blocks from the main train station. In my diary I faithfully described places we saw and things we did. I am disappointed that I recorded only what I saw and not how I felt and what I thought, but that was what I was like when I was fifteen years old: curious, easily impressed, and literal in my descriptions. I was not thinking of this document as a piece of history I would return to in the future. I was merely preserving the moment as I saw it on the day it was happening. These excerpts from my diary bring me back to the last days of 1957 when our trip started: "Immediately they made our soft beds up with clean-smelling linen, a huge soft pillow and thick, warm woolen blankets. It was an absolute luxury. In our wagon there are two Soviet porters, who speak in a beautiful melodic Russian and they are very nice. They are constantly serving huge 'stakany' glasses of tea. We spent the entire day lounging in bed, eating good food. The countryside is desolate and sad."

The trip from Prague to Moscow took a two and a half days. In our case, however, it was longer because of unexpected complications with our documents. In Eastern Europe residents had to carry internal passports at all times. We had papers that allowed us to use special library facilities or that entitled us to medical care at the local clinic and food coupons that allowed us to purchase a limited quantity of scarce foods. We had to have documents that permitted us to make virtually any move. Arrivals and departures had to be documented. Without appropriate papers we could not function in this society. Only those with legitimate documents got past the guards in ministries, libraries, official buildings, workplaces. We were shocked to be kicked off the train when it reached the Slovak border to cross over to Russia:

We were rested and we were getting close to the border village Čierna Nad Tidsou. The border patrol came onto the train and they started their searches. A soldier, who examined our documents pronounced the fatal terrible words that shook us up: "You can't continue on your journey, go back to Prague, you are missing one document from the Soviet embassy." We were forced to get off the train within a few minutes. We had our belongings scattered all over the compartment. We were not able to get our things into the suitcases in such a rush and under our arms we had the things we couldn't get into the suitcase. When we dragged ourselves into the train station we found out some additional wonderful news—in this village there was no hotel.

We slept in an office that was terribly dusty. My parents slept in armchairs and Laura and I slept on a curvy (hunchbacked) couch. In the morning, after a sleepless night we started furious phone calling reproaching Čedok [the Czech travel agency] for not giving us the proper papers. We were already despairing that the trip would be canceled and that we would be traveling back in the direction of Prague and not Moscow. We were so nervous about the whole situation we couldn't even eat. The food got stuck in our mouths from all the worry and nervous tension. Finally they called us back and they told us that we could continue without that fatal paper (document) and they sent a message to Chop (the Soviet border town) that they should let us through. At least we calmed down a bit. We passed through the border control again and we went about 10 km toward the Soviet border. Again the border passport control, but it was the Soviet one and they were very pleasant.

When we reached the Soviet border town Chop, we had to fill out forms and have a customs check that left us three minutes to get back to our coach. The train almost left without us. I was used to functioning in a bureaucracy where the needs of the customer were subsurvient to paperwork, the acquisition of official stamps, and an inefficient system of rules and regulations. Obviously it was going to be the same in the Soviet Union, but instead of being upset that we were forced to run with our luggage so we would not miss the train I observed casually: "When we got to our coach they were pulling up the stairs and closing the doors. We barely made it by jumping up which was quite an athletic feat." The dusty smell of the train station at Čierna Nad Tidsou, the worn-out faces of the travelers, and the heaviness of waiting for something that does not arrive or happen are engraved in my memory. It was a dilapidated, isolated, freezing hole in the wall that accommodated on its few scattered benches the most unsightly collection of scruffy travelers. Local and transient drunks wove through the corridors of the station willing to talk to anybody close enough to listen to their woes. Once we were dumped at this station from our cozy beds on the train my mother was not going to let her two teenaged daughters spend the night brushing off the rough advances of the local drunks. She insisted on getting somebody in charge to remedy the situation. This person happened to be a soft-spoken, mild-mannered man in his thirties with a head that was shaped like a flat pancake. I translated my mother's demands for immediate action for the meek train station manager: "Well if there is no hotel in this town let us into one of your offices; my daughters can't spend the night among all these drunks," and though it had never occurred to him that his office could become a hotel room he obliged my mother. The next day my sister and I went for a walk in the village outside of the station to kill time until the departure of the next train for Moscow. We were grateful that we lived in Prague, the center of civilization, rather than in this desolate sinkhole. But I did not record any of these experiences in my diary. I kept to the positive and upbeat, unwilling or unable to see any faults in the system responsible for the misery that surrounded me.

Once our travel status was reconfirmed, we started again for Moscow. On December 24 (just in time for the Ukranian celebration of independence) we stopped at the Kiev train station:

> Lots of peasant women were sitting here with bundles on their backs and with small children that were so bundled up that you could barely see their little noses and eyes. They were selling roasted chickens here and lemons for 4 rubles 20 kopeks for one. . . . We were surprised to see that the buildings had very expensive and beautiful decorations made out of light bulbs. The light bulbs were constantly changing their colors. We found out that the Ukraine is celebrating on the 24th and 25th of December the 40th anniversary of their independence.

Unaware of the sensitive relations between the Russians and the Ukranians, I could not judge the potential political ramifications of this observance, which acquired full meaning in the 1990s. [*Today I find it most interesting that the Ukranians celebrate their independence from the Russian empire so fervently, because what I recorded was harmony rather than discord and conflict.*] Finally, we pulled into Moscow and settled into the luxurious party hotel Sovetskaya (Soviet). Now the handwritten text in my diary is in the purple ink found in all the inkwells in the Soviet Union:

> In the morning we were impatient for it to be 11:10 AM when we were supposed to reach the Moscow station. We were already expected and we had a ride in a car to our luxury hotel. The name of the hotel was SOVETSKAYA. It is a massive 4 story building. The halls are so huge that I feel like a tiny ant. The stairs and pillars are marble. The dining room is enormous and each setting has several plates and 3 different sized glasses and a cloth napkin. The food in the restaurant is first class.

On the first day of our visit we met our translator, Jedviga, who accompanied us throughout our stay. She translated and got tickets for us to attend major theaters, concerts, and museums. This privileged treatment had to be an indication of the important relationship Abe had with the Russian comrades. Jedviga was a soft-spoken, shy woman in her thirties who performed efficiently, but she never stepped out of her official role. I had no idea where she lived, what her reactions and thoughts were, or if she really wanted to take us around her hometown. Her strong but bookish knowledge of English needed practice. Each day when she arrived at our hotel, on time for the scheduled daily events, she looked as though she needed a few more hours of sleep her hectic life would not permit her.

Moscow made me realize how narrow the small Prague streets were: "One more thing surprised us—how beautifully wide the roads are here. They are crowded with buses, cars and trucks that are enclosed and they have various signs on them like FISH, ICE CREAM etc."

It was obvious that staying at the Sovetskaya Hotel gave us little indication of how average Russians lived or ate. One of the first sights we visited was the Kremlin. The churches inside the Kremlin were converted into museums. I never thought to wonder why there were no church services in these beautiful ancient churches. I was already used to churches in Prague that were used as museums or concert halls. I had studied some Russian history, but I knew nothing about the religious significance of the objects in the Kremlin. This is how I saw the Kremlin:

The Kremlin is like a self-contained city. The Kremlin is an enormous yellow building with beautifully carved gray and white windows. Behind the buildings there is an enormous courtyard with several churches that have beautiful towers shaped like onions. They are golden and silver. We went to two churches. According to their architecture they were from the 14th and 13th centuries, very tall and at the top in the clouds there are pictures of Christ. Tall candles in silver holders are hanging in front of the icons. There are gorgeous silver doors hand-carved. In the other church there was a chair, actually a throne for the Czar and Pope. There are the graves of Ivan the Terrible there and graves of other dignitaries. There is a holy picture there and around it, carved out of metal there are pictures from biblical life.

Far more sacred than the museumlike churches was the visit to the mausoleum, the holiest of shrines in front of which thousands of people lined up to pay their respects to Lenin and Stalin every day. It was not easy to get through the crowds:

> We had planned to go to the Mausoleum. First of all on the subway there was an incredible crowd, because most everybody has off for the holiday. You can't even get close to a store. It seems like lots of people came from the countryside to shop.
>
> When we came to the Mausoleum there was a line that was out of sight. The line extended across the entire park at the Kremlin and it twisted down 2 streets and it was still curved around.

A few days later we actually managed to get into the mausoleum, but not the way Soviet citizens did. We attached ourselves to a group of foreigners:

> Throughout the building soldiers stand guard. The entire building on the inside is out of black and gray marble. Lenin and Stalin are lying next to each other on simple wooden beds and red lights shine on their heads. They don't look like people anymore, but like wax figurines. When we got out we walked along a street by the Kremlin wall where there are graves of various dignitaries for ex.: Gorkij, Potemkin (some foreign men too).

One would never know from my descriptions of our meals in our hotel that there were severe food shortages and long lines in the Moscow stores. We tried hotel, restaurant, and street food: "We bought warm pirozhki with meat for one ruble. A woman was selling them out of a basket. They were excellent." To make sure we spent every last ruble of Abe's honorarium we dined in Moscow's most interesting restaurants, for example, the Chinese restaurant in the Hotel Peking: "It is beautiful there, in the middle of the ceiling there is a powder blue indented center and it gives the impression of having the sky there." We ate in a fish restaurant situated in a boat on the river Moskva, where "we had fish from which caviar comes and which is incredibly expensive, but good. It costs 13.50 rubles for one piece of grilled fish without potatoes or anything else." The Bulgarian restaurant Sofia was "festively decorated and there was a Christmas tree there," and I thought the food was fantastic, whereas the Armenian restaurant Ararat "that is supposed to be terrific isn't anything special." Everything in this country was giant-sized: the buildings, the boulevards, and the portions of food:

Breakfast turned out to be hysterical. Our Russian is not that good and we ordered room service. Daddy ordered pancakes and when she asked how many he wants, he said 3 and Laura wanted to order 2 fried eggs. Instead 3 orders of pancakes came with 2 in each order which could be managed because they were hm hm hm—excellent. Laura was in a worse predicament, she got 2 portions of eggs with 4 eggs in each, thus 8 eggs. So we were punished for our lack of knowledge of Russian. Altogether the Russians eat an incredible amount for breakfast, 4 eggs is a normal portion for them.

Content to be together, the four of us slipped into the New Year feasting on Russian delicacies. The New Year, 1958, would bring unforseeable change and disclocation in my life. But that night I had no worries:

We celebrated the New Year at our hotel in my parents' room. We had wine, vodka, caviar, a chicken, ham, turkey, olives, salami, potato salad and other good foods—and that is how we parted with the old year. We didn't even wait for the Prague New Year's Eve. We played canasta and the winning pair got 4 rubles. Daddy and I won.

While in Moscow my mother wanted the Russians to arrange for me to see one of their doctors in hopes of a cure for my eczema. This was Russia, after all, and anything was possible here. My parents' Russian contacts arranged for me to see a Russian specialist who told me I needed to stick to a strict diet, which excluded meat and chocolate and many grains. In fact, it meant that all I could eat was milk, fruits, and vegetables, all foods that were hard or impossible to get in Prague. The fact remained that there was no cure for my affliction.

We had a chance to see the opera *Boris Godunov* in the Bolshoi that sent shivers down my spine: "The play was historic but I never had such a wonderful time at the opera. All the soloists sang magnificently and the chorus was like one man. The music was serious and beautiful." We went to the Chaikovski hall to see the Alexandrov group (probably folk singing), the Obrazcov puppet theater about which I say, "the puppets are exquisite," and once again to the Bolshoi for the ballet *Swan Lake* in which the leading part was danced by an English dancer, B. Gray. I responded enthusiastically: "I have never seen such a perfect, beautiful ballet. Gray danced outstandingly, the chorus of twenty-four girls danced as if in a dream." I detect a mild case of fatigue with socialist realist art when I express a desire for a hero who is not so completely positive, somebody a bit more real and human perhaps: "We had tickets to the theater of Lenin's Youth League, where they were supposed to play *Years of Wandering*. It is one of the few Soviet plays where the main character isn't completely positive in all respects."

Prague's medieval streets and the above-the-ground tram system made the Moscow metro an exotic yet modern thrill. The Soviets were experts at building underground railroads. In the 1970s they helped the Czechs build the Prague subway. It is efficient and well designed. This is how I saw the Moscow metro:

> We started with the subway station "Dynamo." It is difficult to describe the beauty of the Metro. You enter a building where you buy tickets which cost 50 kopeks. Then there are stands where they sell sweets, cigarettes and the ice cream that is so wonderful. You go down on riding steps so that it is no effort. At the top of the stairs they check if you have a ticket and that is why the trains don't have conductors. When we step off the staircase we enter a rather wide, long hall, where there are either pictures or statues depending on the station. I liked the "Mayakovsky" station the most. It is spacious, white and there are arches there that form a skyline where there is a mosaic picture. Each station is completely different and incredibly clean, nowhere did I even see a piece of paper. The trains arrive with such a speed that they make a dreadful noise. The trains are gorgeous, half green and half blue on the outside. The doors open and close automatically and they stop at the station for a minute. Inside there are soft cushioned seats, good light for reading and ventilators. The windows and the entire train are absolutely as clean as can be. It is warm inside the train. You don't wait long for the train, it is like the trams [the Prague public transportation system], they come one after another quite quickly.

Shopping in Moscow made me realize what an advanced country Czechoslovakia was in comparison. The quality of the products and the selections were inferior here. Now I understood why Russians loved to shop in Prague even though the quality of merchandise in Prague was not particularly high in the 1950s. It is interesting that though in communist countries religious holidays were replaced by secular ones, not all symbols of Christmas were abolished. Officially people were expected to celebrate the New Year and Grandfather Frost replaced Santa Claus, but Moscovites still bought Christmas trees and the big department stores had them on display. I noticed that not all the shoppers could buy things because the prices were prohibitive. Even I could see that the standard of living was much lower than in Prague. These were some of my shopping impressions:

We looked into one of the smaller department stores. The quality of the fabric is unbelievably poor. We were in a store which sold furs—unbelievably expensive. We stopped in a smaller textile store where they didn't have very nice things. . . .

First we went to "Detskij Mir" (A Child's World). . . . They have a large selection of toys but they are quite expensive. A bicycle for a small child costs about 160 rubles. They have charming calendars for 1 ruble with a cat that is standing holding a calendar in its paws in the shape of an accordion. In the center of the store there is an enormous jolka—(X-mas tree), two stories high and around the tree there are animals holding hands circling around. The tree is beautifully decorated and it has electric bulbs. The X-mas decorations are not as nice as in Prague. . . .

We went to look around the market for a while. Mainly farmers are selling their leftover produce. There are lots of potatoes and cabbages for 2 rubles a kilo. There is a lot of cottage cheese and milk but it is quite expensive and so is the meat and poultry.

We spent one entire day at Lomonosov University, where we got the special tour for foreign visitors. I was impressed. The university grounds were so enormous it was impossible to compare it to Charles University in Prague, which was miniature in comparison and which had buildings dispersed throughout the city rather than consolidated:

Today we plan to go to Lomonosov University. It is quite far from the center of town. It is actually a skyscraper with 33 stories and it is terribly long. Of course there are elevators there, otherwise I would feel sorry for the students. On the ground floor there are swimming pools and gym rooms. On the upper floors there are laboratories, libraries, lecture halls and dormitories. Another nice thing is the hotel for guests. There are also stores for the students. We saw the geography department which has several floors. They are very well equipped, they have drafting tables and huge boards with lamps for making maps. They have entire rooms with labeled display cases. Then we saw the dorm rooms they live in, a spring mattress bed, radio, desk, closet and a kettle for tea. A very pleasant room. It has its own bathroom and toilet.

Today I strongly doubt all the students had the spectacular accommodations they showed us.

Museum visits were either political history lessons about the revolution or peasant and folk art forms. Socialist countries promoted folk art, folk music, and crafts, which were glorified as art expressions of working-class people. My parents wanted us to know about the biggest accomplishments of the Soviet era. Visits to these museums guaranteed that we would. At the museum of the Revolution I saw the entire world divided into the socialist and the capitalist ones:

> Today mother, Laura, and I went to the V. I. Lenin museum. The museum is in an enormous building and again there were many people there and groups of schoolchildren and pioneers. His manuscripts are there, his collected works and photographs of his entire family and houses he lived in. There is a chart explaining how he conducted underground work. The coat in which he was shot was there as well as his clothes, boots, the table on which he played chess and which had a hidden drawer for documents. Later during Soviet rule his room in the Kremlin was transferred to the museum after his death. A simple room with a large library with maps on the walls, leather covered chairs, and his large car that he used during the Soviet rule were on display. In a few rooms there were gifts from workers. In the last room there were flags and funeral wreaths that accompanied him at his funeral. . . .
>
> In the morning we went to the museum of the Revolution. There were very many written works and manuscripts of V. I. Lenin, which we couldn't read. There were cannons, guns and outfits of the sailors from the Aurora and outfits of the prisoners. There were many pictures that explained the revolution which had accompanying explanations. There were many pioneers and

older schoolchildren with guides. At the end of the exhibit there were a few rooms with presents received for the fortieth anniversary of the Soviet Union. There were gifts from all countries, from democratic and capitalistic countries as well. For example from Italy there was a tiny fly carved out of metal. From Brazil there was a tray made out of the wings of butterflies.

Moscow would not be Moscow without a visit to the renowned Tretiakov art gallery, where I found the socialist realist art, I am glad to say, ugly in comparison to paintings from earlier periods:

It was a long walk across the bridge to the Tretiakov gallery. There are paintings there from the 11th century to contemporary times. There were many simple people there, soldiers and entire groups of pioneers and schoolchildren wearing their school uniforms accompanied by their teachers who were explaining the meaning of the paintings to them. . . . The paintings from the older periods were more interesting and the colors were more beautiful. The paintings from the year 1954 were ugly and I didn't like the colors.

Russians on the whole were friendly and helpful when we needed assistance, but when they realized we were foreigners they gave us preferential treatment. How did ordinary Russians ever get into choice restaurants, exhibits, and theaters? More than native Russian, the sounds of English worked like instant magic:

On the corner of the street near the Kremlin there was a woman who was selling tickets for three rubles to go into the Kremlin. Some man who heard us speak English gave us purple tickets for free. . . .
We decided to go to the Georgian restaurant and when we got there . . . on the door there was a sign. No available tables. They told us we could wait. So we went inside and when they heard us speak English they took us into a small room with one long table prepared for a feast. We were saved.

On the first day of the New Year I summed up my observations of Moscow as a city. We saw the feverish building going on that was replacing the old Moscow buildings. The Russians told us this was the greatest thing that was happening in the city; they were bringing in the new and getting rid of the old to make room for expansion. Tearing down and rebuilding were symbols of the new Soviet society. I accepted this as a sign of social progress that people were changing, streets were being transformed, and houses torn down and rebuilt. What I see today as horrible socialist housing did not look that bad to me then. As much as I loved the medieval Prague buildings, I had no idea the wooden buildings they were demolishing were old historic Moscow:

> My final conclusion is probably the following. All over Moscow all they are doing is building. Beautiful huge buildings are cropping up all over the place. They are enormous, spanning 2 if not more blocks. On the ground floor there are all kinds of stores and supplies. They even have a post office there.
>
> There are lots of wooden buildings that look like nothing against the new giant buildings. The way they build them is that they first build new buildings right behind the old ones and then they tear down the wooden houses. The city is full of parks and trees.

What I was witnessing was the callous destruction of the past, but what I chose to see was the wave of the future our guides emphasized. That was what Moscow looked like in 1957; that was what I was like at the age of fifteen. And what do I remember now from this Moscow visit that was not recorded in the journal? The outward friendliness of the Russian people on the streets and their readiness to engage in conversation, unlike the reserved Czechs, made a positive impression on me. The Russians freely commented on how one was dressed or if one was putting the exact change into the box when one traveled on the public transportation even if you were a stranger. Whatever one did, there would be an outspoken reaction from bystanders. Throughout the day I was instructed how to do things. The Russians had an opinion on everything. For Russian women, wearing slacks was unacceptable in the 1950s, so in order not to violate their dress code, I walked around in my thin Prague stockings, which made my legs turn purple from the cold. The Russian grandmothers at the bus stop scolded me for not wearing warmer stockings. In Prague people rarely told strangers what they were thinking. More than anything else, Moscow thrilled and overwhelmed me. On the wide Moscow boulevards and in the gigantic buildings I was in a magical fairy land.

I returned to Prague convinced Moscow was like no other city I had ever been to and that there the superhuman was possible. The Russians had a deep pride in their history and firm confidence they had the ability to exchange the old for the new. Though material goods in Moscow were inferior to those in Prague and the standard of living was noticeably lower, I accepted that the Russians compensated for that with an unshakable faith in what they were capable of accomplishing. The Russians convinced me they could remodel cities, change the thinking of the past, even alter the future course of history. In Moscow I felt nothing was impossible or out of reach and the present was exhilarating. I had no reason to doubt that the communist ideal would not come true in this enormous country.

We visited no private homes, met no ordinary people, had no unplanned encounters other than the people we met on the street. I did not even notice the overabundance of red stars and Lenin banners on the buildings, trains, and billboards because I had no concept of a city without them. When I was in Moscow at the beginning of 1958, I did not imagine in my wildest fantasies that I would be spending the last days of that year in the faraway Orient. I had to follow whereever my parents' ideological commitments took them. As their child I had no choice but to continue on their journey to the next destination far away from Prague, Moscow, and New York City.

Chapter 15

. . . .

Leaving Prague to Follow My Parents' Dream

In his essay *Poetry Today in America* Whitman dedicated himself to "fraternity over the whole globe—that dazzling pensive dream of ages!" and called: "That, o poets is not that a theme worth chanting, striving for? Why not fix your verses henceforth to the gauge of the round globe? The whole race? . . . I would inaugurate from America, for this purpose, new formulas—international poems. I have thought that the invisible root out of which the poetry deepest in and dearest to humanity grows, is Friendship."
—Commemoration speech on Walt Whitman by Abe Chapman, presented in Warsaw, 1955

Between 1951 and 1962 my father wrote ninety-two articles and collaborated on nine books. His prolific output was a result of the feverishly intense pace he kept up throughout the 1950s. His days were packed with appointments and lectures, and his nights were devoted to writing and reading. With limitless energy, he raced against time to express his views on current political and literary issues. His clear writing was sharply focused and idea-centered. His interpretation of literature and events was strictly Marxist. Most of his articles were written for the Czech press, but some were published in China, Germany, and France. A random sampling of article titles written in the 1950s shows the themes he concentrated on: "The Struggle for Agrarian Reform in the Philippines," "Karl Marx and Abraham Lincoln," "Michael Gold—Pioneer of American Proletarian Literature," "Walt Whitman, the Poet of the Working Classes," "The American Communists and the McCarran Act."

Deep in thought, Abe periodically returned to his desk from his circular march through the apartment to add a few more lines to the sheet of paper rolled into his typewriter. Throughout the night he sipped strong Turkish coffee and smoked Czech cigarettes that burned throat and lungs. At night he paced up and down the long hallway so that when I slipped into the bathroom I was guided by the red glow of his lit cigarette. While Abe's thoughts journeyed in regions far removed from the enclosed space of our Prague apartment, I was living in the immediate present.

In 1956 Abe wrote two articles for *Rudé Právo* (the Czech Communist Party newspaper), titled "Benjamin Franklin: The Great American Democrat" and "Benjamin Franklin as a Journalist." These articles came out shortly before the International Cultural Conference on distinguished people held in Peking in 1957. As a communist and an expert on American literature and history, Abe was invited to present the opening talk on Benjamin Franklin at this conference. The Chinese conference focused on three outstanding thinkers: Benjamin Franklin and Marie and Pierre Curie.

In preparation for his trip to China, Abe surrounded himself with books on the Orient, Chinese art, literature, and philosophy. Abe had had an ongoing love affair with Chinese art and philosophy that blossomed once he knew he was going to China. Seeing China had been a dream of his since his days of party work in New York City. In the many homes we lived in, as well as in our Prague home, Abe and Belle always hung a wall-sized Chinese rubbing of a majestic horse whose master is removing a spear from its chest. This rubbing had been given to my parents in the 1940s in New York City by their communist Chinese friends who worked with them in the party and who had returned to China by the early 1950s because of the McCarthy persecutions and the Chinese Revolution. This rubbing was the one stable landmark that survived all the changes and moves. It hangs today on my wall in Plattsburgh and continues to keep alive a family tradition that started with my parents and has been passed on to my sons, who have never known a home without the presence of this ancient Chinese horse.

In the evenings Abe read portions of his lecture to my mother. His inspired voice reached me in my bedroom where I was studying. Living through the Slánský trials and dealing with the stifling Stalinist intellectual environment during the past six years shook his faith in the political direction of this country. In Czechoslovakia in the 1950s, people feared punishment for voicing views that conflicted with the official party line. Here there was no open debate. According to reports from China, open dialogue flourished there. Abe left for Peking hoping to find a society that would realize a communist future according to a unique model.

Leaving Prague to Follow My Parents' Dream . . . 159

He stayed in China for ten weeks, seventy-two days to be exact, and returned convinced that China was the communist hope of the future.

Meanwhile, things were going well for me in Prague. At fifteen, I was rooted in my environment, balancing my home life with my Czech one. I had a circle of friends who accepted me. I loved Prague. I was preparing to join the Communist Youth League. I was only three years away from my graduation exams. My studies were going well. I was learning new things, reading voraciously, going to the theater and concerts, and participating in the social and political life of my peers quite independent of my parents. In the summers, I went to pioneer camps in the Bohemian countryside, and in the late summer and early fall I went with my classmates on *brigády*—compulsory trips to the villages to help with the harvests. I loved the Czech countryside with its lush fields and meadows, colorful wildflowers, thick blueberry patches in the woods, and the scent of growing mushrooms after a rain in the predawn hours. I picked the firm, dried bulbs of the poppy flowers to munch on the little poppy seeds stored inside, and I gathered fragrant mushrooms in the damp woods, skilled at finding firm *hřiby* hidden under the leaves or tucked into the roots of the trees. I picked wildflowers and flavorful berries, touching and smelling everything that was growing. When I returned to the city, the smells and sights of the countryside stayed with me for a long time.

All schoolchildren had to help harvest sugar beets, beer hops, and potatoes on the collective farms. We were a source of free or cheap labor to harvest what farmers, who lacked the incentive to work overtime on the collective farms, let rot in the fields. It was common knowledge that if schoolchildren did not help harvest the crops there would be even more shortages in the stores and longer lines. I was content to accept things as they were.

Unlike some of my classmates, I did not mind these *brigádas* to the village. I enjoyed talking with the peasants, who made us hearty lunches and joked with us. On the bus from and to Prague we sang songs, and like most of the girls I was excited to sit next to my favorite boy. By the end of the workday my hands were covered with dried mud, my nails were broken, and my back was sore, but my spirits were high. Pleased that my work was useful, I looked forward to the next trip.

The majority of my friends fantasized about life in the West, the forbidden paradise. I did not. I was not interested in reading Western books or seeing films because I was caught up in the culture around me. Even though there were American newspapers and magazines in our home and friends of my parents traveled to the West, I never thought of asking them to bring me samples of Western culture. Any Western influence was considered harmful to our thinking. I loved Yves Montand's chansons (his leftist politics made him a popular addition to the Prague cultural scene) as much as African musical groups that performed in Prague. I made no efforts to seek beyond the limits set for us. When at the age of twenty-one I reentered the West, I realized how cut off I had been all these years. It is a gap one never makes up.

Abe's glowing letters, written on thin air-mail paper with faint Chinese bamboo designs, arrived from Peking. He described vividly the wonderful people he was meeting and the exotic beauty of Peking's summer palace, the maze of enclosed courtyards, and the noisy marketplaces. He was a guest of honor at elaborate banquets and entertained by traditional Chinese opera performances. It all sounded like an unreal dream. In China he found a perfect match for his radical vision and contact with a culture that fascinated him.

Eventually the letters were followed by telegrams and finally long distance phone calls. The Chinese comrades had invited Abe to move to China with his family. His ideological and writing expertise were just what they needed for the new magazine the *Peking Review* they were planning to launch to inform English-language readers of the changes in China's newly reconstructed society.

The Chinese comrades wanted Abe and Belle to see China for themselves so that they would realize the importance of their contribution to changing backward China to a highly developed society. Visits to communes and the industrial complexes would introduce them to the complex political and economic changes that were taking place. The communist leaders were anxious to show foreign friends like Abe and Belle the rapid transformations that were designed to eradicate the social system and thinking of "old" China. The current Chinese policy, "Let a hundred flowers blossom, a hundred schools of thought contend," indicated that intellectual openness of thought was permitted in China. The offer to work in China revitalized Abe and Belle's faith in the future of their communist ideal. Not Russia but the Orient was the new ideological frontier. When the phone call came inviting my mother to join my father in Peking for a tour of China, she consented immediately.

Leaving Prague to Follow My Parents' Dream . . . 161

Laura and I helped Belle get ready for her trip. She was to take the next Soviet Iliushin out of Prague bound for Peking. Before Belle left, she had arranged with Mr. Svoboda, an elderly Czech neighbor, to sleep in our apartment while she was gone so she would not have to worry that we were alone. In the daytime Laura was in charge of managing things until the grandfather came over to sleep for the night. Each night, before we went to bed, he told us stories about his difficult poverty-stricken childhood and youth. He was happy that his grandchildren would have much better lives in the new communist society than he would have ever dreamed of having when he was young. After telling us the same stories each night, he kept us awake with his loud snoring. But it seemed that his steady snoring kept us protected.

Shortly after Belle's departure, we received a mysterious telegram from Siberia. Unable to decipher the garbled message written in a language we could not identify, we brought the telegram to another American family that lived in Prague to help us figure it out. What if the telegram contained an important message? How would we know what was happening or what we should do? Our parents' American friends exhausted various alternatives, but finally they also failed to make sense out of the confusing telegram. Not until Belle returned from China did we get an explanation of her Siberian telegram. This is what happened: while the Russian plane was being refueled in Siberia, Belle noticed a postal station at the Siberian airport. Looking for some distraction on this long journey, she thought it would be fun to send us a telegram to let us know that her trip was going well. The Russian attendant did not speak English, and Belle did not speak Russian. Belle wrote her message in English, and the attendant transposed Belle's message into the corresponding Russian letters or what she thought they might be, which resulted in a telegram that was neither English nor Russian, but rather a Siberian blend of languages and alphabets.

The mysterious telegram was a minor matter compared to the important news our parents had concerning our future. Before Abe and Belle returned to Prague, where they would be reunited with us, they accepted the jobs they were offered in Peking. That meant the four of us would be moving to China as soon as we could make the necessary arrangements. The offer to work in China was for an indefinite period of time. Abe and Belle could not contain their excitement. Hope and energy were flowing through the house. I was in turmoil. The familiar little world I had established for myself within the last seven years was being disrupted by my parents' all-consuming faith and political idealism. My sole concern, initially, was my desire to complete my schooling in the Czech schools and language.

The first few days after their return I was distracted by the commotion they created in the house. The living room was filled with the clutter of Chinese artifacts: ivory chopsticks, teacups with delicate patterns, rice bowls with Chinese calligraphy, scrolls with paintings of donkeys and mountainous landscapes, rubbings of horses, delicate paper folk art cuttings, shiny brocade with pictures of pagodas, strange-tasting candies wrapped in thin rice paper, aromatic jasmine tea, photographs of sights they visited, and recordings of Chinese music and Peking opera that sounded like the off-key singing of eunuchs. The Chinese objects scattered around the living room had strong, exotic smells. Peking opera was definitely not like Moravian folk music or Czech pop songs. The journey into the Chinese provinces had been an enormous success. Abe and Belle were wooed by the glory of their mission and the insistence of their hosts, who showered them with gifts and lured them into the current thinking on Chinese history, art, and politics. The Chinese comrades succeeded in conveying the impression that life in China would be a purposeful and exciting adventure for both my parents. Laura and I had to fit into the scheme of things.

Abe's description of China had a magical effect on me. My father's voice tumbled forth with contagious energy when he talked about our future life in Peking. Ambiguous feelings struggled within me. The life I had established urged me to stay, but the desire to see the Orient attracted me. I wanted to see China, but the prospect of leaving Prague— perhaps forever—frightened me. Yes, I was told we would return to Prague, but my parents could not tell me when. Right now all that mattered to them were the hopeful challenges ahead. Their optimistic faith in the future was pushing our destiny forward. I had to pack to go.

I knew how much hard work it was to adjust to one new country. What would it be like doing it all over again, and this time in Chinese? I had to leave my collection of books, schoolwork from the past few years, and projects I worked on in neatly labeled boxes we stored in the closet. My childhood mementos remained in New York, my special treasures of my early youth stayed in Prague, and I was moving on to Peking with the necessary clothes and a few Czech books. The only images of China I had were the descriptions from my father's letters and the tales they told us about what they had seen. The Chinese objects they brought back made it obvious that China differed from the world I was familiar with in food, art, music, language, dress, and style of living. The future stretched ahead of me like a blank sheet of paper.

Should I pack my Czech textbooks or would they be useless in Peking? Why did I have to study Czech history and geography if I would not be in Prague to take the final exams? Suddenly what I had been studying the last few years seemed arbitrary and unrelated to my changing life circumstances. What could I do with a few years of Chinese schooling if my parents decided to leave China again? What use would it be to me? Would it be possible for me to switch from Czech to Chinese without losing valuable time so that I could graduate with my current classmates? How long would it take me to follow instructions in a Chinese classroom? Riding high on the crest of their own excitement, my parents were seemingly unconcerned about the practical questions I had about life in a new country. They tried to dispel my anxieties with their optimism that all would be worked out once we got there.

It was not nearly as difficult to pack my clothes as it was to leave behind what could not be enclosed in suitcases: my friends, the city landscape, my school life. My friends envied my chance to go to China and I envied them that they could remain together in the same class. Would Karel, the boy I desperately liked, become interested in someone else even though he told me I was the only one he liked? Nonetheless, I took a photograph of him (subsequently lost), and he had my class photograph in his wallet.

The send-off at the evening train for Peking at the Prague main station was tearful and loud. Firm hugs, final farewells, promises to keep in touch, smiles, tears, and wishes for the best echoed in my ears as our train inched out of the station. The motion of the train reminded me of a previous train trip that pulled me away from the known I had never returned to. The Prague streets were already hidden in darkness as the train pulled into the countryside. I could see the flickering lights of the settlements we passed through and the contours of the thick woods. Passing through the small villages, thick forests, and populated towns of the countryside made me think about the battles that were fought here during the war, right behind these silent trees. I knew from the literature I had read over the last few years that partisans and soldiers who fought to protect the homeland were buried here. Now these were just forests, but then they were battlefields on which one's fate was decided. By the next day I was out of the country, leaving the known behind.

After the first two-and-a-half-day trip to Moscow through Slovakia, the Carpathian Mountains, and the Ukraine, we boarded the Trans-Siberian train, bound for Peking. In 1957, it was an eleven-day journey that covered nine thousand kilometers. We were traveling in the dead of winter. The Siberian landscape was a vast expanse of windblown snow, which had a mysterious, dreamlike quality. For hours there were no settlements in sight, just miles of white land. The white, frozen snow resembled a motionless ocean that had no beginning and no end. Long icicles decorated the buildings along the train tracks. The frozen crust on the snow glistened in the strong sunshine. Coming from a small European country, I was filled with awe of Russia's enormous spaces. In Siberia, where the temperature was consistently below zero, the train had to stop for the railroad workers to defrost the frozen tracks. The strong forces of nature had to be fought like a giant beast. These railroad workers were mostly women, who had to take the place of the men who died during the war to keep the trains moving and the factories and fields producing. The passengers sat in the warm train drinking glasses of hot tea while we waited for the snow-covered path to be cleared so we could continue our journey.

In Siberia our train cut through untamed virgin land, a challenge to the communist Soviet Union. The harsh natural obstacles of the Siberian terrain reminded me of the fat socialist realist novels I devoured during the last few years with titles like *Far from Moscow* in which new socialist women and men struggled to build new cities in formerly un-inhabitable territories. Now I was seeing with my own eyes the regions the Soviets wanted to transform and the rough terrain for which the characters in the novels exchanged their Moscow lives. Here, working under difficult conditions, these brave young people worked on perfecting their moral character under the guidance of the party. The motto of this era was to replace the old with the new and the previously untried. Russia was creating new collective farms, new industrial plans, new relationships, new men and women, and ultimately a new Russia.

I was deeply touched by Russia's striking beauty and powerful presence. I sensed an inexplicable mystery to this place from the landscape and the people I met on the train who loved their motherland—*Ma-*

tushka Rus (Mother Russia) with a passion. On this journey we met talkative Russians who were eager to befriend us and to make us feel at home in their country. My sister and I translated for our parents, in heavily accented and imperfect Russian, but we managed to keep the communication going. Russians believed in traveling in comfort; most of the travelers put their pajamas on as soon as the train pulled out of Moscow, and some of them did not get out of them until they reached their destination. Once the journey started, they set out to rest and have fun. I was one of the youngest passengers on the train, and the Russians pampered me. When they discovered my passion for ice cream, they would get me some at the subzero Siberian stations, proclaiming that the creamy Russian ice cream was the best in the world. It was far superior to Czech ice cream.

The Russians lovingly pointed out important landmarks along the way. They explained the unique regional characteristics, emphasizing the beauty and rich natural resources of the Urals or the industrial importance of Irkutsk. They wanted us to see everything, taste the local foods, feel the greatness of Russia's past, appreciate the vastness and power of their beloved motherland. They pointed to things of interest in the passing countryside, telling me tales of Russia's history and the horror of the recent war. Millions of lives had been sacrificed, they told me, so that this generation had to make up for the crippling losses. They sang touching, mournful songs like "Katiusha" about lovers separated by the war and unfulfilled longings. Deeply moved, I sang along while they nodded approvingly, encouraging me to try the next song. Our people, they said knowingly, have suffered, and now we will make it one of the strongest, happiest countries in the world. I was sure they could.

Our family was squeezed into a compartment with four beds and a small table by the window. The regular hum of the wheels against the tracks rocked me to sleep at night. Restlessly I tossed from side to side on my upper berth hitting the wall as the train moved forward. When the train suddenly turned, I was almost in flight, suspended in space. In the daytime we played canasta, a favorite family game, and did some reading despite the distracting sights of old wooden houses, the Mongolian desert, or the gripping beauty of the passing wintry countryside. The days passed with unexpected speed. The usual measurement of time came to a stop. I was happy in this cozy train, my temporary refuge.

Furthermore, the traveling Russians loved me and I loved them. Russia and the Russians touched my heart.

The Russian travelers invited us into their compartments to share the sausage, bread, butter, pickled vegetables, chickens, and vodka they brought for the trip. Most of the travelers were men on their way to isolated outposts and these were their last days of freedom and rest before they reached their work stations. The mood on the train resembled that of a traveling party. From station to station new travelers, with fresh food supplies and a new batch of songs, replaced those who reached their destinations along the way.

At the train stations women wrapped in long shawls sold local specialties to the hungry travelers. The passengers who befriended us pointed out which local foods we could expect to buy in different regions. When we skirted along Lake Baikal, we flocked to the local women selling baked Lake Baikal fish and Siberian *pelmeni* (meat-filled dumplings) buried in sour cream. The train was ready to pull out of the station when we had just gotten our steaming portions of *pelmeni* and a bowl of thick sour cream. You were expected to eat them fast enough so you could make it back onto the train for departure time. Belle, who heard the warning whistle of our train announcing the upcoming departure, did not want to leave the sour cream or *pelmeni* behind and motioned to the peasant woman to ask if she would sell the bowl with the sour cream and *pelmeni*. Before the peasant woman knew what was happening, Belle gave her a handful of rubles and in a matter of minutes we were back in our compartment with our exquisite Siberian treat and the serving bowl. There were no paper plates or enterprising travelers like Belle in this part of the world. Belle impressed the delighted Russians with her dexterity in deboning fish for anyone who needed help. Removed from our worldly attachments, we grew fond of our fellow travelers.

Most entertaining and memorable were two friends from Moscow, Sergei and Genia, who attached themselves to us. They insisted on sharing their food and vodka. As the toasts between Sergei, Genia, and my parents got more frequent and animated, their cheeks got redder and their voices louder. These two energetic young men analyzed the differences in their personalities. The vodka brought out their unresolved conflict with full force. They confessed, though they were close friends, their biggest disagreement was that one loved Alexander Pushkin and

Leaving Prague to Follow My Parents' Dream . . . 167

the other Mihail Lermontov—both major nineteenth-century romantic Russian poets. Each tried to demonstrate, in a rapid flow of poetic recitations, that his poetic choice was the best. The more they drank, the more melodramatic they became. They wanted us to decide which poet we liked most in order to resolve this dispute. They recited their favorite poems with much flair and feeling. Their repertoire of poems committed to memory was endless. The vodka in their veins helped the poetry flow with ease. Their feelings for their beloved poets intensified with each new poem, each passing mile, each new drink of vodka.

The romantic poetry put us all into a jovial, sentimental mood. My father, who kept pace with the consumption of vodka, started to recite his favorite poet, Walt Whitman, in English. Though Sergei and Genia could not understand a word he was saying, they listened attentively. They respected the big American who joined in the recitations. At this gathering the words of poets were sacred, regardless of the language they were created in. The poetry of one nation was as important as the poetry of another nation. Our Russian friends told us they were able to feel Whitman's power and hear his beat even if the English words meant nothing to them. What mattered was that the poetry was making the journey with us.

We felt we had known these two attractive men for years. Ultimately other travelers joined in this controversy, equally divided over the poetic genius of Pushkin versus Lermontov, adding favorite poetic lines of their own. This poetic ritual took place at least once a day, and Abe nicknamed these two engineers Pushkin and Lermontov. If all else fails, poetry keeps Russians going. Their national poets have captured in words what people genuinely value in life. In poetry words expressed feelings without ambiguity or platitudes. The slogans in the train stations and on the walls of public buildings were static and lifeless in comparison to the lines of Lermontov and Pushkin recited in our train compartment.

We traveled through small villages, enormous industrial cities, along the shores of long and wide rivers, deep lakes, the taiga, and thick forests. The Russian fields were endless, the mountains towering, the cities sprawling complexes. I had come from the land of the Lilliputians to the land of the Brobdingnagians. Most important, I felt at home with the Russians I had met on the train, and I responded to their warmth and energy. Russians did everything with a great deal of ceremony and force. They adopted my father, knowing his spirit was connected to theirs.

The Mongolian desert stretched between Russia and China. When we reached the main city in Mongolia, Ulan-Bator, the facial features of the passengers changed, as did the landscape and architecture of the houses. The Mongolians had protruding cheekbones, narrow eyes, large foreheads, and dark hair. Their physical appearance was a cross between that of the Chinese on one side of the border and the Russians on the other. These physical differences in the appearance of the local people made me realize how far our travels had brought me. China was not only nights and days away from where I had lived but also languages, races, and life experiences away from what I had ever known. The farther the train moved along the track, the more unusual the sights became.

At night, when we pulled into stations to refuel and pick up passengers, I watched the railroad workers switch our train to different tracks. All parts of Russia were connected by this maze of intersecting tracks. The trains carried lumber, metal, industrial parts, trucks, tractors, food, coal, and passengers. On these railroads the constant motion never stopped. The feverish movement of the trains equaled the high-pitched five-year industrial and agricultural plan for production that was the driving force of this nation. Slogans, banners, and red stars proclaiming the goals of the industrial plan were everywhere. The message to "produce, fill the plan, move ahead, forward" was being put into practice along these tracks that connected the industrial centers with the agricultural collectives. On this train I was part of a ceaselessly and frenetically moving world. The entire nation was in action, or so it seemed.

One night our train pulled into yet one more of those many train stations when I woke from my sleep not sure if I was dreaming or awake. I exclaimed: "Look, two moons" at the sight of a lamp that had two big round lanterns. The "two moons" became a favorite family joke. Each time we passed these twin lanterns that were in train stations throughout Russia, my parents pointed at them proclaiming, "Look, two moons." In what I perceived as a mythic land of superhuman achievements even the moon could become two moons shining on the tireless workers busy rebuilding their society.

Eventually the subzero, white Siberian landscape was replaced by the yellow soil of Mongolia and the brown, wintry Chinese fields. At the Russian-Chinese border the Russian dining car was detached, which meant an end to the thick slabs of Russian black bread and sour solianka soup that sustained us for the eight-day journey across Russia. The Chinese dining car was now filled with passengers eating with chopsticks and slurping tea and soup. Gone was the bread and the vodka; here was rice and finely chopped vegetables with slivers of meat. As much as I enjoyed the smells coming from the Chinese kitchen, I could not imagine facing weeks and months and possibly even years without bread. Perhaps if so many millions of Chinese could, so could I.

At the Chinese border large groups of Chinese passengers with bulky bundles and packages were waiting to board the train. The Chinese countryside, so unlike the Russian fields and forests, was divided into neat little patches of farmland bathed in bright, strong sunlight. Water buffalo wallowed in the mud, and the landscape was covered with small huts that did not resemble Western farmhouses. All the Oriental people around me looked alike. Crossing the Chinese border instantly made me a distinguishable foreigner. The train was heading toward Peking, a city of millions and millions of people who did not look or speak like me. I was on my way, almost there. My eyes were glued to the train window for what I was seeing hardly seemed real. Prague? Peking? What next?

Chapter 16

. . . .

A Major Leap:

From Dream

to Nightmare

Man in connection with the general life of humanity appears subject to laws which determine that life. But the same man apart from that connection appears to be free. How should the past life of nations and of humanity be regarded — as the result of the free, or as a result of the constrained, activity of man? That is a question for history.

—Lev N. Tolstoy, *War and Peace*

The Chinese passengers checked out my freckles and the hair on my arms, which their smooth arms lacked. This close scrutiny made me self-conscious. I tried to escape it by turning toward the window. Bright sunshine illuminated the snowless brown fields, giving the impression it was no longer wintry, yet when we walked around the stations when the train stopped briefly for supplies, we had to move at a brisk pace to keep warm.

The Chinese in the train and in the passing villages were dressed uniformly: blue slacks, white shirts, and blue padded jackets. Only toddlers had colorful, thickly padded outfits with bright ribbons distinguishing the little girls. In Russia women wore skirts, even in the bitter winter, but here there was not a skirt to be seen. The masses of people were blue armies, all colorless, all drab. The uninterrupted sight of their identical outfits, short black hair, and black cloth shoes made me long for the exciting variety and color in Prague's fashionable scene, or even Moscow. Draped in baggy clothes, the Chinese managed to make the human body appear shapeless. The women wore no makeup or jewelry. In these revolutionary times such adornments were considered frivolous, even counterrevolutionary. My Czech wardrobe I never thought about much made me suddenly feel like a colorful peacock.

From the train window I watched village women balance baskets on bamboo sticks and little children squat to relieve themselves through a slit in their pants that ingeniously eliminated the need for diapers. Older women hobbled slowly through the village, their miniature doll-like feet wrapped in soft cloth shoes. My father explained that it was a tradition in Old China among the upper classes to bind the five-year-old female child's feet to prevent them from being too mobile and to attract a good husband. Tiny feet were considered sexually attractive. In 1949 the People's Republic of China banned the practice, but the traditions of Old China were still a visible reality, at least for another generation. New sights, smells, tastes and sounds reached my senses.

Spoken Chinese was choppy and jarring to my ear. The tonal variations forced their voices to rise and fall when switching from word to word as if they were moving up and down a musical scale. Chinese lacked the melodic softness of Russian, and in no way did it resemble Czech or English. When we traveled through Russia I could engage in conversation with the passengers, but here I was limited to observations of the stunning landscape and to watching the people around me. The Chinese were as curious about me as I was about them. In the dining car Abe taught me to use chopsticks, a skill he mastered on his previous trip to China. He liked the feel of chopsticks and the graceful maneuvers that captured the food. My first efforts at manipulating the chopsticks were ineffective and awkward. I chased after slippery pieces of meat with my uncooperative chopsticks, which slid around my plate while my mouth was watering. Using chopsticks for an entire meal made me aware of hand muscles I had never used before. By the end of the meal my cramped hand felt as if I had spent the entire day writing. I was, however, highly motivated to eat faster; at each meal I diligently practiced my technique, and in a matter of days I was an expert.

After eleven days of travel, we pulled into Peking. The streets were flooded with bright morning sunlight. I was dizzy taking in the sights. The bustle of the crowds, the bicycle-propelled rickshaws going and coming from all directions, the masses of blue-clothed bodies stunned me. Thick crowds stretched from street to street. People, bicycles, rickshaws, cars, buses, and street vendors fought to claim space among the moving bodies. Voices called out, cars honked, and the ring of hundreds of bicycle bells mingled with human voices. On this first ride through Peking I was too mesmerized by the crowds between the buildings to notice the architecture of the buildings. Leaving the street action behind, we entered the quiet, modest apartment that had been prepared for us. These three rooms were an oasis in the midst of this noisy city.

The first day in our Peking apartment Abe plugged in our small Czech radio. Setting up the radio was a signal that this new place was to be our home. The small brown radio was the only familiar thing in the sparsely furnished apartment. It was ludicrous to hear Chinese sounds in place of the programs I listened to in Prague.

Our living quarters were in the Foreign Language Press compound. From my bedroom window I looked down on a series of *hutungs* (small houses built around a walled-in courtyard). Small children ran in and out of the gates while their mothers gathered in small groups to chat, holding baskets with fresh vegetables just purchased at the market. Our apartment consisted of a small rectangular living room and a bedroom on either side. The beds were extremely hard. What I expected to be a mattress was nothing more than a plain board covered with a thin layer of red cloth. The bed had no bounce and did not yield to the body; whenever I turned to my side, I felt my hip bone hit against the slab of wood. The bed I left in Prague was for a queen compared to this. The bathroom and kitchen had cement floors and no counters, just bare essentials. The coal stove in the kitchen would not respond to Belle's touch.

The grounds of the Foreign Language Press were arranged around a large courtyard. The office buildings were in the front of the compound. There was a large dining room in the office building for the staff of the press. My parents did not come home from work until dinnertime. In the back of the compound there were residential buildings for foreigners who worked at the press. Residing in the compound spared us the trauma of making our way through the crowded Peking streets on a daily basis. The foreigners who lived in the compound had the help of a *bamu* to run their households because marketing without the knowledge of Chinese was difficult and everybody worked long hours at the office. The expert service the foreigners provided for the Chinese was too valuable for them to waste their time on household chores any peasant woman could do. In the hall outside of our apartment there was an ice box that kept the food cold for two days, or until the ice melted into the basin. The ice man dragged the heavy block of ice up the stairs on his back, taking deep breaths on each step. The ice deliveries were too erratic to count on dependable refrigeration.

The unaccustomed smell from horse-pulled carts carrying human waste filled the air throughout the neighborhood. A few blocks from the Foreign Language Press compound there was a crowded food market with unrefrigerated and uncovered food. Covered with flies and insects, vegetables and fruits were dumped in heaps directly on the cement floor. Women did their shopping carrying small children on their backs or hips and with rosy-cheeked toddlers trailing behind. The local market, neighborhood restaurants, exhibits, and parks were filled with three-generation families who lived together and went on outings in large groups. When a local circus troop performed at the marketplace, delighted crowds gathered to watch the acrobats twirl plates on long sticks and juggle shiny objects. Like the Chinese, I munched on sweet, juicy lichee nuts and sunflower seeds.

Belle, who had no time to do kitchen work, had a *bamu*, a middle-aged Chinese woman who did the marketing and cooking. The *bamu* squatted on the kitchen floor when she chopped the vegetables with a giant clever, a habit that mortified my mother. Belle, who could not communicate with the Chinese-speaking *bamu*, demonstrated how she wanted the food prepared. She picked the vegetables off the floor and put them on the little table under the window, showing the *bamu* how to work in a more hygienic manner. This idea did not impress the *bamu*, who watched the demonstration indifferently. As soon as Belle left the kitchen, she was back squatting on the floor with a heap of vegetables by her feet. In this kitchen the *bamu* was in charge, and she did things the way she had learned in the village. She was from a village where they spoke a dialect of Chinese that sounded like atonal singing. Every day she gathered in the hall for a chat with the other *bamus* in the building. I assumed their lively chats were funny stories about the strange habits of the "foreign devils" for whom they cooked and cleaned. When they were together they laughed, shouted, and gesticulated wildly, having a wonderful time. Their faces were full of expression. Once our *bamu* was back in the apartment, she was silent and stony faced.

Peking was a fascinating tourist site, but as a permanent residence it intimidated me. Not only were my new surroundings exotic, but the color white instead of black to symbolize death and red instead of white for marriage indicated that the mythology of the people was unlike mine. Living on the grounds of the Foreign Language Press separated me from the neighborhood on the other side of the tall wall where "normal" life was happening. Here, within the Foreign Language Press walls, there were no families with children my age. This was strictly an adult world. I could see young people my age from my window on the other side of the wall, but I had no access to them. It did not much matter because I could not communicate with them anyway.

Within days of our arrival, my parents started their jobs in the offices across the courtyard. My sister planned to study Chinese at Peking University, which had an intense language program for foreign students. She moved into the university dorms as soon as her program started. The university was located in the outskirts of the city, far from where we lived. I had to take more than one bus to get there, and if I needed instructions to find my way I had to go through a pantomime act to demonstrate my needs. On my visits at Peking University I met the international students with whom my sister studied Chinese, most of whom were from other communist countries. Laura's demanding schedule and the distance to the university made my visits infrequent. As they had promised, my parents investigated schooling possibilities for me with the help of the (once again for me invisible) Chinese comrades who were in charge of their affairs. The search for an appropriate choice was complicated by the language barrier. Peking had no schools for the likes of me; it was a matter of deciding which situation would work best.

Meanwhile, I walked around Peking exploring on my own. I took the pale blue bus downtown, to the marketplace, the winter and summer palaces, and the spectacular Peking parks. I wandered through the narrow alleys in and out of the *hutungs*. Some sections of Peking were nothing more than long rows of gray walls enclosed around the *hutung* courtyards. I could smell the Chinese dinners the grandmothers prepared in the courtyards, but I could not see into the kitchens because the *hutungs* were built facing a courtyard rather than the street. The little children played street games, weaving in and out of the moon-shaped doorways. Small children walked through the streets sucking the sweet juice out of long sticks of sugarcane. I treated myself to the glistening candied fruit on a stick and bean-filled moon cakes. I tried the long dough sticks they fried in vats right on the street for early morning breakfasts and slurped down bowls of flavorful broth with long noodles. When I listened to the language around me, I knew that to learn to read and write in Chinese and to produce the complicated tonal sounds would take me years. I did not know if we would stay for one year or five. I was anxious to start school, any kind of school where I could meet young people and resume a life of my own. I was too old to live in the shadow of my parents' existence and too young to separate myself from the family. I waited for something to happen.

In time the Chinese comrades came up with a plan for my schooling. They arranged for me to attend classes at a Chinese high school where the bilingual daughter (English and Chinese) of my parents' friends was to be my translator. These Chinese friends had lived in the United States in the 1940s when they worked for the party. Their daughter was born in New York City. These might have been the same friends who gave Abe the Chinese horse decorating our living room. Now this family, whose English was flawless, had returned to their homeland to contribute to the building of communism in China. In this fast-changing, mobile world the countries my American parents and their Chinese friends used to live in had been reversed, yet the ideal they worked for remained unchanged.

This young Chinese girl, who was exactly my age, became my personal guide and translator. Her family had been back in China long enough that she had integrated into Chinese society as I had integrated into Czech society. For her this was a permanent return to her native culture. For me it obviously remained unsettled what that culture would be. She was a friendly girl with a round face and a heartwarming smile. Her neat braids bobbed from side to side when she moved her head. She (I do wish I could remember her name, which was something like Little Plum or Rose Blossom in Chinese) was immersed in the political activities at the school. Intelligent, patient, and cheerful, she was a popular pioneer youth leader, an activist, and a natural organizer. It did not take long for me, however, to see that this arrangement was not going to work. Although she was always pleasant and kind, it was impossible for her to be a full-time translator with her demanding schedule. She lived as far away from the school as I did, but in the other direction. I do not remember ever visiting in her home. It is possible that this arrangement was imposed on her through party orders.

Twice a day I took the bus to and from the high school near the center of the city. In class I sat next to my Chinese-English-speaking helper. I watched her fill the pages of her notebook with rows of Chinese characters she produced with impressive speed. While the teacher explained the material, she would wink at me, aware that I was watching her closely, barely stopping the flow of her speedy note taking. The rest of the class formed neat Chinese characters in their notebooks. I wondered, with growing concern, how I was going to learn anything at all in this setting. How many years did it take them to learn the thousands of characters that were like intricate pictures? How long will it take me to follow this class? Where do I start?

In class I was a mere observer, unable to participate. The school day dragged. I knew only what I could see: the classes were large and the students were obedient. Hearing Chinese spoken all day long did not help me understand it. In between classes the students gathered in the huge courtyard for group calisthenics, *tai tchi chuan*. That was the only activity that required no words, just gentle body movements. But even here I felt awkwardly out of place. Next to the graceful, petite black-haired youngsters who recreated these ancient movements of their arms and legs with natural grace I was a clumsy elephant, an alien. The movements of my classmates were like those of the wings of birds and swaying branches of a bamboo tree. The children studied me closely with friendly curiosity because I was the only Westerner in the entire school. It was a heavy responsibility to represent all those absent Westerners.

My classmates tried to include me in their circle. They would take me by the hand and show me places around the school and things they brought from home waiting to see my reaction. Pleased at how surprised I usually was, they would laugh in a warm, friendly way, and I would laugh along with them. At least laughter, smiles, eye-to-eye communication, and hugs were international. A group of them accompanied me to the bus station at the end of the school day, trying to teach me Chinese words along the way. If I managed to repeat the word so that they could recognize it, they laughed and clapped their hands, happy with my little accomplishments. My informal language lesson went as follows: they would grab my hand, pointing to a man walking down the street carrying a fish on a strand of straw strung through its head. Together they shouted loudly, "Yi, Yi," which I took to mean fish, waiting for me to repeat the sounds. For a few weeks I had a Chinese teacher who taught me character writing. He dressed in a long black robe. He had a stern face, a scraggly beard, and glossy, beady eyes. Patiently he painted beautiful characters with a small paint brush while I watched. I repeated his motions, but I had no idea what I was writing. He spoke only Chinese. He reminded me of a character who had stepped out of an ancient Chinese scroll.

When I realized that I needed to learn three to four thousand characters in order to read a modern Chinese text I panicked and then rebelled. I explained to my parents, with tears of frustration running down my cheeks, how absurd, absolutely unworkable my school situation was. I wanted to continue my education and actually learn something and not passively watch what was happening around me. Assuming we would return to Prague one day, I worried about how I would pass my graduation exams if I remained in this Chinese class too much longer. I demanded that they consider some alternative to this arrangement.

Because I read exclusively in Czech, my supply of reading material soon dwindled. After I had read all the books I borrowed from the one or two Czechs I met in Peking, I felt cut off from friends, learning, and reading materials—everything I desired at that point in my life. I was beginning to outgrow my Prague clothes, which had to be replaced with Chinese clothing. I would look out of place in my Prague classroom in these outfits. Watching the crowds celebrate the Chinese New Year in the Peking streets or tasting food at banquets that were art creations in themselves could not substitute for peers or experiences of my own.

I met many interesting people in the foreign community. One of the first foreigners we met was Sid Rittenberg, an American GI who stayed in China after World War II. He was devoted to the goals of communist China. He introduced us to this bustling city which he knew extremely well; his affection for China was contagious. He spent a generous amount of time showing Laura and me the sights of Peking, patiently explaining the local customs. He bought us unrecognizable foods—local delicacies from street vendors. He wanted us to respond to the special foods and sights of Peking and the Chinese culture and to feel at home in this enormous city. Sid spoke perfect Chinese. His Chinese wife and small children spoke no English. He swept through the city with long, confident strides, finding his way through the *hutungs* that all looked alike to me like a cat familiar with back alleys. Though he had been born in the American South, this was his home. He maneuvered his large-framed body with grace through the crowds of Chinese who were much smaller and shorter. I had never met such an American before who spoke perfect English but whose thoughts and mind-set were Chinese. He was an American who adapted to this country so thoroughly that one could almost think him Chinese, except for his physical appearance and his southern background.

[*In 1993 Sid Rittenberg's personal memoir* The Man Who Stayed Behind *was published in the United States. In the book he gives a detailed account of his commitment to the Chinese communists. He was the only American trusted by the Chinese to be included in the top revolutionary circles. He was in their wartime headquarters in Yanan, joined in overland marches, and lived alongside revolutionaries, taking part in secret meetings. He argued dogma with Mao Zedong and discussed philosophy with Zhou Enlai. Later he spent a total of sixteen years in prison because of false spy charges and for being mistrusted during the Cultural Revolution. His story is a devastating account of the psychological manipulation of human thought for the sake of ideological power. It is at the same time a story of the making and unmaking of a revolutionary in which Rittenberg traces the darkest moments his misguided thinking took him through before he arrived at the realization that the world should be changed through "measured more modest ways" rather than through "the glorious tumult and clash of revolution" and that to learn to question is better than absolute answers.]*

It was simpler to orient ourselves around Peking than it was to assess the changeable currents in the political climate. It was difficult to get a grasp of the present situation; to predict the future outcome of the ongoing political debates was virtually impossible. In the political conversations my parents had with people like Sid Rittenberg, Israel and Elsie Epstein, Jack Chen, Ruth, Janet, and others they expressed no doubts; they spoke with authority. During the frequent evening visits they talked about the China of the past and the rapid changes that were taking place now. Enthusiastic about what was going on, they had faith in the future. Some of these communist sympathizers from the West had been living in China for a long time, and each had a uniquely personal connection to the country. They shared a common devotion and loyalty to communist China. My parents became a part of this group.

The Eighth Chinese Party Congress in 1958 coined new slogans for the Great Leap Forward to ensure greater, faster, better economic results. The party goal was to create "a world rid of exploitation, a brave new world of new men!" The accelerated political demands for change altered people's lives. Within a year of our arrival, political mistrust of intellectuals, whose thinking did not conform to the accepted doctrines, put a stop to the open debates. China was moving away from the Soviet version of communist leadership and developing its own.

Independent-thinking, educated professionals were sent to the country-side to undergo a corrective education. Several colleagues of my parents disappeared without farewells. One of the two men my father shared an office with vanished from Peking overnight, sent to the countryside to do forced labor while his wife and children remained in Peking. He was expected to confess "old crimes" to demonstrate that he had corrected his deviant thinking before he could return to his family. At the office, my father did not dare mention the name of his bright, witty colleague, who disappeared and whom he had grown fond of, but at home he talked about how painful the separation was and how concerned he was for his frail health and his family.

The disappearances at the Foreign Language Press were the first signal that the political currents were changing drastically. Within months of our arrival, the political atmosphere deteriorated to such an extent that it resembled the oppressive atmosphere of Prague's political scene in the early 1950s. The Chinese party, to tighten its control, was particularly merciless in condemning those who had been educated in the West and who were fluent in several languages. They mistrusted anybody who had foreign social connections or access to information through the knowledge of Western languages. My parents rationalized what was happening for as long as they possibly could; they could not, however, postpone indefinitely the reality that the hundred flowers were no longer in bloom.

The new official policy was to focus exclusively on what you thought and how you thought. Employees had to make public confessions at the workplace defending their political positions. The previously bare walls of the Foreign Language Press building were covered with hasty, handwritten confessions. Swelling groups gathered to read them. Long sheets of paper on which intellectuals confessed their sinful thoughts flapped in the wind. New ones instantly replaced those that fell to the ground. When there was no wall space left for the new supply of confessions, written for public scrutiny, clotheslines were added to accommodate them. Everywhere on the walls, in the corridors, on clotheslines, on trees, there were public declarations of loyalty to the party. At meetings held during the workday everyone was encouraged to bare his soul, confess, tell all. To preserve their jobs and to stay with their families, people confessed. Chinese comrades Abe had intimate discussions with just a few weeks ago now looked away when they passed him in the hall, uncomfortable to be seen with a foreigner. He was devastated to be isolated from the very same comrades who brought him to China. The happiness and hope that launched my parents into the year 1958 turned into despair and sadness by 1959.

Abe and Belle invited all their Chinese colleagues for a New Year's Eve celebration at the close of 1958. They prepared drinks and food for them, hoping everybody would fit into our small apartment. Nobody showed up. Earlier that day none of their colleagues indicated that they would not come. The chopped-up food shriveled on the plates. We welcomed midnight by ourselves without a word of explanation or an apology from the otherwise formal and polite Chinese. For the first time since we had arrived in China, my parents were scared. That New Year's Eve my parents drank to escape their fears rather than to celebrate the arrival of another year. Last New Year's Eve in Moscow had been festive and happy, a shocking contrast to the final hours of 1958. The mood in our apartment was more like a vigil in a funeral parlor than a celebration. The newly implemented official antiforeigner policy forced the Chinese to disassociate themselves from us instantly. We had become too dangerous for their own safety. What were we doing in this country?

Every morning the loudspeaker flooded the Foreign Language Press compound with music and recorded announcements. One song in particular was played throughout the day all over the city. It had a simple nursery-school tune. Having heard the song so many times, I was able to sing it until one day I asked for a translation. What I was singing turned out to be "Socialism is good, socialism is good." I forgot what followed that line.

Since relations with Chinese were forbidden, Abe and Belle were restricted to socializing with their Western friends. My mother started to drink a bit more than usual. In the evening, thoroughly exhausted from a day at the office, she lacked the energy or desire to do much. My father continued to read and write for long hours after my mother went to bed. Initially, my father remained hopeful that this might be a passing phase. Characteristically, Abe continued to seek long-range positive ideological solutions. My mother, firmly rooted in analyzing the practical consequences of events, saw no hope.

The atmosphere my parents worked in became progressively more tense and foreboding. Abe and Belle still shared hot water from the thermoses of their Chinese colleagues for the green tea they sipped during the day, but they no longer exchanged ideas. Yet the Chinese still used the skills foreigners contributed to the workplace. The more formal the relations became, the more unsettling life was. It was no longer possible for us to live at the Foreign Language Press. The Chinese wanted the foreigners segregated as much as possible, and for that they had a perfect place in the outskirts of Peking. I was about to find a school to attend and a completely different environment to live in that was like no other place in China. It was a replica of Soviet life within Chinese walls. It was time to move across the city, where we were removed from the China the Chinese lived in.

Chapter 17

Life in Druzhba

SELF

Not knowing which world to call home,
He chose an arbitrary tongue and creed,
Pitched an improvised tent of sand.
Beneath the canopy of a little star,
He began his heart's commerce with
things:

   was that the real me?

—Mu Dan, Chinese poet

Early in 1959 our family was moved
out of the Foreign Language Press compound to a newly built mini-city
called Druzhba (friendship in Russian, it was the same name as the day
care center I went to in Prague). The Druzhba was built for the families
of Soviet experts who had come to help train Chinese industrial personnel. Soviet engineers were sent to China to develop the backward
Chinese industry when the Soviets and Chinese still shared a common
political ideology. When the political rift between China and the Soviet
Union widened over the next few years, the Soviets started to recall
their technical staff back home. The system of reward and punishment
always worked according to political guidelines: if the Chinese cooper-
ated with the Soviets, they received help; if, however, they wanted to
follow a deviant and independent political path, help was withdrawn.
The communist governments functioned like a benevolent parent who
rewards obedience and punishes disobedience.

In 1959 there were still hundreds of Russian families living in Peking.
At the Druzhba, as at the Foreign Language Press, foreigners were
segregated from the Chinese on the other side of the Druzhba wall.
Furthermore, the Russians kept away from other non-Russian nationalities within the walls of the Friendship complex. Soviet technicians and
specialists who were dispersed at work stations throughout the Chinese
provinces left their wives and children at the Druzhba, where there was
a Soviet school, shops, Russian bookstores, dining halls, movie houses,
concert halls, a swimming pool, and libraries. Situated in the outskirts
of Peking, the Druzhba provided the Soviet version of a privileged life.
Every few months the Russian husbands would return to Peking to visit

their families for a short time before they left for another three-month work period in the provinces. The wives and children who remained in Peking carried on their lives, speaking nothing but Russian, only occasionally venturing out of the Druzhba to see some of the Peking sights and to shop. The Russians residing in the Druzhba had no social contact with the Chinese. Though we still lived geographically in China, we were so isolated from the Chinese that we might as well have been living in the Soviet Union. This walled-in complex was my final home in China.

There was only one small building by the outer wall of the compound that was set aside for the small group of non-Russians who lived here. The Russians did not mingle much with our small group, which consisted of French, Arabs, and Spanish. The three of us, my parents and I, were given living quarters in this building for "other" nationalities. We lived right above the Spaniards. Abe and Belle had an apartment of their own and I had one that was a bit smaller, next to theirs. For the first time in my life I lived by myself. I liked the freedom to read late at night, but during the day or in the evenings I would have enjoyed some company. I saw my parents when I joined them in the communal dining room where we shared a large round table with other residents of the compound. I was by myself in this heavily guarded fort when my parents traveled outside of Peking to visit model communes and factories.

The name of this residence, Friendship, was ironic because I did not see any Soviet-Chinese friendships develop here. My bedroom window faced a tall gray wall under which a Chinese guard paced day and night. In the entrance of the building there was a small room with another guard who kept a detailed log of our arrivals and departures. We were watched at all times. I watched them watch us. To get into the Druzhba one had to have a pass, and visitors had to go through cumbersome procedures before they were allowed to enter. This tight security system discouraged spontaneous contact with those who lived outside. The presence of the guards indicated that nobody was trusted, neither the Chinese nor the foreigners. In place of the bustling *hutung* life outside my window at the Foreign Language Press, all I could see from my window at the Druzhba was the wall that blocked everything out and the solitary guard pacing back and forth, twenty-four hours a day.

Here, in our building for foreigners, I met the Spanish Lacasa family who lived in the apartment underneath us. Their daughter Amaya became my only friend. This friendship helped me endure the isolation I felt in this city of four million people. She was the daughter of Spanish communists who were exiled from Spain in 1939, when they settled in Moscow. Amaya and her older brother Jorge had been born in Moscow, where they spent their early childhood years. Jorge, very much like his mother, had a kind face and a warm smile. I was always comfortable in his presence.

Amaya's father worked at Peking Radio. Amaya attended the Russian school in the Druzhba. She spoke Spanish with her parents, but her Russian was rich and sophisticated. She was bright, well-read, introspective, and sensitive but a loner. She spent most of her after-school hours reading in her tiny bedroom. Amaya's mother did not work outside the home. The soft features of her face folded into an apologetic smile. Her light little steps barely seemed to touch the floor. Her slumped, skinny shoulders gave the impression that she was carrying a heavy burden. Amaya's father, a short, chubby man, ruled the household with a temperamental, authoritarian hand. He was a communist who applied progressive ideas for change to the outside world, but in the privacy of his home he was the ultimate master. He demanded his meals on time and quiet for his work. Amaya's father provided for the family and made all the important decisions. Her mother took care of the home, the family, and her husband's wishes.

Amaya's face was intense and intelligent. She had large, inquisitive, but rather sad eyes. She loved books, ideas, discussions. We talked endlessly about all kinds of subjects, chief of which was our sense of displacement. Having experienced so much disruption in her short life, she was far more mature than an average sixteen-year-old. She understood longing and deprivation. She lived through the energy of her mind. Concerned about Amaya's solitary life, her parents embraced me warmly and lovingly, a respite from the Russian school she attended at which she was able to continue the education she had started in Moscow.

I was enrolled in the Russian school at the Druzhba. At least the language of instruction, Russian, was much closer to Czech than Chinese. At this school the staff and students were all Russian except for the small group of Spanish political exiles who came to China directly from the Soviet Union, never having lived in Spain. Their Russian was perfect. The Russian teaching staff taught us from the Soviet textbooks used throughout the Soviet Union. All the pupils had to wear Russian school uniforms. The girls had dark brown dresses and black smocks they brought with them from the Soviet Union. I was told by the uncompromising vice-principal that I would have to have a uniform made by a Chinese tailor, for under no circumstances was I to attend classes in my street clothes. At this school, in the outskirts of Peking, there were no flexible rules or alternative ways of thinking.

It was not easy to find a Chinese tailor who could make such a uniform. When I explained the kind of outfit I needed, he shook his head in disbelief over why one would want to wear something like that. I never liked the unattractive, dark uniform. In class we all looked the same outwardly, but there were diverse personalities: Valia, the shy, skinny girl I sat next to who moved slowly and cautiously, never getting involved or expressing an opinion; the class clown Andrej, always saying and doing silly things; determined and serious Tamara; and flighty and frivolous Tania, who had a winning, coquettish smile and who teased the boys mercilessly. When we walked quietly through the halls in our identical dresses, with different styled white collars, one would not suspect there were such differences underneath these uniforms. Our Russian teachers taught much more than the assigned subject matter; along with math, geography, history, and chemistry we were taught the fundamentals of a communist moral system, just like in the Czech schools.

The Russian language classes I had in Prague since fourth grade were something of a joke reminiscent of the popular Czech witticism: "Do you know the difference between a brother and a friend? You can choose your friends, but you can't choose your brother. The Soviet Union is our big brother." Not all Czechs wanted to make an effort to learn the language of the big brother whom they did not want to have in the first place. The Czech teachers' negative attitude toward the Russian language allowed the students to learn as little Russian as possible. Now that I was in this Russian school, I desperately wished I knew more Russian so I could follow the classes without having to strain and guess. I launched an intense campaign to master Russian. I had always loved the sound of Russian, a language I genuinely wanted to learn. There was no Kamilka Svobodová here among the Russian teachers who was willing to help me out. But there was Amaya.

The language of communication between Amaya and me was Russian. Hers was fluent and mine was elementary. We had so much we wanted to talk about, but I had to grope for words to express my thoughts. Amaya patiently instructed and guided me to read Russian articles and stories aloud, while she corrected my pronunciation and explained new words with a professorial seriousness. Her excellent Russian vocabulary and her astute instincts made it easy for her to find a substitute Russian word to help explain what I could not initially understand. We spent our evenings in her bedroom reading, talking, and creating a mutual language. She was the master, I was the student. Amaya coached me through the Mendeleev system of elements and math formulas, helping me prepare for my exams until I was able to study the material on my own. While we worked together on the Russian language, our relationship blossomed and deepened. Meanwhile, I acquired the skill to communicate my complex thoughts in Russian.

We both knew what it was like to live as daughters of exiled communists growing up far from our native countries. We were spiritual soul mates whose friendship broke the isolation our circumstances imposed on us. Dislocated, we relied on each other to struggle through our teenage confusions and strivings. We both had to cope with unique cultural conflicts our own parents never understood. Amaya's parents were as thoroughly Spanish as mine were American. But what did our life experiences so far make us? As children of rebels, we lived without the presence of stable, constant family role models. Our unprecedented life circumstances provided no tradition we could follow. Together Amaya and I sought a connection to the adult world and a sense of belonging that would define us.

Amaya, only sixteen years old, succeeded magnificently at her first teaching job. She helped me become functional in the Russian school in a relatively short time. It was ironic that a Spaniard and an American living in Peking had Russian as their common language and in so doing formed a close bond. We hardly ventured into Peking together. I mostly remember spending time with her in her bedroom and on the Druzhba grounds. We were both sixteen, and we had no idea how much longer we would be together in Peking, for we knew we were not in control of our destinies.

The Russian I heard all around me at the Druzhba further aided in my rapid language improvement. One day I got into a conversation at the communal pool with a friendly Russian woman who was watching her two little daughters play in the water. She was a teacher of Russian literature who was temporarily living in Peking while her husband, an engineer, was working in a factory in the Chinese provinces. I explained that I was learning Russian so I could follow my classes at the Russian school. She asked me if I had ever read Tolstoy's *War and Peace*, her favorite novel. When I said no, she literally commanded me to purchase a copy at the Russian bookstore, and she set up a time for me to come up to her apartment while her children were napping so she could introduce me to this novel. It was inconceivable to her that one could go through life without reading Tolstoy, the master of the Russian language and visionary of the human heart.

I did as I was told. I bought the book, and on the appointed day I knocked on her door on the third floor of the large building for Russian residents. She was awaiting my arrival, anxious to turn to the opening pages of the novel. She told me about Tolstoy, his life, his works, his characters. She made me read the opening scene of the novel out loud—a scene set in a nineteenth-century salon, where we meet the Russian aristocrats whom we come to know intimately in the thousand-page novel. My teacher, Anna Petrovna, talked about these characters as if they were people she had known for a long time and who were a part of her twentieth-century life. At the end of this spellbinding introduction to Tolstoy, I was given a lengthy assignment for our next session and detailed instructions about what to concentrate on in the plot development.

When I returned to my apartment, I immediately opened the first of the four volumes of this panoramic novel to do my assigned reading. When I became frustrated, I thought of my self-appointed teacher's animated face when she talked about Pierre's search for a meaningful life or Elena's cold nature. I hoped that I might eventually feel as excited about the strangers I was meeting in Tolstoy's novel as she did. With my Russian/Czech dictionary beside me I worked patiently night after night. When I needed a rest, I paced back and forth, stopping at the window. The Chinese guard, also solitary, paced along the back wall of the Druzhba while I paced from one end of the apartment to the other. Restricted to our confined spaces, we never smiled at each other.

When I returned to the pages of Tolstoy's novel, I forgot where I was and became engrossed in the lives of the characters whose destinies had a completeness my life lacked. Engrossed in the happenings of their lives—births, marriages, deaths—I stopped wondering about my own problems. I was riveted by the intense passions and human trials of their daily lives. The further I got into the novel, the faster I was able to turn the pages until I could read entire passages without the help of my worn dictionary. Tolstoy's novel thoroughly exposed me to the Russian vocabulary I needed to master to become proficient. My three teachers, Amaya, Anna Petrovna, and Lev N. Tolstoy, made the remaining days at the Russian school much easier.

Each time I came to the apartment of my Tolstoy mentor, Anna Petrovna relived her favorite scenes, lingering over every detail of Natasha's first ball: her gown, the dancers who courted her, and the youthful excitement she felt experiencing love for the first time. She projected her own hidden passions into the love between Andrej and Natasha and later on Natasha and Pierre. In this novel, which was life itself, I learned the meaning of living, loving, dying for the motherland. She initiated me into Tolstoy's world by showing me how it moved and stretched her imagination. From now on I could live beyond the walls of my little apartment, beyond Peking, beyond the present room or the present time. I joined those who loved, hurt, dreamed, and lived what I had not yet fully experienced myself.

Chapter 18

. . . .

Peking:

The Sparrow

Shall Fall

All I knew was that I never wanted to see a sparrow war again. But then, I never wanted to see these starving skeleton forms again, either. Was it true that one or the other had to be, that the sparrow must fall so that man might live? Was it true that always, somehow, in Asia one had to choose? I did not know.

—Han Suyin, "The Sparrow Shall Fall"

The revolution is not yet Completed. Our comrades must Strive on.

—From the will of Sun-Yat-Sen, epitaph to Israel Epstein, *The Unfinished Revolution in China*

Finally I was learning new material and following my classes at the Russian school with relative ease. I could rattle off the Mendeelev system of elements in Russian, and I understood the readings and assignments in my math, literature, history, and geography classes. Glad to see an end to the months of mental inactivity, I worked hard. No longer in limbo between schools, countries, and languages, I was busy memorizing new material. Daily my Russian vocabulary expanded. During the schoolday I chatted freely with my classmates, who were marginally curious about me but not sure of the wisdom of inviting me to their homes. Russian schoolchildren were trained from the earliest years to believe that capitalism is evil. Capitalism equaled America. In private, my Russian classmates were interested in associating with me, but in public I was a liability, a foreigner who did not fit into the protective enclosure of their Soviet cocoon. In this school I was treated as an odd American, not a peculiar Czech. The Russians were insular and unlike the Czechs, arrogantly proud of their unique grandness. They always maintained a strong sense of cultural superiority which isolated them from the foreign and the unknown. Amaya, my Russian-speaking Spanish fellow foreigner, remained my only friend.

When I met my parents at dinner, I switched from Russian I used throughout the day to English. The big round tables in the dining room made socializing easy and privacy impossible. Most evenings we dined with a charming young Arab who was single when we met him. He was in his thirties, soft-spoken, shy, and an engaging conversationalist. One day he announced he was getting married. We were surprised for we had never seen him in the company of a woman. Who was she? Where was she? He explained that his family in his native village selected his bride and that a proxy wedding was about to take place in his home town. How could this sophisticated man consent to an arranged marriage? He did not seem concerned that he did not know her. After the elaborate wedding, she was sent to Peking to meet her husband and to start her married life. I could not wait for her to arrive. Our Arabic friend was visibly excited on the day of her arrival. We met her the very next day at dinner time. I would never had known from the wedding pictures she brought with her that the groom did not attend his wedding. It looked like any other elaborate wedding celebration, with a bride in a floor-length gown, a layered wedding cake, and a proxy groom (who could have been taken for the real groom) dressed in a tuxedo.

The new wife was a beautiful woman. She had a shapely figure and gorgeous soft brown eyes that reminded me of a gentle deer. She was extremely quiet and shy, and our friend, usually a lively conversationalist, was subdued, even shy in her presence. But after a few weeks they both had a vibrant glow, and they looked into each other's eyes for long periods of time unaware of what was happening around them. I was certain they had fallen in love. I was monitoring the situation very closely, leery of arranged marriages, but the outcome was far better than I had anticipated. I was watching their love blossom. Was it their will, their different expectations, or luck that made the marriage work? Puzzled, I wondered if perhaps love could be cultivated rather than an uncontrollable magnetism that controlled us?

Wearing the prescribed school uniform was no indication that I belonged in this Russian school. There were frequent reminders that I was a tolerated outsider. In a history class the teacher was giving a typical "capitalist America is terrible" lecture to the class, and as he was enumerating the capitalist evils—unemployment, crime, prostitution, poverty—he fixed his weary eyes on me: "Well, Anja, why don't you give us some examples of what it is like in America? After all, you did live there, right? Go ahead, tell us how terrible it is there!" I attempted to explain that I knew much more about life in Czechoslovakia than in America. His request invariably led to more questions I did not know how to answer. Which country could I truly represent? It was not America, a country of fragmented images, but Czechoslovakia, which held the memory of my most recent life experiences. In this classroom of Russian youngsters in the heart of China my American birth counted more than my years in Czechoslovakia, though what counted for me was how I felt inside. I could not explain myself to outsiders in a few sentences. In the Soviet school if I said, "my parents are American communists," it granted me a degree of social prestige, but it did not put an end to the questions I wanted to avoid.

The very first composition I wrote for my Russian literature class was on the character of a greedy old man in a Gogol story. I worked on it for a long time, agonizing over each sentence. This was my first attempt to compose in Russian. I wanted to show my teacher that I could express complicated thoughts and feelings in literate, perhaps even elegant, Russian. I was excited about this assignment because I loved Gogol's idiosyncratic quirky old man, who was selfish but at the same time touchingly human and pathetic. Gogol's phantasmagoric, hyperbolic descriptions created more than just a wonderful lifelike character; they showed me what the Russian language could do in the hands of such a master. I was, at the time, reading the collected works of Balzac in fifteen volumes, which Abe bought me at the Russian bookstore at the Druzhba as a birthday gift. I shared my love for Balzac's world of characters in his *Human Comedy* with Abe. He suggested that I approach my assignment as a comparison between the Gogolian and Balzacian characters. Balzac also had a story of a greedy old man, which reminded me of Gogol's character. Enthusiastic about Abe's suggestion, I portrayed both characters in my essay, concluding that Gogol was, in comparison to Balzac, the ultimate master of his craft. With great care I copied the final version of my essay, making sure my Cyrillic letters were clear and neat. I was proud of my first composition in Russian.

When I got the composition back, there was a lengthy note from the literature teacher and a failing grade. I was informed that nowhere in the assignment did it state that I could compare a Russian author to a French one. The teacher reprimanded me for coming up with such an absurd idea. The teacher expressed hope that in the future I would follow directions I had been given. Neither Abe nor I deserved a passing grade in the Soviet school system. If I wanted passing grades in this school, mastering Russian was not enough. I had to learn to limit my creativity.

My entertainment was limited to what was available in Russian in the Druzhba movie houses and library because I could not function in Chinese. The movie theater in the compound showed current Soviet films to an extremely small audience; at times during afternoon showings I was there by myself. I could not understand why there were empty seats when so many Russians lived at the Druzhba. While I was learning Russian, I wanted to see films in Russian to improve my language skills. After I had seen a few films I was no longer surprised. How many times can you watch happy *kolchoz* workers make phantasmagoric strides in the crop yields, the entire village cooperating to transform the countryside into a massive agricultural wonder—all to the tune of ecstatic violins? Another variation on the same theme was the plight of the miner and the industrial worker striving to overproduce, overachieve, to surpass the previous records. In these socialist realist films, everything functioned according to a smooth formula. When characters deviated from the expected norm, they were punished or retrained to protect the interests of the socialist state. Evidently the Soviet films shown in Prague were higher-quality ones. Here I had a chance to see the "B" as well as the "C" ones. I was also getting older and less willing to accept this formula as representative of real-life situations and feelings. I was coming to recognize how terrible these films were. It did not take long before an evening of Peking opera was a refreshing treat.

I met young people whom I would have liked to have known better, but we had no common language to communicate with each other. I still have a photograph of a smiling, energetic French girl whom I met at the Druzhba, who spent most of her time in the swimming pool. She swam back and forth with great skill and speed. We were the same age. I have no idea what school she went to, or why her parents were in Peking. We liked each other, but we could never get beyond smiles and pantomime gesticulations. Between French, English, Russian, Czech, and a couple of Chinese words we exhausted our resources without learning much about each other. Ultimately we had to give up. Though we could never communicate our thoughts and feelings, I knew I would have loved to have this bubbly girl with a thick braid of chestnut-colored hair and the most natural, warm, open smile as a friend.

I did not date while I lived in China. I had typical teenage attractions and desires, but the circumstances were not conducive to developing relationships. When we first arrived in China, there was a Chinese man who accompanied us on several trips I took with my parents. I tried to stay close to him whenever I had a chance. We looked at each other a great deal, joked in a nonverbal way, because he did not speak much English, but we never touched. I liked his eyes. It was exciting to be around him. I dreamed about him and hoped something would or could happen. Nothing did. After a few months I never saw him again. And then there was the unexpected invitation from a young, single Soviet engineer Genia, to celebrate New Year's Eve with him in one of the halls at the Druzhba. Was I excited! When I came to the appointed room to meet him at ten o'clock that New Year's Eve, his friends were seated at a large table, but Genia was not there. I was told that Genia had been taken to his friend's bedroom, unable to walk or talk. He had consumed too much vodka too quickly. I danced with his friends, but it was not the same. Genia was too embarrassed to look me up again, especially when he found out I had seen his friends trying to get him back to his room early that morning, still incapable of walking on his own. And that was the sad ending to a romance that never was!

During our second year in China, our family took a trip through the country, as far south as Canton. We traveled with Elsie, the wife of Israel Epstein, called Epie by his friends. Epie and Elsie Epstein lived in the Foreign Language Press, one building away from us. Epie and Elsie were a most unusual looking pair. He was short and small-framed. Elsie was tall and large. She towered over Epie whenever they walked beside each other. I am not absolutely sure about their backgrounds, but I believe Elsie was British. Epie spent his boyhood in China and spoke fluent Chinese. He was a correspondent who had traveled a great deal in China. The political conflicts Epie escaped when he left America are documented in the same volumes of the congressional hearings in which I read about my father. He was a strong supporter of the Chinese communists. He was accused of justifying the new communist Chinese policy to the West in his highly controversial book, *The Unfinished Revolution in China*, published in 1947.

Both Epie and Elsie were dedicated to furthering China's communist cause. I remember them as kind, caring people. Their apartment was filled with books, magazines, and newspapers. They had no children, and they lavished a great deal of attention on me. Epie frequently took me into his study to show me his library. He suggested things I might enjoy reading. It was Epie who told me to read the *The Diary of Anne Frank*, which I bought at the Russian bookstore. The book had a profound effect on me. I believed these communists I spent time with wanted to make sure Anne Frank's fate would not be repeated. Epie discussed *The Diary of Anne Frank* with sincere passion and feeling. When he got carried away, his metal-rimmed glasses would slide down his pointed nose. He was oblivious to how comical he looked. Ideas played a dominant role in Epie and Elsie's lives, something I was used to from my own family.

For days we planned our trip to the south of China. I was delighted Elsie was coming. She was fun and she loved to try new things. Nothing would stop her from going to the marketplace, where she talked with the local people about their regional specialties. Elsie loved Chinese food. She was looking forward to tasting a particular fish soup made only in the southern provinces. When the bowls of hot fish soup Elsie ordered were brought to our table, she was the first one to dip her porcelain spoon in the thick broth. Unfortunately, a little fish bone got caught in her throat before she could have a second spoonful and her eyes filled with tears. We had to give Elsie a drink of vinegar, a Chinese remedy to help dislodge the fish bone. As soon as Elsie felt the fish bone slide down her throat she finished her bowl of soup. No little fish bone was going to get in the way of Elsie's enjoyment of a culinary delight she had been anticipating since we left Peking.

Six of us set out on this trip: our family of four, Elsie, and an assigned Chinese interpreter/guide who watched our every move. We traveled by train, exchanging the pleasant northern temperatures for the steamy southern tropics. During the trip I got the flu. Because of the high fever, I was not sure at all times if what I was seeing was a dream or reality. In Canton I watched the boat people navigate up and down the wide Pearl River on their traveling homes in which multigenerational families cooked, washed clothes, and raised their children. On the streets families slept on the sidewalk on straw mats to escape the oppressive heat of their apartments. Toddlers with distended, naked bellies played in the packed streets. At night, when the heat prevented sleep, the images of beautiful banana trees covered with the heavy yellow fruit and the ever-present crowds that filled the streets, parks, restaurants, markets, and riverways haunted me. All these millions of Chinese people had to be fed, clothed, housed, employed, and entertained. The enormity of the task was staggering. This was China's challenge.

The beauty of the glistening tiles and statues on the roofs of old palaces and Buddhist temples contrasted with the disturbing sights of poverty and overcrowding. I could not block out the human misery around me and concentrate exclusively on the architecture of the buildings. China was much more backward than Czechoslovakia and Russia. The stunning palaces of the former wealthy class were now government buildings or museums. Most of the people lived with three generations crowded in one or two rooms. What I saw on this trip confirmed the seriousness of China's economic struggles.

In the South the heat and humidity were so excruciating that when we were outside sweat dripped down our arms and slipped off our elbows. When we walked around the southern cities and visited communes in the villages, we were surrounded by hordes of small children who gathered within minutes of our arrival. They tried to touch the hairs on my arm, or they stared right into my face, exclaiming excitedly to each other things I could not understand but could easily imagine from their faces. They could not get over the physiological differences between us—the freckles, the hair color, the manner of walking. The faster I walked to escape their curiosity, the more children joined the crowd, turning the initial group of twenty into forty and fifty. There was no escape from the crowds of children studying my body, my walk, and the sounds I made. There was no place for me to hide to escape this zoolike examination of my body.

One night in our hotel I accidentally discovered that on the other side of one of the doors at the end of the hall there was cool air. What was this, a division of hot and cold floors? Who are the cool corridors for? We were evidently not among the privileged who deserved the cool air, but neither were most of the millions and billions of Chinese people outside. In this hotel I was as uncomfortable in the unbearable heat as were the Chinese outside. But now that I discovered this air-conditioned section of the hotel, I knew what a difference that contrast made. Before, in precommunist China, it was the rich who had special privileges; now it was the party functionaries. When I returned to Peking from our trip, I doubted that the communists in power could overturn China's past as quickly as they thought they could. There were many more hurdles to leap over, far more than the Great Leap Forward campaign could ever accomplish in the time frame that had been set. This big country needed so much improvement it was impossible to envision a revolution that would reverse centuries of poverty in five or even ten years. The unrealistic gap between party slogans and projected goals and what I could see with my own eyes made me suspicious. Words were dangerous weapons between a desired truth and reality, and I had to distinguish between them and decide what I believed.

My sweet sixteen birthday was celebrated in glorious style in the company of my parents' friends. It was a royal feast in one of Peking's renowned restaurants. As the celebrant I had the honor of choosing my own eel, which was still swimming in a barrel in the restaurant courtyard and was to be cooked for us. The eel was on its way to the kitchen while we started with the hundred-year-old eggs and shredded slivers of pork and cucumbers in a spicy sauce. After the exquisite but formal dinner, we gathered in Mania's *hutung* to continue the celebration. Mania wanted my birthday to be memorable.

Mania was an old-time American communist who had lived in Moscow for many years before she moved to China. American communists, who could not return to the United States, worked as writers, journalists, or editors in their host country. Practically all the communist refugees hoped to return to the United States when the fierce anticommunist sentiments subsided so they could reestablish their legal status. The expatriate community did not live in constant political harmony. Anna Louise Strong, for example, a well-known communist who had worked with Chairman Mao, lived in Peking while we were there. My parents had no contact with her. There were vague references to political differences and disagreements. But Mania, loved by my parents, was my favorite.

Mania lived by herself in a charming old *hutung* in downtown Peking. Before she moved to Peking, she had lived in Moscow for a couple of decades. Her rooms were filled with stacks of books, papers, magazines, and manuscripts in both English and Russian. She was short and chubby, her round face framed with thick straight white hair. Her face came to life when she got excited about the ideas we were talking about. We had one thing in common. I was learning Russian, a language she already knew well. We both loved Russian literature, even though she knew far more about it than I did. I was just discovering Russian writers she had known for a lifetime. The main topic of our lengthy discussions was life: just like the heroines in Russian novels, I wanted to know the meaning of life and love. Mania's patience and knowledge were inexhaustible.

As often as I could, I traveled by bus across Peking to visit her in her peaceful *hutung*. She was ill when I met her, even though she hardly ever discussed it with me. I knew from Belle that she had terminal cancer. Every once in a while during our conversation she would take a deep breath and put her arm across her breast as if she was trying to stop the pain from claiming her. When she recovered from the sudden flash of pain, she immediately continued the conversation. She never complained, never sought sympathy. She was interested in people, literature, ideas. Mania knew she didn't have many months to live. I was sixteen, she was sixty. She had much to teach me, and I had much I wanted to learn. My life was ahead of me, and she was living out her final months. She talked about her childhood in America and her family with reserve. Remembering the past always made her sad. She talked about Russia and the Russians with deep feeling and a sorrow she never explained. Turning the conversation to my life and goals cheered her up right away. Her political commitments led to painful separations. I could identify with that. Mania was convinced her devotion to the party was not in vain. Her faith remained unshaken. When I listened to her talk, I believed she had no regrets, but when I looked into her sad eyes I had doubts.

The discussions with Mania stimulated me to wonder about my own future. What was I doing in Peking? Where was my life leading me? Would I always remain an outsider? Would I have a life like Mania's— dignified, purposeful, but lonely and homeless? At sixteen I had the pressing urge to know my forgotten family name and the facts about my past. I had no anchor to steady my inner chaos. Mania and I never discussed my confusion directly. Instead, I listened to her stories about her life and the lives of other dedicated communists, and we discussed my life through the veil of literature. She wanted me to be strong and independent and to have confidence in my future. Her steady voice had a strong impact on me.

Eventually, my unsettling emotions erupted on the pages of a long letter I composed for my parents. I feared my emotional turmoil would upset them, but I could also no longer live in silence. My letter was a desperate plea for the truth. At first, I declared my love for them. I thanked them for all they had done for me and for being the wonderful people they were and for the experiences they introduced me to. At the same time, I wanted them to understand that my needs for a stable home base and continuity differed from theirs. I insisted that at sixteen I was entitled to know why we had left America and why we could not return. I wanted to know my original family name. I wanted, in short, the taboo of silence broken. My life was a mystery that stifled my individual choices and options. Just this one time I wanted my needs to be granted equal importance to the party cause. I wanted them to level with me and trust me as an equal so I could sort things out in my own way.

In this letter I poured my heart out, explaining my conflicting emotions of love, despair, confusion, loneliness, and loss. I needed to have this information and their confidence right now, not later, not never, but *now!* I was worn out being a pawn. No longer a child but still vulnerable, I demanded more than just the fabricated story, more than the party line. Surely I had to be worth it! The letter was written in phonetic English because I could not spell. I wanted to be freed of the burdensome secret that bound me to them. Under these circumstances it was impossible for me to perceive myself as separate from them. As keepers of secrets, they controlled my destiny. Confident with the power they had over me, they loomed large, almost saintly, towering over ordinary human beings who lived their lives out in the open bound by shared conventions and rules.

I held on to the letter for several weeks, frightened it would devastate them. We were vacationing at the seacoast when I slipped the letter into their bedroom. The next day my parents asked me to go for a walk with them on the beach. They both looked serious, aged. I was full of anticipation. Perhaps today is the day I will be able to say the name I had when I was born, perhaps I will learn about their thoughts and hidden feelings and the meaning of many things that puzzled me. It was a gray, windy day. We walked in silence until we reached a huge rock near the edge of the water. We sat on the rock for a long time. I felt the ocean spray on my cheeks. My mother broke the silence with a few words. "It is safer for you not to know, for what you don't know nobody can get you to talk about. We cannot tell you anything." My father, always overflowing with words, sat hunched over, gently rocking his body. I was crushed. This was not what I hoped to hear. With grave looks on their faces, they expressed the hope that one day I would come to understand. Slowly the two of them, arm in arm, walked back to the cabin. Thus they had fulfilled their parental obligation.

I sat on that rock for a long time. Crying and screaming, I called to the ocean and the clouds above me for help, for guidance, for peace and calm. The wind carried my cries to the ocean, where they dissolved and dispersed. The cries subsided, filling me with numbness. Cursed by fate, I was different from others and alone. But I also felt a strong love for life and a passion to feel, to know, to experience. I had to harness that passion and learn to deal with the inexplicable without the help of religion, peers, parental support, an extended family, or a society of my own. I had to make sense out of what I was living on my own terms. Like a soldier returning from the battlefield, where he saw things he could not communicate to others, I was separated from those who had not been there. In our family we never talked about my letter again. We all had to learn to love each other knowing there was hurt and things we could not talk about or change. I broke my childhood chains that day.

Meanwhile, efforts to implement the Great Leap Forward were taking on frenetic proportions. China was speeding ahead, mobilizing the manpower of the nation to carry out previously untried campaigns. To improve the overall industrial output, the party encouraged the construction of small furnaces all over Peking to melt down metal for the production of steel. Everywhere in Peking they were building little smokestacks and primitive furnaces that changed the Peking landscape. This campaign did not last long. It did, however, make a mess of the courtyards, a lasting reminder of a failed attempt to accelerate production at an unrealistic rate.

By far the most outrageous campaign was the war on the sparrow population of China which was part of the campaign against Four Evils (rats, flies, mosquitoes, and sparrows). The theory was that the sparrows had to be eliminated to salvage the grain they consume for the Chinese population. In the choice between sparrows and people, it had been decided that people needed the grain more than the sparrows. Based on this deduction, the campaign was going to be carried out in the following manner. The radio, newspapers, and loudspeakers all over Peking announced that sparrows would be poisoned, shot at, caught in nets, and prevented from resting from their flight so they would have to drop to the ground from exhaustion. The governing slogan was "Keep the sparrow flying." For three days the entire nation participated in the campaign. People lined the streets armed with long poles with strips of cloth flapping at the end, gongs, and firecrackers. Everybody made as much noise as possible to scare the sparrows to death. The morning newspapers reported the numbers of sparrows killed each day. People waving their poles in trees and schoolchildren standing on rooftops were encouraged with slogans blasted from loudspeakers and banners on trucks to "fight the sparrow to the death" and to "bravely struggle forward, eliminating the sparrow pest!"

Pioneer groups advertised the numbers of sparrows their troops killed, and the nation bragged about the amount of grain that would be saved. Sparrows dropped from the sky, their population wiped out, destroying the ecological balance of nature. The great leader who devised this campaign was not thinking about the long-range effects of a country without sparrows. Everybody was obligated to participate in this campaign. Millions all over the country hollered, waved flags, and waited for the sparrows to fall from the sky. During the campaign I too sat in a tree with a long pole, madly waving down exhausted sparrows. I never hesitated or stopped to think that something was not right with this campaign. Without deliberation I believed it was the right thing to do whatever the collective did. So did most of the Chinese.

On the third and last day of the campaign, roads were filled with carts heaped high with dead sparrows. Processions of schoolchildren carrying banners telling of the number of sparrows their units had killed marched between the carts. Some eight hundred thousand sparrows were killed. In the war against sparrows the proletarian dictatorship was the victor. In the battle with people who opposed the ruling regime, who was going to survive? What a show of unity and strength this campaign was!

Wu Ningkun in his 1993 book, *A Single Tear*, recalls the long-range effect of this campaign: "It was reported much later that the extermination of sparrows had contributed to the crop failure in the next two years, as insects injurious to crops, freed from the threat of their natural enemies, ate their fill at the free Communist mess."

The political lies and the repressive atmosphere that spread at workplaces and the university made my sister wish for one thing only: immediate removal. Older and more independent than I was, she demanded her right to leave Peking and fly back to Prague to resume her studies at Charles University. As the economic and political situation worsened in China, she could no longer watch the diet of rice and sweet potatoes the Chinese students lived on while the foreign students were fed dishes with vegetables and shreds of meat. The party issued imaginary production figures trying to make it seem that things were getting better. What we saw, however, was that the daily lives of the people were consumed with long work hours, political meetings, self-criticism, and deprivations. And there was fear in the eyes of the people and in the way they walked by you without looking directly at you. By the 1960s relations between the Soviet Union and China had deteriorated drastically. More and more of my Russian classmates returned to the Soviet Union when their fathers were given orders to leave the plants at which they worked. Belle, the master strategist and the ultimate poker player, realized the safe days for foreigners, even reliable communist sympathizers, were numbered. Explosive political forces were coming together, but the moment of attack had not yet been determined. Belle wanted us to get out of China, fearing that if we waited too long it would be too late. She was right. Both my parents had been working in an agency that had access to information, a dangerous commodity in those days. It was safest to know nothing, and they definitely knew too much.

The drama of hope and expectation had played itself out, bringing to a close the dream for a perfect ideal. When we boarded the train for our return to Prague, where life was much safer for refugees like us, Belle collapsed into the cushions of her seat exhausted from the weeks of pent-up tension and genuine fear. Drained and pale, she let the following words quietly slip out of her usually clenched mouth: "I wasn't sure we were going to get out in time. This was a dangerously close call. I won't feel better until we get past the border." She was right, for a few years later all the non-Chinese communists we spent time with, some of whom worked with my parents, ended up in prison. Sid, Elsie, Epie, even the most loyal, were behind bars for knowing too much or not being trusted enough and for being foreigners. The loyal foreign communists who believed in China's communist future and who worked hard to make the dream a reality were betrayed by the very thinking that brought them to China.

On this return trip, two years after our arrival, the Trans-Siberian train crossing was quite different. My parents, exhausted and worried, were trapped in the communist world, the one they had hoped to help create. Regardless, they had to get on with their lives without hope that the dream that set things into action was going to succeed with the leaders who were currently in power or, worse yet, as a workable social system. Only two years earlier they could not wait to get to China, and now they were desperate to leave alive and free. Instead of following a dream, we had our personal lives to contend with and the problems of reconstructing them once we returned to Prague. At least in Czechoslovakia, sparrows were still flying and eating grain as they had always done. Our train pulled into Moscow late at night. We had boxes with Chinese furniture and Chinese paintings and rubbings my parents had bought during happier days. The drunken Russian porters handled the boxes roughly, and a few boxes came apart. Some of the furniture got damaged. My parents tried to negotiate with the porters. The porters brusquely replied: "*Malo, malo*" (Too little, too little). What had happened to the glorious communist brotherhood? Even Moscow appeared changed. Now it seemed not one for all but one for himself. We got back to Prague to an empty apartment, from which everything we left behind had been confiscated by the state. We were once again free to resume our lives in these barren rooms.

Chapter 19

· · · · · · · · · · · ·

Returning Home

I climbed the moonbeams of desire
In the midnight of misty quests,
Mind's midnight dawns of hope and
    expectation.
And slid down the solid sunrays of raw
    reality,
In the noons of unslaked quests,
Lost ladders and shimmering shadows
And parched shadows of the sun-drenched
    day
And darker than the shadows of the night,
The midnight dawns of quests and
    questioning
In the answerless sunlight
Of reality unfathomed
—Abraham Chapman, written in the Intensive
Care Unit in Wisconsin, 1976

You're not getting me involved in anything, are you?—I ask with a smile but
with some concern.
—No. Not unless having a past is a serious
crime.—
—Anton Shammas, *Arabesques*

My sister informed us that she had re-
turned to an empty apartment when she arrived in Prague several
months before we did. During our stay in China, Czech government
officials confiscated the belongings of the defected Czech pilot and his
family. They took everything they found in the apartment, unaware or
indifferent that our things were mixed in with those of the defectors.
Routinely the state repossessed private property defectors left behind.
State warehouses were full of furniture, art objects, and personal treasures that were officially the property of the people or more accurately
the communist government, which was the uncontested owner of all
property, the holder and manager of national wealth. Everything I had
neatly packed in boxes before our departure for China ended up somewhere in those state warehouses. Our things were never returned to us.

The officials also opened and removed the contents of the sealed vault in our bedroom, which had been the source of many wonderful childhood fantasies for my sister and me. In place of spinning dreams about the unknown contents of the vault, I had to face the reality of resuming my existence in Prague. Despite my barren bedroom, I was relieved to be back in Prague. I did miss Amaya and our long talks, but otherwise Peking held few attractions for me.

In the rooms we were occupying our footsteps sounded hollow on the carpetless floors. We had to start all over again to make these rooms a livable home. We borrowed blankets and sheets and set ourselves up on the floor. I thought of the Gypsies who camped out in apartments instead of hampering themselves with furniture and civilized conveniences. Belle decided to have furniture made to order, accepting the reality that we would be in Prague for an indefinite time. After a decade of exile, this was to be the first sincere attempt at setting up a home that reflected their taste. It took a couple of months before we could sleep on beds and sit on chairs again. There were, of course, the crates with odd pieces of Chinese furniture, scrolls, and rubbings that my parents accumulated while we were in China, but in these empty rooms the handsome pieces of furniture looked more like museum pieces than aesthetic additions to a home. Anyway, at eighteen, I had more important things to worry about for I had to complete my education and graduate before I could think of going to college. I had to make up the two lost years of Czech education.

I was in a panic about whether I could graduate with my class. Overwhelmed by the challenge, I was nonetheless determined to do it. It was a straightforward situation: I had to learn what my classmates had covered these last two years in two months, or I would have to repeat another year of school. I worked day and night, switching my attention from one subject to another. I was determined to have this plan succeed. I had to postpone reentering the Prague social scene until the end of exam time. I paced through the apartment cramming facts and formulas the way my father did when he wrote his articles. I got up at six in the morning to study while the rest of the family was still asleep. I drank strong coffee and munched on thick slabs of rye bread without taking my eyes off my textbooks and notes. In the bath or when traveling on the tram I memorized poems and read Czech novels that I might be questioned on during the exams.

I had no time to dwell on the significance of the experiences of the last few years. I had to immerse myself in my studies if I was going to get on with my life. I had to pull into the finish line by the spring or I would be the oldest student in the history of the Koráb school. One by one I passed my exams in the individual subjects before I was granted permission to take the final *maturitní zkoušky* (graduation exam) with the rest of my class. In preparation for the exams, we had lists of questions for each subject. On the day of the exam we picked a question from the list we studied in each subject area, trusting our luck in getting the question we knew best. Before we were examined, we sat at a *potítko* (a sweating table) for half an hour to prepare our answer. We were examined orally by a committee of teachers and outside examiners. At oral exams, nothing escaped the attention of the examiners.

The matriculation exams were in math, Czech, Russian, and a subject of one's choice, in my case chemistry because I was planning to continue my studies in chemistry. I loved chemistry chiefly because I loved my chemistry teacher, Mr. Krupka. He was a young man in his early thirties with a boyish, honest face, thick, straight brown hair that covered his forehead, and silver-rimmed glasses. He lived for chemistry. He discussed the relationships between chemical elements with a passion. His enthusiasm and genuine interest in my performance made it impossible for me to arrive at our study sessions unprepared. Krupka made me believe that chemistry was crucial for industrial progress and that chemical research had limitless potential in a socialist state. I dreamed of becoming a scientist who would discover unknown chemical compounds that would bring our nation into the modern world. If it had not been for Krupka's encouragement and faith in my abilities, I am sure it would have never occurred to me to select chemistry as a field of study. My family was surprised to see my sudden commitment to science. They had always assumed literature and the humanities were my true love.

Preparing for the math exams petrified me. There were great gaps in my knowledge of math, because of multiple schools and language disruptions. I had to be tutored to get through the math exams. My mother found a young man who came highly recommended, a math genius. This extremely shy math whiz stuttered uncontrollably. He could not look me straight in the eyes while we worked. Karel patiently explained the math concepts I could not understand. We exercised all the mathematical formulas I needed to learn. He wrote out the solutions on a piece of paper, sometimes filling an entire page with numbers before he could finish his sentence because of his stuttering. He wanted me to master math, and I wanted him to stop stuttering. Once the numbers and formulas started to work for me, I was able to solve problems, amazed at my breakthrough, which proved more realistic than overcoming Karel's stuttering.

Preparing for the Czech and Russian exams was much easier for me. There were grammatical rules I had to know and literature questions I had to study, poems to memorize, and Marxist ideological interpretations that I could rattle off with little thought. I hardly had to prepare for the Russian exam after what I learned at the Peking Russian school and from Amaya, but I had volumes of reading to make up in Czech literature. As nervous as I was on the actual day of the exam, once I pulled out my questions I felt confident. I was going to show this committee that I was ready for college. I passed in all subjects along with the classmates I had studied with since elementary school and despite the disbelief of some of my teachers that I could not do it because of my two-year absence in China. Now that the exams were over, I was ready to emerge from the bedroom in which I had isolated myself. I wanted to live!

My neglected wardrobe desperately needed updating. Having lost out on two years of fashion trends, I wanted to shed my Russian school uniform and Chinese clothes for the latest styles. Prague was much more stylish than Peking. It was a thrill to get my first pair of thin high-heeled shoes as well as skirts and dresses that made me feel feminine. I did not care that the high heels got caught between the cobblestones when I ran to catch a tram or that they were squeezing my toes. If that was what elegance felt like, it was worth it. I bought glamorous lipsticks and costume jewelry. I had to purchase a ready-made gown (there was not enough time to have one made by a seamstress as most of my classmates did) for the graduation ball downtown in the elegant Obecný Dům.

My friends, who had attended the formal dance classes while I was in China, had lined up their partners to escort them to the dance. I had no escort, but it would have been socially unacceptable for me to attend this ball unescorted. My sister's fiancé offered his services. He was determined to make this big night a special one for me. He picked me up at the house dressed in a dark suit and with a corsage to decorate my rustling nylon gown. We set out for the ballroom, where after a few initial dances with my attentive escort, I danced the rest of the night with my classmates and friends. It was intoxicating—the musical tunes of the band, the lights of the crystal chandeliers that twirled in front of my eyes as my partner moved me swiftly along the shiny parquet floor, and the feel of my partner's hand around my waist. I had a grand time.

Most of the students in my graduating class were eighteen years old. Few were planning to continue their studies at the university. Even the best students who wanted to go to the university could not apply if they had the wrong political credentials. Some students were entering the work force, and many were going to *průmyslovky*, vocational industrial schools where they would be trained for skilled jobs. High heels, makeup, stylish clothes, and the Charleston were in; communist slogans about production, collective goals, and positive moral character were necessary jargon we did not apply to ourselves. We said things we did not fully believe in so we could get into the university or get a good job. We were trained to function within these political limitations and to set our sights accordingly. During that summer my friends and I gathered in local wine cellars and pubs to drink, dance, sing, fall in love, and talk late into the night. We had completed our compulsory school years and our future was ahead of us. I was young and ready for anything.

In Peking I became friends with Hana and Miroslav, a young and talented Czech couple, both fine musicians from Brno, the capital city of Moravia. The husband was an oboe player for the Brno symphony and the wife was an accomplished pianist at the conservatory. In Peking they played with a Chinese orchestra and taught music. They wanted to improve their conversational English. In the evening I visited their apartment at the Druzhba so we could talk in English, after which we had a good long visit in Czech. Hana was beautiful, dark haired, and graceful. She was Jewish; her husband was not. I was extremely fond of them. They were well-read, and music was central to their lives. After I returned to Prague I received a phone call from Hana. She was calling from Brno. She had left her husband in Peking and returned temporarily to Brno to care for her elderly mother, whose health was failing. She wanted me to keep her company for a few weeks that summer because, as she explained, she was having a difficult time. I knew from Hana that her mother had been an accomplished musician, spoke six languages, and had taught music and concertized before the war. During the war she was in the concentration camp at Terezín. I packed my bag and took the train to join Hana in Brno. When I got to Brno I was sad to see what had happened to Hana's mother.

In the last few months Hana's mother had deteriorated rapidly. She was confused and incoherent. She switched from language to language unconcerned if she was understood or not. If I started a conversation with her in Czech, she would switch into German and French, both languages I could not speak. She put things where they did not belong: we would find cookies in the silverware drawer and canned goods in the bedroom. Several times a day she hid from us in the bathroom dressed in several outfits of clothing, one on top of the other, clutching her shabby purse, afraid we would take it from her. Hana could not recognize her bright mother in this frightened, deranged woman. At night she talked out loud to her former camp mates as if they were in the room with her. We heard her relive the horrors of the war years as she recreated conversations with people who had died but were still living in her mind. One night, with sobs breaking through her words, I heard her whisper gently, "Don't worry my little pigeon, my dear Sara, I will protect you from harm," after which she mumbled something in a mixture of Yiddish and German. Day by day she retreated further and further into her past. We were unable to comfort her. It was not true that the war was over; for some it never ended.

At night Hana and I talked about their family past. Hana showed me albums with photographs from the days when her beautiful mother was playing piano in major Czech concert halls. Then came the war. In one of the albums Hana had money the Germans made for the prisoners in Terezín. The Terezín money could not buy anything; it was used to impress the world that Terezín was a "model" city. Now, years later, Hana's mother was back in Terezín, far away from us. I still have the crisp Terezín bills Hana gave me. This worthless money is a tragic reminder of the way those experiences changed the lives of those who lived through them.

My father, back at the Academy of Sciences, had continued to write and work at the same feverish rate he always had. He seemed troubled, even more absorbed in his thoughts than usual. My mother, working again for an international organization, had trouble adjusting to the hardships of daily life. The constant scrounging from store to store and from line to line for meat, vegetables, or toilet paper were no longer a source of jokes and witty strategy. They were exhausting, frustrating annoyances. In Peking, she did not have to run the household or cook. Here she had to return to the full responsibility of providing meals for her family and working long hours at the same time. And in Prague these were two draining jobs. Once a week Abe went to a small downtown restaurant, Rotiserie, where he met with Czech writers. They discussed literature, which as everything else in this society, was inseparable from politics. Much of Abe's writing was devoted to literary subjects in these years.

My father frequently helped those who needed his English expertise. An older Czech gentleman translating Thomas Wolfe's novel *Look Homeward, Angel* came to our home to consult with Abe about some of the American terms in the novel he had trouble understanding in their proper context. Over several cups of Turkish coffee, they could discuss one particular word for an entire hour. My father's voice caressed the words he used to evoke the uniquely American scene the word described. The translator asked questions to help clarify the distinctions between the Czech and the American ways of perceiving things. Their conversation made me realize words were far more than denotations; they implied feelings, attachments, connections to a world that had created them. That is why this Czech translator, whose English vocabulary was far better than mine, was sitting in our living room. He needed the unfamiliar context clarified. So did I. The only difference between him and me was that he was interested in learning about this larger context for American words. I remained stubbornly indifferent.

Abe and Belle had Czech friends who, in order to survive, tolerated the communist system even though they despised the ideology and the limitations it imposed on them. My father, who was optimistic by nature and who lived in a world of abstractions, fought hard to see the good around him, but my mother, who functioned in a concrete world of realities, did not disguise her bitterness and disillusionment. Abe escaped into literature and art while my mother had to keep the family afloat under trying circumstances. Any regrets or sorrows they had about our prolonged exile they discussed in private. Every once in a while a strange comment, a suppressed memory, or a desire for a change in our situation slipped out. The cure for their homesickness was not in their hands.

Just a few months after our return to Prague, we moved to an apartment in Vinohrady, much closer to the center of town. Kobylisy was a beautiful residential neighborhood with gardens and trees, but the more urban Vinohrady district was conveniently located. I do not remember why or how the apartment change was negotiated. I had many wonderful childhood memories connected with the Kobylisy streets and back yards. But no matter. Life was busy and exciting. I had been accepted into the Chemical Engineering University. My sister started her first editorial job at a news agency. That summer before I started my studies I was appointed to work as an official translator for the ČSM, the Czech Communist Youth Organization (the Czech equivalent of Komsomol).

At eighteen I spoke and wrote perfect Czech and fluent Russian, and I had a native oral command of English with a limited vocabulary and no writing or reading skills. My new job was a good match between the main headquarters of the Czech Communist Youth Organization and me. I was honored to have important work during which I learned translating skills. My first translating job was to work with a delegation from Ghana hosted by ČSM. Lída, who trained me and arranged my assignments, was an overworked, overweight, pudgy-faced woman with thick glasses and straight black hair that was always in disarray. She was considerate and competent. I followed her orders, nervous about how I was going to handle my new responsibilities. Lída guided me through my first assignments until I was comfortable on my own.

I traveled throughout the country with four (two men and two women) high-ranking functionaries from the Ghanian Communist Youth organization for an entire month. They were guests of the Czech government, and the goal of the visit was to show them how the Czech organization was structured and how it worked in practice. The Ghanian representatives were to meet people, see the country, and learn about the communist accomplishments in factories and villages. I was well paid for my work by Czech standards, which was a new thrill. I had to translate efficiently while the meetings were in progress so we could get through the scheduled activities for the day. In the three summers I worked for ČSM, I learned how to translate simultaneously and how to deal with different people in unpredictable situations. I adjusted to the stress of public appearances, improved my skill in negotiating delicate social situations and in the art of converting ideas from one language to another without losing the quality of the original. I met people from all parts of the world, fascinated to discover similarities and mutual points of interest. Furthermore, dealing with foreigners forced me to define my own identity.

One night, on my first month-long job with the Ghanian delegation, I had an encounter with Ben, one of the two male African delegates, which challenged my naive notions of innocence and communist morality. My sexual preparation for the real world was inadequate. Not only had I had no sex education in school, it was considered immoral and socially unacceptable to have sex if one was young and uncommitted. In the media there was no sexual advertising or hype of any kind. That is not to say that young unmarried girls did not get pregnant, but society scorned such behavior. (Once in high school we went on a field trip to a border town, Aš, for two days. Why we went there I will never know; there was nothing to see or do there. One night word got around that Jitka was in the bedroom with one of the male teachers. The news spread with the speed of a ripple from a stone gliding across water: Jitka and Mr. X were having *sex!* We all gathered in the hotel hall outside their bedroom to confirm the reports. From the sounds that were coming from the room, something had to be happening; two healthy people would not need to breathe so loudly. Everyone in our class stopped talking to Jitka. Nobody would sit at the same table with her during mealtime. She was publicly shunned, but in private we admired her nerve.) I guess that was our sex education.

That night, at a villa where we were staying, which belonged to the ČSM organization and was used for foreign delegations and was cared for by an old Czech woman, Ben, the important representative from Ghana, came into my bedroom. He grabbed me in a tight embrace and carried me over to the bed. Not expecting this from an important visitor, I did not know how to react. He got as far as pulling down his pants when the noises from my room alerted the old lady who lived in the villa. She flung open the door to my room. I slipped out of Ben's arms as soon as he loosened his grip at the sound of the slamming door. Ben remained on the bed in an immobile position with his legs spread wide open and his genitals fully exposed. I thought he was in a trance of sorts. The old lady, who saw the horrified look on my face when I looked at Ben in his frozen position, took me firmly by the hand and pulled me out of the room, saying, "One day you will understand, there is nothing wrong with him. Don't ever let him into your room again." In the future when I stayed at this villa with other delegations I knew why the old watchwoman suspected I needed her help. There were coerced and willing sexual unions behind the closed doors in this villa that sealed international friendships for at least one night.

The work varied from delegation to delegation, and though it was fascinating, it was also demanding. One of my assignments was at a factory that made train wagons. An English delegation had been invited to tour the factory and to consult with the Czech engineers. Because I did not understand how wagons were made, I had to spend my nights studying factory manuals while in the daytime I struggled to translate the technical terminology. I did not understand the technical terms in either language, but I managed to satisfy the basic needs of the good-natured engineers who understood each other on a higher, nonlinguistic level. Assignments such as this (including taking the foreign visitors to the best restaurants and cabaret shows in town) made me aware of how much energy and money the Czech government spent in presenting to the outside world a picture of a successful, relatively problem-free economy. I went from assignment to assignment without time to unpack my bags. By Prague standards, I was living in the fast lane.

My first encounter with Indians for whom I had to translate at a large press conference turned out to be my most embarrassing moment in public. I met the delegates on the morning of the press conference in the lobby of their hotel. I spent a brief time with them at breakfast, and then we were taken by car directly to the conference room. When the first Indian speaker got up to deliver his speech, I was to translate. I could not understand a word he said. I had never before heard English spoken with such an accent. Fortunately, after a few agonizing moments, a middle-aged Czech journalist, who spoke excellent English, volunteered to translate in my place. I was never so grateful to receive help. Eventually I became adept at dealing with the many versions of spoken English and foreign accents I heard in the course of my translating days: Indonesian, Chinese, Indian, Ghanian, Australian, working-class British English, and Norwegian.

During my years as a translator I had a chance to meet traveling Americans, which in some instances turned out to be a foreign cultural encounter for me. Sometimes they were Americans my parents had met who wanted help to get around the city. Other times they were Americans who had been told by acquaintances to get in touch with me. I was glad to oblige. I loved showing off my city. I remember one family in particular, who were staying in the newly built exclusive Hotel Yalta on the upper part of Václavské náměstí and who had a daughter my age. Her father, a successful businessman, told me the story of how well he made out in America, starting with a mere $1.29. Through hard work and shrewd business sense he had become very successful. I had not met Americans like this before, definitely not in my parents' circle. They invited me to dine with them at their luxury hotel, unconcerned about the prices.

Their slender daughter ordered a light meal of fish and vegetables she hardly touched. Her mother, worried about her diet, wanted her to stay away from rich and starchy Czech dishes that filled the menu. I had never heard the word *diet* used in this context before. I thought she might have a special disease. I ordered the richest and most interesting dish on the menu without any concern for calories, if I even knew what that word meant. When the two of us went for a tour of Prague by ourselves after dinner, she asked me where we could buy some chocolate candy. I was surprised because we had just finished eating. She told me her mother wanted her to diet so she would be thin and presentable. In her mother's presence she did not dare order the rich dessert I had in the hotel restaurant. Living in a country with severe food shortages, I was unaccustomed to such thinking. I was also not as slender as she was.

The more we talked throughout the afternoon, the more obvious it was that we belonged to dissimilar worlds. She had not read any of the books that I discussed with my friends, and I had not seen the movies and TV shows she mentioned. I did not have a television in my home. She asked me questions about my life in Czechoslovakia which made it clear that my experiences were alien to her and more than a translation from language to language was needed to convey their meaning. By evening I was glad to part with her. We were strangers to each other in ways I did not feel with Russians and other East Europeans. No doubt this was the environment where I could function best, adept at the rules that made me self-sufficient.

One day I returned home from my university classes expecting my parents to be home. But nobody was there. The neighbors told me that my father had been taken to the hospital in an ambulance. What had happened was serious: in the middle of the day while at his typewriter my father collapsed with severe chest pains. He had a massive heart attack.

The speed with which he was delivered to the hospital made it possible for him to live. He was placed in a military hospital at the other end of the city because my parents had a friend who was a doctor at this hospital known to be one of the best in the city. In a crisis like this, connections were a big help. While Abe was struggling between life and death, visiting restrictions were strictly enforced. Each night my mother would drag herself back from the hospital ashen-colored and drained. She was like a ghost, going through the mere motions of existence.

"Now we will be here for life. We will never get out of this country!" Belle despaired. But Abe was a fighter. He mobilized all his mental and physical energy to return to the living. In those days heart patients were hospitalized for many weeks, and doctors restricted their activities. I had never seen my father ill before. He always lived without sparing himself, driven by a powerful inner force. But now his typewriter sat on his desk untouched. He did not pace through the apartment during the night. The mail piled up on his desk, and the apartment was lifeless. The generator that put it all into motion had come to a standstill.

When he returned home after his long hospital stay, he was weak. He rested for long stretches of time, read, and thought about things he was not ready to discuss. Gradually he got strong enough for little outings to the park down the street. Together Abe and I would sit on the bench and talk while soaking in the sun and watching the neighborhood people. We could spend more time together now that his mad whirlwind of ceaseless activity had come to a halt. He took time to notice nature and the children and old ladies in the park. I found the following poem on a yellowed piece of poor-quality Czech typewriter paper, the same paper his articles were written on, among his files after his death. I suspect it is about the ladies he saw in the park when he was recovering from his first heart attack. From this poem I can tell that Abe's attitude toward time and life changed drastically after his illness.

THREE OLD LADIES
Three old ladies
    on a park bench
    in the fall.
One, felt-slippered, tall, formless.

The second, raisin-faced, shrivelled, all nose.
The third, thin-haired, pink-scalped,

the features of the face knocked
by the years into a shapeless pulp.

Victims and victors.
Linked in their separateness
Each flaunting her silver hair
like the insignia of their
conspiracy against time.

Three old ladies,
Now chatting on a park bench,
Nodding their heads in unison,
Like three puppets on a single string.
Pooling their loneliness
In a mutiny against time,
Making common cause
Out of their common grievances:
      The sun is now buried in the clouds
      the chill of this October afternoon
      the fear of wind
      the time-cooling of the blood.

Three old ladies
      on a park bench
      in the fall
Warming their backsides on the wooden bench
Nodding their heads in unison,
Conspiring against time.

Abe's heart attack occurred one year after his return from China. He had to learn to listen to the signals and warning signs his stressed body was sending if he wanted to live. While he was recovering, he turned from the external world of events that had usurped him to his private inner world to regain his strength. This was a difficult time for both Abe and Belle. Unsure of how much time he had left to live, Abe no longer concealed his desperate desire to return to America. The hope that one day he might be able to return became a driving force in his recovery. His personal journey was unfinished. He was not ready to give up on life, not so far away from his homeland, not before he had a chance to sort out the meaning of the last decades. Abe's brush with death made me realize how irreversible and dangerous the consequences of his communist faith had been. Shortly after the first near fatal attack, he suffered two more severe attacks. He fought fiercely each time. Once back in the United States, he wrote the following poem about identifying the symptoms of a heart attack that nearly killed him in Prague:

I didn't know
It took so much knowing
To know the difference between
  a pain in the chest
      and
  an aching heart
(No rhetoric) a paining heart.

Voice of known
And sounds for the knowing.

The certainties he lived by in his youth no longer worked. His rebellious heart led him to confront how much of the unknown he still had to discover within himself.

Chapter 20

. . . .

University Years

There is farce because the world is far-
cical, the world is a joke that God has
played on man. We enter His game, we
join His game.
—Eugene Ionesco, *Defense of the Absurd*

The big lecture halls at the Dejvice
Chemical Engineering University were filled with note-taking students.
For the first time I had no humanities classes, just science, math, and
the obligatory lectures on Marxism and political economy. As a beginning chemical engineering student, I was most concerned about managing the demanding math and chemistry material. Ironically, the most
inspiring experience my first college semester turned out to be the very
math lectures I had feared so much. The professor was a short, older
man who looked like a conductor. His white hair in disarray, he paced
energetically between the lectern and the blackboard. He lectured with
a passionate intensity and absolute clarity. His delivery was charged with
vitality, and the force of his words affected me, although I could not
understand everything he said. His lively eyes scanned the heads of the
students crammed into the lecture hall without focusing on any one
face. I'm not sure he even saw us. His sights were set on what was going
on in his mind instead of on the audience; his mind was imaginative and
thriving. It had never occurred to me that math could be so exciting.

It took five years to complete the engineering degree. During those
five years all students had to spend two semesters working at a factory,
leaving the comfort of the Dejvice lecture halls and labs. The rationale
for sending students to work as factory laborers the second semester of
the first and fourth years was simple. Students were expected to learn
how the actual production operated from the bottom up. The experiment was intended to improve our understanding of the work process
and to sensitize us to the needs and ways of the workers. In a socialist
society, engineers were hypothetically expected to service the people.
And the people were the workers and farmers, not the professionals.
Living in the vicinity of the factory and working with ordinary workers
taught me things that had nothing to do with factory management or
socialist production.

After completing a semester of tough theoretical courses, I left Prague for the factory plant in Mostecko, in northern Bohemia. Mostecko was nothing like scenic Prague; in fact, the area was incredibly ugly. The town was a series of factory plants, canteens, and workshops with unpaved paths that instantly turned into messy mud puddles when it rained. I had not expected the variety of languages and the range of nationalities I found among the factory workers at the Mostecko plant. Wooden barracks behind the factory buildings housed migrant workers who were Czechs, Hungarians, Romanians, and Gypsies. These workers, both men and women, were rough characters, not at all like the smiling workers I had seen on the posters who wore clean work clothes and shook the hands of the young pioneers. I was now in the company of real workers with scruffy beards and sweaty, dirty clothes, not mere creations of socialist realist artists.

The workers I saw at the canteen intimidated me. In theory, it did not sound like such a terrible idea to "get to know the working class," but in practice it was virtually impossible. First, the men checked me out from head to toe to see if I had a pleasing shape. I was a sexual possibility, not a future engineer. In the enormous canteen the starving men sat at long tables shoveling dumplings and gravy into their mouths at rapid speed with a couple of beers. After a few cigarettes and some coarse jokes, they returned to their work. What did I have in common with these men? What could we talk about? I did not trust them without the protection of my friends. Our engineering class was scattered throughout the factory for work assignments, and I was left to my own resources.

I did not work in the major plant where the heavy work was done. I worked in a print shop connected to the factory, and I took direct orders from a boss, comrade Novák, who was in charge of the entire operation, which involved more than twenty workers. During our break, I gathered with the other workers for conversation, a much needed diversion from the monotony of our jobs. Some of the employees were nice to me, even though I was not one of them. Most of the workers were indifferent. Nevertheless, every day I joined in the friendly bantering that helped pass the time.

Faithfully and naively adhering to the high moral code set for the proper sexual conduct of young people, I was surprised, even shocked, by the frequent talk about the exchange of sexual favors and the sexual teasing that went on among the married and unmarried workers. I had read too many socialist realist novels that were divorced from the way people actually lived. There were two young girls I worked with, not at all like the heroines from the novels, one chubby and large-framed, the other scrawny with unkempt straight hair and bad complexion. Each morning they started their day describing the guys they slept with the night before, boasting about how many encounters and drinks they had the night before. They joked about the sex (a relief from their boring daytime routine) they had with men whose names they did not even remember the next day. How could I find a way to relate to these two girls who thought I was too serious and boring because I could not share tales of my own sexual exploits?

We were housed in an isolated country spot several kilometers from the plant, in a castle called simply Castle, the *zámek*. For Europe, it was a rather contemporary one, about two centuries old. It was a large stone construction built around a spacious courtyard. We were bussed or trucked to work, and if we had to work overtime we had to catch the local bus or hitch a ride. The owners of the castle had left the country after the communists took over, and the confiscated property belonged to the state as our Kobylisy home did. That is how we came to live there. The *zámek* was located in a small village that had a JZD (a State Agricultural Cooperative) and the fields stretched far beyond the horizon from the castle windows. The castle garden, now sadly neglected, had crumbling garden statues of mythic figures and cracked stone bird feeders. The interior of the castle with its long corridors and cold stone floors, enormous rooms with oversized carved doors, and heavy brass door knobs was designed for spectacular social gatherings and a large service staff. It was never meant to be used as a dormitory. Our rectangular bedroom had fifteen beds close to each other lined up against the wall. From the outside the castle appeared romantic and otherworldly. But for us, it had no charm. It was just plain uncomfortable.

In the winter the tall-ceilinged rooms were freezing. The tile stoves in the corner of each room could heat only a small portion of the space. We had hardly any storage for our clothes and personal things so we kept our clothes in boxes under our beds. Boženka, who slept in the bed next to me, seldom spent the night by herself. She did not care about breaking the rules to sneak her boyfriend in for a couple of hours. The squeaky rattles of the metal bed frame and the hushed squeals of the lovers made me wish I was back in Prague where I only had to share the bedroom with my sister. Boženka did not care that her love life was exhausting me.

We were not really learning what it was like to live in a working-class environment in Mostecko. We were learning what it was like to live with each other. Exhaustion and overcrowding fueled minor irritations and frustrations. Most of us were so tired at the evening political meetings we would doze off and wake up at odd intervals so that the speaker's voice trailed off into a stream of senseless sounds. Halfway through that winter I developed an uncontrollable cough, which developed into pneumonia. The factory doctor placed me in the small hospital on the edge of the factory complex. It was a low, two-story building with about twenty rooms. None of the patients were so sick that they could not enjoy company, and everyone was thrilled to be sick enough not to have to work. Without television, our only source of entertainment was conversation. We talked for hours.

By far the most engaging conversationalist, from the room across the hall, was a handsome, single young man in his late twenties who was not unlike the storyteller in the *Arabian Nights*. He kept his audience enthralled with descriptions of his passionate nights of lovemaking. I thought his girlfriend had to be a sex goddess. His elaborate descriptions made it easy for me to imagine what I could not see. We were eager for the next night's installment. I believed each and every one of his tales. But his beautiful sex goddess never came to visit him in the hospital.

In the hospital I also became friendly with a kind, middle-aged woman, Věra, a mother of four nearly grown children. She was a short, shapeless woman with premature wrinkles and worn-out eyes. When her husband came to visit her, he walked toward her bed with brisk, long steps without noticing any of the other women in the room. His face beamed when he looked into his wife's eyes. When he reached her bed, he lifted her into his arms and gave her a long, passionate kiss on her lips. I had associated passionate love and desire with good-looking young people, not with worn-out, middle-aged, plain-looking couples who had been married for several decades. The passion I witnessed between Věra and her husband made me see her through the eyes of her adoring husband. And that made her forever beautiful.

When I returned to work, my boss asked me to make up some of the time I had lost while I was sick. The request seemed reasonable, so I arranged to stay at the print shop extra hours. When the day shift was over, I noticed that the boss and I were the only ones left in the workshop. The boss walked up to me to explain the work he wanted me to do. He grabbed me firmly in his arms and squeezed me tightly. I had not expected a married man, who was also a manager, to abuse his position this way (as I had naively not expected the African representative, Ben, to take advantage of his position). It was time to take life as it was and not as it was supposed to be. I managed to get away from him, but I feared he might resent my unwillingness to accommodate him. From then on I counted my remaining days at the shop. Only thoughts of my life in Prague sustained me. The lecture halls at the university provided the protection our factory environment lacked. Here it was raw life, as it is, not as we were told it would be. As soon as our working hours were over, we returned to our castle and the surrounding countryside, keeping our distance from the workers. Perhaps this social experiment worked in a way it was not intended to; it maintained and confirmed the unbridgeable distance between the students—the future professionals—and the workers.

Back in Prague I was busy preparing for my summer job as the translator for the Czech Youth League Delegation at the International Youth Festival in Helsinki. The members of the Czech delegation spent a week in training sessions at a resort outside of Prague. At these sessions we were coached in how we should present Czechoslovakia to other countries and what answers we should give on sensitive political topics and how we should behave in a Western country as model communist youth. We were discouraged from expressing excessive enthusiasm over flashy displays of Western merchandise. We were told the temptations of the seductive West should be tempered by the strength of our communist morality and the knowledge that our society was socially superior. Of course, those selected to go abroad were the most dependable and loyal. Measurements were taken for the light blue suits and white shirts that were made for all members of the Czech delegation. This was my first trip to the West since I had come to live in Prague. On this job, I was representing Czechoslovakia and translating at encounters between "our" country and other nations.

When our delegation gathered at the Prague airport for our night flight to Helsinki, we were too excited to care about losing a night of sleep. I shared the curiosity and excitement about seeing a Western country with my own eyes. It was like opening gates to a forbidden territory where unknown dangers had seductive powers. We flew into Helsinki just as the sun started to rise over the city. Not having slept an entire night might have contributed to the euphoria we all felt riding through the quiet, clean city streets that had no banners or large posters with political slogans and no red stars on the buildings. It was amazing how different a city looked without them. Lush green lawns contrasted with the blue waters of the Baltic Sea. The Finnish language had a system of declensions like Czech, but in Finnish there were fifteen cases and in Czech only seven. Now that made me respect the language of this country! There were well-supplied, tastefully arranged stores advertising the owner's name and the products they were selling in place of the drab state stores we were used to. Not only were the advertised products actually in the stores, but there were no lines and the shoppers could make a selection from a large variety of brands. Shopping was a luxurious fantasy.

We had been given some pocket money, but we discovered within the first few hours that the prices were astronomical. All I could get was a Coca Cola (which I longed to taste) and a handful of fresh oranges to bring back to Abe, who was recovering in the hospital from his second heart attack. We walked through stores filled with beautifully packaged merchandise we could not afford to buy because we came from a socialist country. We could not exchange our Czech crowns for the local markka; there was no official trade between a socialist and a capitalist country. The economic superiority of a capitalist society was glaring; even if we were morally and politically superior, would we ever be economic equals?

At the Youth Conference I translated at small gatherings from English- and Russian-speaking countries. To simplify things for all the Soviet bloc countries, Russian was the official language of communication at this conference. In an effort to establish friendly ties with other nations, we exchanged token gifts and pleasantries. We made toasts and delivered optimistic speeches. When I translated for the Americans they were puzzled by my connection to the Czech delegation because of my American accent. Most of the American delegates who came to Helsinki were supporters of the Left. I met, for example, the daughter of Morton Sobell's wife. Sobell's family was still waiting for his release from prison in connection with the Rosenberg case. It was a strange quirk of fate that both of us, children of communists whose own family destinies were still unresolved in 1962, met here in Helsinki. Twelve years of history are not the same as twelve years in one's personal life. Those twelve years gave me time to grow up and develop a life of my own; they made Sobell's stepdaughter angry at the American government for unjustly destroying their family life. For the children of American communists, at home and abroad, the McCarthy era was not over yet.

The Americans asked me questions I could not or was instructed by my parents not to answer. This made the encounters with the Americans far more disturbing for me than the sessions with the Yugoslavs or Russians, where we made speeches and drank toasts to celebrate the eternal friendship between our nations. During the festival I sang romantic Russian songs by the ocean with the Russians and danced in the streets enjoying the rapport we established because we were young and together. The Helsinki white nights made it impossible for us to contemplate sleep, for we did not want to miss out on the organized and chance encounters that were taking place. Here in Helsinki I made friends with bright and politically active Czechs in our delegation with whom I remained friends when I returned to Prague.

I was closest to Slávka, who had been selected to come to Helsinki for her loyalty and hard work for the Young Communist League. She was completing her studies in political science at the university. Devoted to the communist ideal, she was a perfect choice to represent the Czechoslovakia of 1962. I do not think, however, that this is what attracted me to Slávka. She was tall, large-framed, a bit stocky, but soft and feminine. She had thick, short, curly hair and sharp brown eyes. At times she had a devilish twinkle in her eyes, but most of the time she was serious. She was soft-spoken and shy, and she blushed easily but did not lack the courage to express her opinions or to speak up on issues that mattered to her. She was hardworking, caring, and highly principled, demanding exemplary standards of performance and conduct from all, but mostly from herself. Slávka radiated a powerful spiritual strength. She loved literature, philosophy, ideas, people. We had intimate discussions about building a strong character and being useful to Czech society. Those were my exclusive goals at the time. During my last year in Prague, I spent as much time with Slávka as I could.

When Slávka was preparing for her final exams in Marxism, she went to the countryside for a few weeks of solitary study. She asked me to visit her for a couple of days to discuss the ideas she was studying. When I arrived, I found her at her study table stacked high with books and note cards. She was rereading Marx's *Capital* and studying its relationship to the works of current Marxist economists. After days of isolation, she was anxious to share her reactions to the complex material she had been studying. She explained the relationship between Marx's theories and the social structure we had now. Her enthusiasm was pure. I often wonder how she weathered the political and moral changes in her country over the last decades. What happened to the sincere faith that Marxist theories were applicable and workable in a communist society? And what are her thoughts today?

The Indonesian and Australian delegations that had been at the youth festival in Helsinki were invited for a tour of Czechoslovakia. I was their translator. This job kept me busy until the start of my second academic year of studies. A few weeks into the semester, while doing an elaborate experiment in a lab during which I had to run gas from a tiny hose into my test tube, the faucet malfunctioned. I fainted and in the process crushed a glass test tube in my hands while the gas filled the closet-sized lab room with fumes. When I was found sprawled on the tile floor, I was minutes away from death. I was instantly dragged out of the lab into the fresh air to recover. Friends walked me to a local clinic, where they diagnosed a brain concussion and a broken collarbone. After putting me in a cast from my neck to my waist they sent me home on my own. Our Vinohrady home was on the other side of the city. On the tram I nearly fainted. Luckily, concerned strangers made sure I got off at the right station. When I rang the bell at our apartment late that evening, I collapsed at my parents' feet. They had no idea what had happened to me; they were never notified by the university of my accident.

My mother made my case into something of a cause célèbre, a chance to fight indifferent university officials and the disinterested doctors for sending me home by myself and for unsafe lab conditions. In a socialist state, she complained, nobody could be held responsible; nobody in particular was in charge. My mother was irate over the lack of concern for the safety of the individual, who in this case happened to be her daughter. My mother's attempts to find justice were futile. My recovery took a long time. My parents wanted me to consider switching to a safer field of study. I did not return to the Chemical University; instead, I became a student of Spanish language and literature at Charles University.

That winter I went to East Berlin with my parents to visit their American friends who lived and worked there. Originally the arrangement was for me to work at the broadcasting station for a few weeks over the holidays where they needed American-accented voices for broadcasts to the West. Media warfare on the airwaves on both sides of the Iron Curtain was intense during those years. The Americans persistently broadcast Voice of America, which the Czechs consistently jammed.

On the wide downtown Berlin *strasse* boulevards I felt the oppressive presence of recent history. Faces of Germans old enough to have participated in the war and who might have even killed Jews, the sound of German language, the destroyed buildings that made the war a reality were images I was trained to associate with evil Nazis. The uniformity of the bland yellow Christmas tree lights that adorned each tree and the impeccably tidy hotel rooms made me long for the presence of individual expression. I was, frankly, overpowered by the flow of painful images I had accumulated over the years from films and books that portrayed Germans as evil. And now visiting in this country I was suffocating.

I flatly refused to stay any longer in Berlin. I could not handle it emotionally. The staff at the radio station was not really interested in using my services as they had originally planned. I could not wait to return to Prague—a city that was friendly, alive, and human in comparison. The day before I left Berlin I purchased fifty fresh eggs—a precious find. It did not seem fair that the East Germans had eggs, which we could not get in Prague. I carefully wrapped each egg in newspaper, hoping the border guards would not discover what I was bringing back in fear they might confiscate them. The guards checked my papers and searched my suitcase, but they ignored my bulging handbags. I distributed these prized eggs to my friends in Prague, glad they would eat them instead of the Germans. I was not ready emotionally for the impact postwar Berlin had on my sensibilities as a Jew and as a Czech who had been taught to love the Russians and hate the Germans. I still functioned in a restricted world of dogmatic formulas. I needed time and life experience to sort such things out.

One of the summers during my university years our family went on a vacation to Bulgaria. We stayed at the International House for Journalists, which was on the shore of the Black Sea, outside of Varna. The only other time I had vacationed on such a large body of water was in China, when I spent time at an ocean resort and had loved it. Czechoslovakia had its own vacation escapes—beautiful countryside forests for mushroom hunting, mountains in the Tatry and Krkonoše, but no ocean. We traveled to Varna by train, stopping in Bucharest for a day. Bucharest was like a mideastern city with a lively street life, open markets where people bargained loudly and aggressively, and beggars who were not too shy to touch and address travelers. The Romanians were far more outgoing and physical than the Czechs. In Bucharest, dressed in Czech-made clothes, we were approached like Westerners who came to Prague; we were followed and envied for our "classy" appearance. I could not make sense of how there could be such an enormous difference in language, culture, and the standard of living between two countries that were so close to each other geographically. When we got to Bulgaria we were overcome by the smell of ripening peaches, vineyards weighted down with heavy grapes, and the tang of strong salty sea breezes.

Abe befriended the local Bulgarian fishermen, who took him out on fishing expeditions with a bottle of wine, crusty local bread, and salty cheese. Though he could not speak their language, they had a wonderful time. Belle and Laura soaked in the sun and relaxed, and I fell in love with a local Bulgarian by the name of Kostia, a student at Varna University and in the summer a waiter at our resort. I could not speak Bulgarian, but its closeness to Russian, a language we both spoke, made it easy for us to talk about almost anything. We became inseparable. My parents were not concerned about the outcome of this relationship because they knew that in a few weeks we would be returning to Prague and I would never see Kostia again. We felt otherwise.

Kostia took me to the small fishing villages along the coastline, proudly telling his friends and relatives I was his fiancée. I was living a dream. We spent evenings walking the streets of Varna munching on sardine-sized deep-fried fish wrapped in a paper cone, laughing, talking, and looking into each other's eyes. Late into the night we drank wine and strong Turkish coffee at a little cafe nestled in the rocks right by the ocean, run by a rotund old Turk, who had seen many couples like us. But the day came when I had to leave Kostia. A correspondence started between us in a mixture of Slavic languages but with one overriding message: we were miserable without each other. International travel was difficult in the Eastern bloc, even between the socialist countries. One had to have money, passports, visas, and in some instances letters of invitation. Kostia wanted me to invite him to Prague, and he wanted to marry me. My parents were frantic. They would not let me invite Kostia to Prague. And I was not a rebellious young woman. They voiced their concerns with questions I tried to answer: "What, settle in Bulgaria? What kind of a life would that be? What would that do to the future of our family?" From now on they desperately wanted to get me back to the United States before I got involved with a young man with whom I would contemplate establishing a permanent home in Europe. Their race against the tides of history was now in conflict with my biological readiness for a male partner.

My social life in Prague was active. Charles University was located off the Old Town Square, an area that had at least a pub or cafe on each street, and I got to know all of them. After classes I debated crucial life issues with my friends over wine and coffee, which helped distract me from the memory of Kostia. Between my parents' objections to the possibility of a Bulgarian marriage and the complicated official red tape between countries, the hope of ever seeing Kostia again was fading. Meanwhile, I met Bohouš Smrčka, who became part of my everyday life. Subtle signs of liberalization I welcomed were beginning to appear in Czechoslovakia, which ultimately led to the events of 1968.

On one of those typical university days I had just come out of a late afternoon lecture on Marxist dialectics at Charles University, during which two hundred students had been struggling to keep awake. I went straight to the coffee shop on the ground floor of the large stone building, right behind the wide marble staircase that led to the largest lecture hall in the building. Charles University had been founded in 1348, but these obligatory lectures on Marxist theory dated only from 1950.

With a cup of black Turkish coffee in my hand, I went over to a small table where my friends were seated. "I did not understand a thing at today's lecture," Karla said. "I didn't even try to make sense out of it. This weekend I'll cram for the test and hope for the best," I replied. Quickly the conversation turned to the latest issue of *Plamen* (Flame), a new literary magazine that had published some daring short stories challenging the limits of censorship. Excited about the slight change in the otherwise tightly controlled political climate and what it might bring in the future, we decided to continue our conversation in a nearby wine cellar. We shared our personal hopes and dreams over several glasses of wine.

I told my friends about a new translating assignment I had for that summer. I knew that I had a talent for interpreting. I wanted to become a trilingual interpreter at international conferences, maneuvering between Czech, Russian, and English. Willing to take risks and fast at switching from language to language after years of informal training between my home and school life, I was a natural for this work. I was proud to explain Czech history and culture to foreign delegations; they were things about which I knew a great deal. On the tram ride home I thought about Bohouš, who had asked me out dancing that Saturday night and whose companionship I was beginning to depend on. He was kind, funny, sexy, and intelligent. We both loved wine, dancing, talking about books, and walking around Prague late at night. Whenever he looked into my eyes and held my hand he called me "Anička," the endearing term for Anna in Czech. I found myself dreaming about him.

That night when I got home, the light in the living room told me my parents were waiting up for me. I feared something might have happened to Abe, who had recently had three near fatal heart attacks and was still recuperating. When I entered the room, however, I heard my father's clear, strong voice: "Ann, sit down. We must talk with you." My father looked animated in a way I had not seen in years. "We have just had word from the party that we can start the process of negotiations to return home, to America. I've been waiting for this news for so long I thought it might never happen in my lifetime. Imagine. We'll finally return home, back to the States." His eyes shone in the dimly lit room, and with a trembling hand he caressed my stiff shoulder. My mother quietly smoked one cigarette after another.

I was speechless; the effects of the wine instantly evaporated. I did not want to believe this was happening. I felt complete panic; the days ahead looked dark. Slowly, I got out the word "When?" and my father, who could hardly contain his excitement, said, "Probably within a year. There is a lot of paperwork that needs to be done. It will be complicated, but it will happen," he assured me.

I stumbled out of the room, and though it was late, I called Bohouš. "Listen, Bohouš, something has come up. I must see you, talk with you, hold you. Everything is crashing in on me. I'm lost. I'm about to lose everything and everybody."

Chapter 21
· · · · · · · · · · · ·
Preparing
to Leave

People are always shouting they want to create a better future. It's not true. The future is an apathetic void of no interest to anyone. The past is full of life, eager to irritate us, provoke and insult us, tempt us to destroy or repaint it. The only reason people want to be masters of the future is to change the past. They are fighting for access to the laboratories where photographs are retouched and biographies and histories are rewritten.
—Milan Kundera, *The Book of Laughter and Forgetting*

Milan Kundera opens his novel *The Book of Laughter and Forgetting* with a description of a speech Premier Klement Gottwald made in February 1948, when the new communist government was formed. This crucial moment of Czech history was preserved for eternity in a much publicized photograph of the communist leader Gottwald standing on the balcony of a baroque palace addressing hundreds of thousands of citizens. In this photograph Gottwald stood next to the foreign minister, Vladimír Clementis, who took off his fur hat to cover Gottwald's bare head to protect him from the cold February flurries. Four years later, during the Slánský trials in 1952, Clementis was charged with treason and hanged. In the novel *The Book of Laughter and Forgetting*, Kundera shows how history was retouched to obliterate the memory of Clementis's presence: "The propaganda section immediately airbrushed him out of history and, obviously, out of all the photographs as well. Ever since, Gottwald has stood on that balcony alone. Where Clementis once stood, there is only bare palace wall. All that remains of Clementis is the cap on Gottwald's head."

To remember what we were forced to forget was an act of courage in a socialist state. I know from personal experience that the government tampered with historical, political, and personal information. Our own family history was recreated in the offices of the Ministry of Internal Affairs, possibly even in the same building where Clementis was lifted out of the famous photograph. What remains of my existence as Čapková is merely a memory of a tarnished reality comparable to Clementis's cap accidentally left on Gottwald's head. Like the cap, which is proof of a denied fact, I have only a few books and an old school map of Czechoslovakia, which are signed *Anna Čapková* in my schoolgirl handwriting. Otherwise I have just my memory.

During our last year in Czechoslovakia, our personal documents were processed to change our family name, Čapek, which had outlived its use, to the one I could no longer remember. Now the identity we had lived under had to be reversed; I could only return to America converted once again into who I had not been during my Prague existence. My life as Anna Čapková had been destroyed. When the time was right to terminate our exile, I was guided through the necessary procedures of reinventing a thirteen-year family history that would make me once again a legitimate American. Yet, to become an American I had to deny I had spent my youth as a Czech citizen. The only way to undo our illegal status as Czechs was to take further illegal measures to abolish the papers under which we had lived. Arranging our return to the United States took close to a year. My father filled out forms he had been sent by a lawyer from America (an old comrade from his American communist past) to negotiate the intricate paperwork involved in acquiring valid travel documents for our return. This stage of our transformation from Czechs back to Americans took months, during which application forms, documents, and letters of explanation were mailed back and forth. All my documents—school records, graduation certificates, whatever had been done and accomplished during my short life under the name Čapková—had to be annihilated or falsified to my original name.

It was explained to me that by 1962 it was finally possible to negotiate our return because of what my parents referred to as a "change in the political climate in the States." With John F. Kennedy as president there was a more liberal attitude toward former active American communists, which made it possible for those who had been persecuted or hiding abroad to return to the United States without the danger of imprisonment. Furthermore, enough time had elapsed for the statute of limitations to free my father from any danger of imprisonment or persecution. I was powerless to stop the delicate proceedings set in motion to bring our migrant lives to a close.

I tried everything possible to get my father, a veteran of three heart attacks and still in precarious health, to understand that I wanted to stay in Czechoslovakia. My studies, my translating future, my friends, and my roots were here. I had nothing left that would draw me back to the United States. Discussions on this subject invariably brought out violent, uncontrollable, and painful emotions. At this crucial juncture in our lives, my parents and I belonged to different countries pulling us in different directions. I fought to keep mine; my father fought to bring me back to his homeland that had once also been mine. Emotionally he could not accept that there was a cultural and language divide between us. I knew that my connection to Czech and the world it represented was my true and only homeland. The deep love we had for each other made this conflict a nightmare.

In the end I had to go along with the unfolding of the drama that started back in 1950. I had no documents of my own that would separate me from my parents and their complex political history of intrigue. I was bound to my family's predicament. There were no legal means for me to keep my Czech papers. My parents argued, and passionately believed, that I would eventually be grateful to return to the United States. I could not possibly imagine that ever being the case.

Abe would turn red in the face and gasp for air when the exchange between us would get too upsetting and the emotions too heartwrenching. I feared he would have another heart attack. Paralyzed, I stopped the flow of hurtful words, realizing the futility of my attempts to reverse things. For the first time in my life I felt my father was my opponent who was taking something precious away from me. How could I get him to understand that my years in Czechoslovakia were not a casual addendum to my life, as he might have wanted to believe, they were my life. In this situation he remained the all-powerful parent, and I was the helpless child, even though I was long since passed my childhood years. My parents treated me the way the party treated them—one had to obey orders for a higher, larger cause. To destroy all the documents we had under the name Čapek/Čapková (the masculine/feminine versions of the same name) we worked closely with the Czech communist authorities.

When my parents told me the family name withheld from me for thirteen years, I no longer desired to know it. I had disassociated myself from this name. Once denied access to my past, I created a life beyond it. At age twenty-one I was no longer the fragile wanderer I was at sixteen. I was now firmly established as Anna Čapková, a person with a connection to that name and a short-lived but genuine history of my own. To become a Chapman I would have to give all that up. At this point, being a Chapman was an empty void that would annul my current life. For me the issue was not politics but culture, language, relationships; in a word, my entire identity. I wanted my right to remain in what was my home country. I wanted my freedom to be independent from my parents' political lives. I did not think of staying behind because Czechoslovakia was a communist country and it reflected my political beliefs. It was simply the only society I knew how to function in. I had no desire to go back to a country that conjured up frightened feelings (maximized by the not altogether unsuccessful communist propaganda), fragmented images, and memories of loss. America was a foreign world, a country where even my family were strangers.

I have come across only two documents in my father's files that show how the Czech authorities tampered with the facts of our lives to create a history the American authorities would find acceptable and that would brush over the illegality of the Czech status we had lived under for over a decade. One document was issued to prove (falsely) that we had a "foreign" status while we resided in Czechoslovakia:

Ministry of Internal Affairs:
No. VB-1601/801–1963

Prague April 29, 1963

VERIFICATION

The Ministry of Internal Affairs confirms on the request of Mr. Abraham Chapman, who resides at Prague 3, Slezská 125, that he and his wife Isabelle, born 11.7.1915 and daughters Laura, born 7.5.1938 and Anna, born 19.5.1942 are foreign citizens who live in Czechoslovakia on a residency permit for foreigners and for that reason they could not participate in elections.

Head of the department
Monsportová

This document looks official. It has a big red stamp of the Ministry of Internal Affairs of the Czechoslovak Socialist Republic on the bottom of the page. Was this memo true to the facts of our lives? The reality is that as Czech citizens living with Czech papers we had to vote; it was one in a series of factual realities that was being wiped out. The other document denies that we had ever been in China because American citizens were not allowed to travel to China in the 1950s. We did, but not as Americans. But if we were never those Czechs in the first place, how could we have been in China at all? The undoing of one lie led to several new absurdities. My parents were bringing back a few pieces of Chinese furniture they had purchased in Peking, and some of the pieces were damaged in Moscow when transported from Peking. This is the document that the Czechs prepared to cover up the two years we spent in China:

Ministry of Education and Culture
Prague, January 6, 1958

No. Sine 65/58

Mr. Abraham Chapman
Slezská 125
Prague 12, Vinohrady
Concern: The purchase of Chinese furniture

The Ministry of Education and Culture, in response to your letter of 19.12.57 informs you that as a foreign citizen you may purchase the Chinese furniture which is stored at the castle KONOPIŠTĚ. The pieces of furniture itemized below were damaged during the occupation by the Germans and they need repairs.

You have placed a deposit of 2.000 crowns for: 1 Chinese linen chest, 1 low coffee table, 1 higher coffee table, 1 nest of tables (4 parts), 1 nest of tables (3 parts), 2 night tables, 2 tables for plants.

All further arrangements will be directly done with the Old Czech Market, Prague 2, Nekázanka 17, where you will kindly complete your negotiations.

Head of the department
[Scribbled signature]

In this document, instead of comrade, as he had always been called, my father is addressed as Mr. The document has several revealing untruths. The forged letter is dated 1958, but we did not return to Prague until 1960 (how could he have purchased furniture he acquired two years later?) with furniture that was never purchased at the castle, and we did not move to the above-mentioned address until 1961. An entire situation and sequence of dates was invented that never took place. What does the truth matter when it interferes? All they needed to create the desired version of our lives was a typewriter, an official ministry stamp, and a signature.

I had to leave the university while our documents were being redone. I had to drop out of public life because I could not function without valid papers or an internal passport. During this transitional period, I was suspended between the life I had to give up and the one I was not yet living. A Czech secret agent, a tall, thin man with a narrow neck and a melon-shaped head, worked closely with our family on the "retouching" of our documents. He was a liaison between us and those invisible authorities who were handling our case. Laura and I disliked him, and we called him "the worm." I cannot remember his name, if it had in fact even been his real name. He also coached us in what to say in compromising situations and the safety rules we had to abide by while we had no legitimate papers. I could not reappear in public until my new documents, making me a Chapman, were issued. (In some strange way "the worm" became quite fond of my parents, and as a parting gift they let him walk away with a handsome set of wooden bookcases. Why not?)

At first, I stayed in the apartment in a sort of house arrest status. It was depressing. The tensions between me and my parents grew as time dragged on. They arranged for a country retreat for Laura and me in a remote village outside of Prague, where we could wait until our papers were prepared for us to apply for passports at the American embassy. Every few days we called home from the local post office to find out if it was time for us to return to Prague. It was the only phone in the village. Here at least there was the wide expanse of country paths and the woods to walk through and peaceful silence. I could face my pain without the raw anger and resentment I had toward my parents in the loving company of my sister. I needed to adjust to my new circumstances in my own way. Here I could yield to my sadness and despair. This was my last chance to be with my married sister, who was not returning to

America with us. I did not know when or how I would see her again. The future was a frightening black canvas. Events were turning my life around without consideration for my wants. I was still bound to the collective destiny of our family unit. When would I be free of this bond?

We stayed in an old farmhouse and ate our meals at the local pub. Brisk walks in the rain brought momentary relief. And it rained for days. Everything that was happening to me seemed unreal—the village we were waiting out our time in, the predicament I was in, but the hot sun and the rain drops were soothing and real. When we were given the signal to return to Prague, we took the first train we could get out of the village. I noticed that one of my teachers from Charles University, Professor Nosek, was sitting by the window in the train we had boarded. Fearing I would be seen, which would lead to questions I could not answer, I quickly switched to the next car. My heart was pounding; beads of sweat covered my forehead. I reentered Prague like a thief no longer entitled to my previous life. I thought about the days I spent in Mexico and about the hotel room in Prague thirteen years ago—all part of my nonlife. I hated the secrecy and deception with a passion.

I dreaded the appointment we were about to have at the American embassy. This was the first time I had ever stepped into the Prague American embassy building. Over the years I had demonstrated outside the building with my Czech friends to protest American imperialist actions. At the embassy I was grilled about my life in Czechoslovakia. I had to lie about my Czech past so that I could return to a future in America my parents wanted me to have. The embassy officials made the interrogation unpleasant. They did not trust or like our kind, but they had no concrete reason to refuse us our papers. That did not prevent them from making me feel like an undesirable American. My parents did not expect to be treated nicely. As long as the outcome was positive, they did not care. They never feared enemies. All they wanted was the victory of getting their papers. That day, in front of the embassy official, was the first time I signed the name Chapman. I felt like a traitor, betrayed and betraying at the same time. My jubilant parents took my sister and me to a fancy restaurant with a view of the Prague rooftops and bridges to celebrate their victory over fate. I was not even interested in seeing the menu. Before me was the city in which my existence had been terminated with one sweep of a pen, one fatal signature.

The plan, once we had our papers, was to leave Prague in the fall of 1963. After a flight to England, where we would separate from my sister, who stayed in Europe, my parents and I were to travel from Southampton aboard the SS *France* to New York City. Separating from my sister, the only person in the world who shared and understood my unorthodox childhood, was excruciating. The American embassy did not give the three of us individual passports. My parents and I traveled with a letter of explanation typed on a single sheet of thin paper with the letterhead of the Foreign Service of the United States issued at the American Embassy, Prague, Czechoslovakia, September 27, 1963. This document said:

TO WHOM IT MAY CONCERN:

This will certify that Abraham Chapman, Isabelle Chapman and Ann Chapman were issued Certificates of Identity Issued Under Section ##360(b) Of The Immigration and Nationality Act at the American Embassy in Prague, Czechoslovak Socialist Republic on September 5, 1963. These certificates are travel documents valid for return to the United States after extended residence abroad.

James Guy Gwynne
American Vice Consul

This was the sole document with which we reentered the United States. My fate was linked to that of my parents as long as my name was on that single piece of paper. I was Ann, the daughter of Abe and Belle. I was not Ann with my own passport, which would have granted me the freedom to have a destiny separate from theirs. From now on my life and my sister's life would continue in separate countries neither of us was familiar with and with a wide ocean dividing us. I was twenty-one years old. More than thirty years later, as I write the concluding pages of this book, my sister and I are still living on different continents, still a divided family.

Shortly before our departure, I arranged everything I had accumulated over the years on the floor of my bedroom in a large circle. My friends divided these possessions among themselves: my personal library, artifacts from China and other travels, my wardrobe. When my friends came over to choose what they wanted, the atmosphere in the bedroom was solemn. I felt much better knowing that my favorite books, my radio, and my mementos would remain with my friends instead of strangers. I had to spend all the money I had in the bank from my translating work because Czech crowns were not convertible to dollars. With that money I bought things I thought would have lasting meaning for me: a 1961 edition of *A History of Czechoslovakia* (written by a Marxist historian, proving to me now how seriously history was tampered with; for instance, the Slánský trials are not even mentioned, and how terrible the ideological rhetoric was, for example, "the young socialist intelligentsia is freed from the oppressive ideological burdens of the past, completely raised on a historical-materialistic scientific worldview"—that was me and my generation!), a sampling of my favorite Czech authors, and some hand-made glass, two garnet rings, and a delicately carved silver pendant. On the day of our departure all that was left in our apartment was our luggage because our furniture had been distributed among my parents' friends. The empty rooms were no longer a home. My friends did not leave their addresses with me, for they could not get letters from America without damaging their own political and career prospects. I was on my way to the other side of the Iron Curtain and could only bring my memories. This parting was final, absolute.

The fatal departure day arrived on a crisp, sunny October morning. I had known about it for a long time, but none of the preparations could make me ready. The private farewells with friends had already taken place in homes, wine cellars, or on long walks through my favorite city spots. Severing my ties with this life was the final performance of a play that was no longer going to be staged, at least not here, not in this way. I did not have the script for the next scenes.

Nobody came to see us off at the airport. My parents feared drawing any attention that might ruin things at the last minute. They just wanted us to get out of this country without any delays or complications. We slipped out of Prague as quietly as we had arrived (only this time it was my mother, father, and me, not my mother, sister, and me) on that cold night in 1950. At the airport I listened to the boarding announcement. This time I understood every word. All my thoughts were in Czech. Drained by a sleepless night, I found my head throbbing, my stomach in turmoil, waves of nausea. The unsteadiness of my legs compelled me—perhaps fortunately—to concentrate on the physical self rather than on my mental state. I had to find the energy to take those last steps leading me to the aircraft. There were just minutes, seconds left before the metal door would close, permanently separating me from the city in which I had grown up. The last glimmer of Prague's medieval skyline with the prominent Hradčany castle above the Vltava River soon disappeared under the clouds.

I tried to close my eyelids, swollen from a night of crying, but a stream of tears made even this simple act impossible. Once I buckled myself into my seat and the plane rose above the Prague skyline, a flow of tears poured out of me which lasted until we landed in London, a short distance from Prague in miles but the end of the world for me. My entire body resisted the inevitable motion of the airplane: sporadic sobs expressed what words could not. I was too worn out to rest, too sad to fight the despair. For me this departure was a funeral; for my parents it was a return from the dead, a resurrection. It was something the three of us could not discuss.

When we landed in London, we found ourselves surrounded by the sound of English, the bright, garish billboards advertising cigarettes, alcohol, and underwear—all of which confirmed that I had landed in an alien reality. The one-hour flight had transported me from a communist society, characterized by material deprivation and political slogans, to a capitalist world with its focus on consumerism and personal comfort. This was the first part of our return journey to America, my final separation from the known. I walked through the London streets consumed with sorrow and loss. I would not, absolutely could not, speak to my parents for days. I was too hurt, too angry to forgive. I was alone and desperate.

The voyage on the elegant SS *France* would have been exciting under other circumstances. I watched others dine, dance, have drinks, but I was disengaged and numb. For others life went on. The ship sailed through the tail end of a storm that forced the steward to close off the open decks where passengers sat in lounge chairs sipping strong bouillon. During the storm the bottles at the bar swayed from side to side, and in the dining room waiters had to secure the plates to the table. I admired the force of the storm. It resembled the feelings flowing through me that I could not express. After five days the ship pulled into New York Harbor, passing the Statue of Liberty. The skyline of New York City glowed in the strong sun, showing off the beauty of the modern buildings, which did not convey the centuries of history the Prague castle and the old city did. The tall skyscrapers represented the dream of the New World where the sky is the limit. This is where my parents' dream started. I was not ready to enter the New World; I did not have a dream to pursue.

When the ship docked in the harbor, immigration authorities came on board to check the passengers' passports. When the officers saw our travel documents they made us wait until all the other passengers were processed. The immigration officers questioned my father at length in a nasty, brusk manner. I pretended I was not listening to this hostile welcome. Hours after our arrival, the officials let us off the empty ship. We passed through the iron gates where there was a large group of people waiting to greet us. "Here they are, Abe and Belle are back!" some of them screamed when they saw us emerge after their long wait. Complete strangers hugged and kissed my parents and me. Tears and laughter expressed long-suppressed feelings. Gradually among the unknown faces I recognized some of my parents' friends who over the years had visited us in Prague.

For the old comrades who greeted us at the ship, our return was a faint victory after a series of major failures and setbacks for the party. My father was surrounded by people who used to know him well but who no longer knew the thinking of the forty-eight-year-old man, a survivor of three heart attacks, who had been stripped of those communist ideals which he had once fought to realize. The old-time communist and organizer Abe, his feisty, supportive wife, and his non-American daughter were back on American soil. One daughter never returned. The experiences we had been through and the world we had lived in not only transformed the history of nations, it changed my parents' outlook on life and my identity. Not all the teary-eyed comrades who greeted us on the day of our return were able to understand how and why our exile changed Abe and Belle so much. There was no adequate vocabulary to describe what they had survived.

My parents were too worn out to explain to people who still held the convictions they once lived by themselves what they had learned in their practical apprenticeship in the communist world. All Abe and Belle desired now was to resume their private lives, not as a brother and sister in the communist family but as private citizens. Everybody was on his own in figuring out why, if, and how the communist dream had failed. Our return signaled a major movement away from the tight-knit collective togetherness of party membership to the solitary struggle of each individual to make a life for himself.

Chapter 22

. . . .

In Retrospect

In early 1957 John Steuben, one of the old Communist leaders who had helped build the party among the steelworkers and in the industrial areas of Ohio, lay on his death bed, a forgotten and shattered man. Gasping for breath, he announced his break from the politics that had consumed his entire being and with a humility rare among former Communists said: "I want to live the rest of my life in agony and silence." It was the last word.

—Irving Howe and Lewis Coser, *The American Communist Party*

Communism was not defeated by military force, but by life, by the human spirit, by conscience, by the resistance of Being and man to manipulation.

—Václav Havel, 1991

Our family's exile that began at Grand Central Station in the summer of 1950 did not end when we pulled into New York Harbor thirteen years later. We had to deal with the drastic changes that had taken place both in us and in the United States during our absence. There were no shortcuts for the adjustments each of us had to make. For my parents there were the practical matters of finding a home, getting a job, and creating a new life without the moral, economic, and political support of their comrades and the party. My parents had to live for the first time by the rules of "regular" society, which demanded legitimate degrees, a permanent residence, and a steady income. At the age of forty-eight my father and mother had no home, no job, no savings. Belle had used many organizational and editorial talents in party activities, but how could she market her "degree" as political activist at an employment agency?

Abe sought his first "regular" job armed with a Ph.D. from Charles University in Prague, where he had written a dissertation on his beloved poet, Walt Whitman. His other accomplishments were not valuable assets to his marketability. Initially we took up residence in Chicago because my father had family there. We moved in with my aunt Adele and her family and lived with them for a couple of months. My parents had nowhere else to turn for help. Afterward, when Belle got work, we moved into a furnished apartment in an old Hyde Park hotel. I had a small bedroom, and my parents slept on a Murphy bed in the living room. Our living quarters were cramped and uncomfortable, but at least we were on our own again.

My mother supported us with a job at the Encyclopedia Britannica doing editorial work. I recall that she spent three months just editing citations under the letter "O" before moving on to the letter "P." Belle's strong point, however, was doing what had to be done for the survival of the family. Abe too tried to plug himself into the job market, but it was more difficult for him to find an academic position in which he could use his Ph.D. It took an entire year for the employment agency he had registered with to find him a teaching position. When Abe's first job in America came through, it brought my parents to Stevens Point, Wisconsin, the middle of the Midwest. It was not until Abe and Belle moved to Stevens Point that my mother learned how to drive a car and find a way to blend into American life again. Belle realized that she had to make herself marketable, and so, in her mid-fifties, she enrolled in college and began a new life as an undergraduate, surrounded by teenagers amused by the "little old gray-haired lady" whose eclectic life experiences were from another planet. After graduation, Belle found a clerical job at the public library and later a more challenging position as librarian at a Catholic high school. Dinnertime conversation, which used to dwell on the latest twists and turns of party policy, was focused on the new superiors, the Brother Patricks and Sister Maureens. The students at Pacelli High enjoyed Belle's spunk, her sharp sense of humor, and especially her liberal and, for them, daring views. If only they had known how she had toned down those views compared to her radical days, they would have been even more impressed by her boldness.

Belle lived for nineteen years after she returned to the United States. During that period she accomplished and experienced many new things: she earned a B.A.—the only older student in her class at that time—found employment, passed her driver's test on the fifth try, and helped purchase the only house my parents ever owned with a peaceful wooded back yard, traveled to California, New Mexico, New Orleans, Cape Cod, England, and Ireland, made new friends, and became a thrilled grandmother. But her feelings about her past remained deeply buried and unreachable. Wrapped tightly in a shroud of pride were disillusionments, hurts, disappointments, self-accusations, and guilts. The memories she loved recalling were the funny and benign ones, such as the time a Chinese comrade, whose English was difficult to understand, asked if Abe and Belle wanted a snack. When they got to the restaurant, they were served snake, not the snack they expected. They had to eat this snake meat, which was a local delicacy, so as not to embarrass their Chinese host, who never suspected they were surprised.

The wall Belle built around her private inner world made the feelings she wanted to conceal strictly off-limits. In her radical days she hoped and struggled for the impossible; in her later years she had to live with the results of where the commitment had led, the reality of a dream that turned into a nightmare. Despite her private anguish, her fierce pride, her advancing age, and the difficult readjustment to a life without all-encompassing political ideals, Belle courageously started over again. The intoxicating days in the movement were over, and life would never be as thrilling or dangerously exciting. In Stevens Point her days were productive but uneventful; her nights were sleepless. Abe, on the other hand, probed the darkness she tried to avoid. He was intrigued by the mysteries of human nature and its bizarre paradoxes as portrayed in literature. In his examinations and analyses he communicated what Belle kept silent. Belle's past left a void she could find no way of filling. Belle's emotional impasse resulted from the same devastation I noticed in her contemporaries who had been politically active. The quiet contrasts of private life outside of a powerful political movement did not compensate for the need for something more meaningful, more significant. My father's restless mental energy, in contrast, found new outlets when he shifted his focus from politics to art and literature, both more tolerant and illuminating in dealing with the irrational in life and human nature. Abe would not let his past consume him. There was still too much for him to explore and discover about life and living to allow regrets and sorrows to dominate his powerful life force.

In the classroom Abe challenged his students intellectually, and they flocked to his classes to experience his enthusiasm and knowledge. He arrived in class with a briefcase bulging with books so he could quote from the original texts. Animated, he pulled students into his own as well as an author's world of ideas with a compelling magnetism and urgency. I know from personal experience that his classes energized and engaged the mind for when I sat in on his course in American literature, the world outside the classroom ceased to exist. He met writers and poets whose works he studied and who invited him to lecture on college campuses. For Abe, the former Marxist and party functionary, literature became a means of social and individual change, a rediscovery through self-realization and understanding. His lifelong identification with the needs of minorities and the oppressed became the subject of his literary studies of American black, Indian, and Jewish writers. Literature enabled him to switch from the collective political vision of "we" to the individualistic, personal "I."

My father's language and thinking during the peak of his Marxist days was hackneyed and ideological. In the articles he churned out throughout the 1950s the message and choice of language were combative and utilitarian, aimed at defending a political position. In the article about book burning in America that he wrote in 1952 for *Literární Noviny* (a leading Czech literary newspaper) his militant communist voice is representative of other articles he wrote during that decade:

> The summaries of the most widely circulated books in the USA during 1952, now appearing in the American press, reflect the sickly depths of degradation of contemporary bourgeois American culture in the straitjacket of Wall Street's war drive. For years, now, the arbiters of the American literary marketplace have been doing everything in their power to coordinate and subordinate the content of all the American cultural media to suit the program of American imperialist aggression. Sadism and brutality, aggression and conquest, chauvinism and mysticism, sex perversion and anything that can dehumanize the reader and force his attention away from the realities of life have been extolled and promoted. Everything human, honest, democratic, expressing man's desire for peace, has been condemned as "subversive."

The rigid thinking in the introduction Abe wrote for the 1958 Czech anthology *Black Poetry* is in striking contrast to the introduction he wrote for the American edition of *Black Voices*, a book he wrote ten years later. In 1958 his words were weapons in the fight against American imperialism:

The anthology *Black Poetry* is not only a literary event for the Czech readers, but also an expression of solidarity and friendship and identification with the freedom movement of the blacks. Czech translations of black poetry are a contribution to the anti-colonial fight which always inspired World literature. . . . The freedom movement in Africa and the anti-racist struggle in the Western hemisphere are directed against one enemy, which is imperialism.

Ten years later, at his desk in Stevens Point, Abraham Chapman wrote a very different introduction for *Black Voices*. After having survived Prague, Peking, and three heart attacks, he finds meaning in capturing the individual's inner world instead of attacking the invisible imperialist enemy:

We would consider America as a whole a very static, drab, and regimented country without the very deep and fundamental differences of opinion which mark our national and cultural life. . . . Conflict of opinions and values is the way of life of every thinking and human community. . . .

The literature in this anthology takes us into the inner worlds of black Americans, as seen and felt from the *inside*. Literature as a way of knowing and perceiving probes beyond the conscious, the fully known, and the fully thought out. With contrast and analogy, imaginative ways of ordering images and values, with metaphor and symbol which suggest and imply the shapes and intimations of things and conditions sensed and known in the psychic subsoil, literature searches and captures human hopes and fears, dreams and nightmares, aspirations and frustrations, desires and resentments which do not register on the computer cards and statistical surveys, and government reports.

The need to understand man's irrational uniqueness gradually replaced dogmatic Marxist thinking. Two years before his death, in his *Anthology of Jewish-American Literature*, Abe voiced concern about the depersonalization of the individual and the struggle to maintain a sense of self in a modern world plagued by fragmentation. His language is far more personal and analytical than in his Marxist days:

Literature, by its very nature as human expression and explo-
ration, is many voices, illuminating simultaneously both the
uniqueness of every person and the common humanity of all
people. Literature . . . represents manyness, the infinite manyness
of human individualities and the manyness of the diversity of
cultures of humanity created by communities of individuals.

In our age of fragmentation and depersonalization, when the
pressures of conformity and homogenization are so perilous to the
human personality, writers have found it increasingly difficult to
hold together self and community. At one extreme of nationalism
and total collectivism, war has been proclaimed against the self
and the individual, to be voluntarily or involuntarily subsumed in
a controlled collective: the death of the "simple separate person."

Abe's later, post-Marxist thinking shows the emergence of a new understanding filtered through past experience. Painful disappointment with
communism's vision of a more perfect world liberated him to see life
outside of formulas. Abe's mind was alive and growing to the very end
of his life. During the thirteen years he lived after returning to America,
he edited five books. One was dedicated to my mother, one to the memory of his father, one to my sister and me, and one to each of his grandsons, Daniel and Michael. The fruits of his new intellectual world were
his gift to his family; he gave us what he valued most—perceptions
showing his genuine love and awe for man and life. Literature became
his medium for exploring a significance larger than the self and cer-
tainly absent in political ideologies.

During the last year of his life, Abe talked about two books he wished
he had time to write: one was an analysis of America's diverse cultures
as reflected in ethnic literatures (in the broadest sense); the other was
an autobiography. The idea for an autobiography, he told me from his
hospital bed, came to him in the emergency room while sucking in
oxygen to revive his failing, depleted heart. He saw a large white shape
against the tile walls of the hospital room that beckoned him to enter
a spiral tunnel. The friendly shape that appeared before him was not
frightening. When he reached the entrance to the tunnel, he knew with
absolute certainty that he was ready to examine his own life. After a life
devoted to the study of works written by others, he wanted to author an
original work of his own. The presence of the white, ghostlike shape

inspired a flood of memories and images. He told me he composed the opening page of this unwritten book as he lay on the emergency table. He felt he was back in Palestine listening to the rhythmic sound of chimes coming from the bells on the camels walking down the road. When he regained consciousness, he realized he was not in Palestine but in the emergency room and what sounded like the chimes of the camels was the emergency room equipment. The past surfaced with a sharp clarity as the present was receding. Abe was only sixty when he died. Instead of an autobiography, he left behind fragmented poems he wrote on scraps of paper during his last months in the Intensive Care Unit as he went from one heart failure to another. I found these poems in his files six years after his death. He scribbled them in haste in between breaths from an oxygen tank and being given blood tests. He never stopped probing, searching, or expressing himself:

In the midnight dawns
Of moondrenched nights
I have climbed the moonbeam
Searching for the morning sun
The womb of suns
The meaning of the sound of light

   Wanderlust
   Wander lost
   Wonder lost

The distance between life and death, time past and present, dreams and realities, and a sense of limbo, neither life nor death, reality nor dream, are important themes for him:

Between from and to
Between discharge from the hospital
And the fullness of life,
Between last stations on a trackless line
Between where I was and where I want to be
Between the unripened seed of my fulfillment
And the intimations of decay

(Definition: Between is a time and space
              relationship, reality,

not neutrality, impartiality,
evasion of choice)

Between is the sweet mystery between her thighs.

But above all by the end of his life Abe moved from certainties to searches:

Seascape

Tide out
A single gull
Standing one-legged
on a rock jut
lost in water
When the tide is in.
Out east?
Nonconformist?
Seeker?
Welcome!

His questioning poems intimate what he might have discovered in his personal writing if his heart had let him write. The white shape appearing before him in the emergency room urged him to jot down these unfinished poems, which took all the time and energy he had left. In these poems he roams the seas, the interior of his body, and the timelessness of being:

Masked with tubes,
from nose
from throat,
a breathing machine beeping oxygen
oxygen tube where my voice should be
clamped wordless
inarticulated words fetuses in my mind
seeking birth
language languishing in my clogged larynx
looming silence of the breathing tube
my life the extension of a machine
Can there be human meaning
With language buried in the brain?

. . . .

each mortal, finite moment absolute
mind and waning, dubious body
summoned
to add beat to beat
to keep the rhythm moving
beat by beat
to find the drumbeat of my heart
to make time in the dim timelessness
heartbeat by erratic heartbeat
my rising, falling, rising, pounding rhythm, my dance
my pact with life
circles of love
the drums of my blood beat, my lifeboat
heartbeat by erratic heartbeat
past the past, far from the future
repeated and repeating rhythm
second after pauseless second
All.

Fearless, Abe confronted those dark voices within himself, transforming them into life-affirming images. Abe's writing in the last years of his life became humanitarian and questioning. From crushed hopes and flights with "broken wings" a new unknown opened up to him.

Ever proud of his American heritage, he always wanted that part of himself transmitted to me. When I was thirteen, in 1955, he wrote the introduction to the first Czech edition of Walt Whitman's *Leaves of Grass*. He inscribed the copy he gave me as a gift with the following wish:

TO ANN—
> something about our greatest,
> and my favorite, poet
> good Old Walt
> With love and hope that you
> will get to know and appreciate
> our American culture.

> Abe, Prague, July, 1955

Not until decades after he wrote this did I realize what a struggle it has been for both of us to have his hopes come true.

In 1976, when I was living with my husband and two children in Binghamton, New York, I received an early morning phone call informing me that Abe had had another serious heart attack and that he might not live through the night. I took the first available flight, not knowing if when I arrived he would still be alive. I found him hooked up to oxygen tanks, which made it impossible for him to talk. He had not been warned that I was coming because my mother did not know which flight I would be able to get. When he saw me enter the room, he became extremely upset, thinking I had been summoned by the doctors for a last farewell. With pleading eyes he scrutinized my face. Am I alive, dying, almost dead? Once we managed to calm him down, he held my hand in his and closed his eyes. He was exhausted. My mother, who had been by his bedside the entire night, left the two of us alone. After a sleepless night of travel and filled with fear that he might not be alive when I got there, I was soothed by the warm squeeze of his hand.

The only sound in the room was the beep of the monitor and the regular suction of the oxygen pump. I wanted him to feel at peace and to show him how deeply I loved him. Neither the past nor the future was important now; only the present moment mattered. We were both frightened, sad. I held his hand, and without consciously thinking I started to sing to him the way I did to my infant sons when I put them to sleep. But I knew no English songs. I sang the Czech and Moravian songs I used to sing with my friends in Prague, songs Abe had always responded to but could never sing himself. That moment the tunes of my Czech songs brought our two cultures together and made them feel like one.

The last two songs I sang before he dozed off had particularly beautiful but mournful melodies. One was an old Carpatho-Russian song I learned from my husband's mother that was sung by newcomers to America, depicting their search for a center and the faith that God would somehow protect them; the other was the Czech national anthem which celebrates the homeland. The Carpatho-Russian song is about a wanderer like Abe, like me, like the millions who have been uprooted in search of a dream:

As we wander
where shall we go?
Through the mountains and forests,
everywhere God is with us.

What will we drink?
The water from the Danube
in the green meadows
As we wander
what will we eat?
Stuffed cabbage and fried chickens.
As we wander
where will we sleep?
In that green Paradise
where the birds sing.
As we wander
what will we cover ourselves with?
With those leaves that are above us.

I could still feel the restless movements of Abe's fingers in my hand when I continued to sing the Czech anthem:

Where is my homeland?
Water rushes through the mountains,
Forests roar in the valleys,
Spring flowers bloom in the garden,
It is an earthly Paradise.
Is the Czech land, home of mine,
Is the Czech land, home of mine.

This was a moment like no other; our guard was down. We had run out of time to defend or reproach. All we felt was the strength of our love. By the time I sang the slow tunes of the anthem, his irregular breathing had calmed down. I remained seated by his side for a long time singing softly as I watched him sleep. I had much to remember and to hope for. I had much to accept.

For ten months Abe struggled between life and death, becoming the longest resident in the history of the Intensive Care Unit in Stevens Point, Wisconsin, a medical miracle, a human victory. Born to fight, Abe held on to life. Abe showed me what a wonder it was to be alive and what a struggle it was to be human. Belle taught me one needed strength, humor, and flexibility to survive. Both of them showed me the human extremes of their powerful strength and tragic weakness of believing in a vision that was larger than life itself. What I experienced with Abe and Belle is a permanent part of what I am today. It is not possible neatly to package one's years of growing up into twenty-two chapters, an introduction, and an epilogue. We all have the potential to live many lives; I happened to live mine in more than one culture and location, which complicated their harmonious integration.

The black poet Michael S. Harper, a close friend of Abe and Belle, wrote the poem "Abe," which was published in 1975 in *Nightmare Begins Responsibility*. In his poetic account of Abe and Belle's long history of struggle for social change he also captured the ambiguities and complexities that have become a permanent part of our family history.

Abe

— 'I lost my last name at Ellis Island' —

When you came back after your heart
stalled on the Chinese steps,
what street name in Prague,
does not matter;
what matters is your song
of great strain in our 30's
called hard times,
when great men of art
were workers from breads
their mothers made to sell,
and when they ate
they laughed, and what cheese
they got they paid for twice
in the same day
to the same man;
what roads their fathers
walked for work
we'll never know.

What we know is the price
one pays for indifference,
the shoed nail bent
into each soul to kick
at the arched movement,
each yarmulke poised to crow
on your wife whose name
comes clear as the belled charge

of Coltrane we will listen
to in the room of your daughter,
her son the book
written as your heart
pours liquid fumes
of the life he must know,
and what the bread cost,
what you paid
to keep the stairwell
unchambered, unbypassed,
a red road open
at the crossroad
of scarred hands.

                    for Abe and Belle Chapman

Epilogue

When asked how her patients were responding to the revolution and the new society it had ushered in, she [Czech psychologist Helena Klímová in Prague, 1989] told me . . . "The psychotics are getting better and the neurotics are getting worse." How do you explain that? I asked. With all this new freedom, she said the neurotics are terribly uncertain. What will happen now? Nobody knows. The old rigidity was detestable, even to them, of course, but also reassuring, dependable. There was a structure. . . . To the neurotics the change is very unsettling. They are suddenly in a world of choices. And the psychotics? Is it really possible that they're getting better? I think so, yes. The psychotics suck up the prevailing mood. Now it's exhilaration. Everybody is happy, so the psychotics are even happier. They are euphoric. It's all very strange. Everybody is suffering from adaptation shock.
—Philip Roth, "Return to Prague," *New York Review of Books*, April 12, 1990

On my first return visit to Europe in 1984, I visited Warsaw (still under martial law), a city demolished by the Germans in four successive bombing raids. Because it was the historic capital of Poland and the center of the Polish resistance, Hitler had ordered it leveled to the ground after the 1944 uprising. At the end of the war, the Poles decided to restore to its prewar state the medieval center of the city, the Stare Miasto. In a daze I walked through Zamkowy Square, restored from rubble, and toured the old town museum containing drawings of the ancient Warsaw streets. I was also amazed at the newly restored classicist palace in Lazienki Park, a symbol of Poland's noble past. In the palace I watched a group of twelve-year-old pioneers tour the splendid rooms in which the last Polish king, Stanislaw August Poniatowski, had lived. The teacher proudly described the careful work behind the restorations, the marble pillars that had been faithfully reproduced from eighteenth-century originals, the hand-made crystal chandeliers that were exactly like those first crafted for the extravagant palace rooms. The restoration had cost the state an astronomical sum of money. For this new generation of Polish children, history was visible; it could be touched and committed to memory for future generations. These landmarks of the past restored to the present connected the children to their ancestors in a way only tangible images can. The palace affirmed that the Poles evolved from a culture that was centuries old and filled with unique achievements. The Polish youngsters entered the mysteries of that past gliding from room to room on oversized felt slippers that all visitors had to wear to protect the shiny parquet floors.

The impressions of that day overwhelmed me. It was suddenly clear that a nation, like an individual, has a past to which it needs to be connected in order to function in the present. I realized it was vital for the Poles to restore Lazienki palace to its former beauty, despite the effort and cost. Within me I felt a deep connection between the destruction of this city and the broken continuities of my own family that could never be restored. The rebuilt streets and buildings of old Warsaw forced me to confront my own disconnectedness and made me wish to recapture what had been lost.

Historical and geographical continuity parallels continuities in our personal lives, our sense of place, and gives us a sense of belonging, pride, and self-worth. Those unbroken patterns are a source of strength and wholeness that sustain us during moments of loss and confusion. Reconstructing Warsaw's historic landmarks clearly affirmed the Polish nation's continuity with itself and became a source of pride and hope during the long years of communist domination after the war. Poland's tribute to its past also made it feel there could be a future. As difficult as it would be, I, too, had to uncover the meaning of a past that had been torn away and shrouded in pain.

That summer, when I also returned to Prague, I was unprepared for the emotions the familiar streets and city landmarks triggered in me. Twenty years of longing and remembering sights like the Old Town Square and Charles Bridge dissipated quickly as soon as I arrived in Prague, but they were replaced by a dull ache that was more difficult to deal with. As much as Prague was a return to a dearly loved and greatly missed landscape, it also reminded me of the cultural and linguistic ties I had to a people who knew me when I was Anna, a young "Czech" woman with dreams of a future among them. In this city of one million people, after these twenty years, there was not a single person to whom I could return. I was a complete outsider to those who lived and loved in the streets, cafes, and wine cellars of Prague, as I had done in my youth. The familiar surroundings only reinforced the alienation from what had once been my home, my people, my language, my country.

It was not until six years after my mother's death and my gradual recovery from that loss that I desired to confront the disturbing memories of my past. The visit to Warsaw, my first return to Prague in 1984, and the persistent questions of my children about my childhood urged me to evoke the memories that led to the writing of this book. I did not know any other way to overcome the sense of uprootedness with which my parents' life had left me. After my parents died, I felt homeless and abandoned. The decisions they made in life severed me from extended family, while the tenuous sense of place and belonging they had created to replace all we lost disappeared with them in death. All that was left to me now was my life with my husband and children. But there was no homestead to return to, no city I belonged to, no relatives who knew me as I was growing up, no country I could really feel was mine. My moorings were afloat.

I had to dig my way out of the burdens of conspiracy and secrecy imposed on me as a child to start the slow process of self-restoration. Not until I had shattered the silence and taboos demanded by my parents could I restore what had been lost. I was the only one who could rebuild my history. Patching together strands of my past was a way to fill the void. Breaking the secrecy dissolved a web of fears. The more my story unfolded, the easier it was to retrieve good memories that overshadowed the bad. Remembering what had been stored in darkness allowed me to illuminate the multifaceted meaning of isolated memories. Writing helped me remake the past and understand the nature of myself separate from the person my parents wanted me to be. Like other children of American communists who lived in exile, with phony identities, forced to lie to protect their parents' cause, I had to shed the mystique of secrecy I inherited in order to discover who I was and what held meaning to me.

My sister and I have dealt differently with these problems. For me, memory and writing have been salutary, but she has found her balm in privacy. Since I love and respect her, I have tried to mention her as little as possible in this book and allow her story to remain with her.

In adjusting to America, I had to reconcile the clash of Czech and American cultures and communist-capitalist values. I experienced all the stages that any new immigrant adjusting to America goes through — from being overwhelmed by the variety of choices as I purchased my first bar of soap to the realization that I had to decide what direction my life would take. I was forced to become the master of my own destiny and not expect, as I had in the past, that the state would make decisions for me. I was a private individual and free to discover myself. In a communist society I knew the kind of person the state and the party expected me to be. There was never a chance to explore who I really was or who I wanted to be. But when I was back in America I had to learn to follow the voice of my own will rather than the directives stemming from a particular ideology. I had to struggle hard to retrain my heart and mind to think and feel in English. I was expected to function as an American without the training my American peers had been given. I had to learn a new set of skills to survive in an unfamiliar setting. I lost all continuity with my sense of Czechness that came alive for me only through the Czech language.

I went to college, married, raised two sons, made friends, found employment, mastered the art of shopping, learned how to drive and use a computer, and in externals became an American. But I did not always react or feel like an American. My non-American self still lives within me. There are important parts of me that come alive when I have a chance to speak Czech, see a Czech film, and read articles on Czechoslovakia and Russia in the *New York Times*. This hidden self emerges when I go to a Czech dance or gather with people with whom I can sing my favorite Moravian folk songs or when I read a new novel by Milan Kundera, Ivan Klíma, or Josef Škvorecký. It comes alive when I make *medvědí tlapičky* (bear's paws) cookies for the Christmas holidays or listen to Dvořák or Smetana. Powerful emotions flicker on and off inside of me, according to the setting I am in.

I am at ease with Jewish friends when we engage in the teasing banter that underscores our intimate conversations, having been well trained by my mother in the philosophy that "if I don't tease you, how would you know I like you?" I am in tune with the expansive and unpredictable Russian soul. I respond to the tonal sounds of Chinese and the exotic flavors of China's food, and I have maintained a lasting interest in events in that country. But my upbringing and experiences make me a foreigner in a Jewish temple, and the pursuit of the American dream is distant to me. When I am among Czechs, however, I feel as if I am entering a dark room, and although I know where the light switch is, I do not need to turn it on. I can see through the darkness.

It has taken me a long time to understand the cultural diversity of America that my father was so fond of. So what does it matter if I do not know what to call the combination of cultural and linguistic associations that evoke responses in me? Members of my husband's family, whose background is Russian Orthodox, consistently refer to "our kind of people," who do things this way as opposed to the way others do things, which implies that there is also "your kind of people." This reinforces their continuity with tradition and their sense of identity. I may be a person who lives in that twilight zone between "our" kind and the "other" kind. Unknowingly and unintentionally, my parents contributed to this uniquely American predicament, making me a stranger in their own land and mine as well.

I have compassion for Abe and Belle's dream to improve the human condition. I also have compassion for the political disillusionment they endured and the consequences the undoing of that dream had for me. I am no longer haunted by my past but enriched and strengthened by it. When I started to write this book, I had written a dedication in memory of my father that emphasized the ill effects his political commitments had on my life. By the time I finished the book, however, I had to change the dedication. Reality is more complex than assigning blame or unraveling injustices. Although Abe made some grievous mistakes in his life and paid dearly for them, he was also a man who refused to accept defeat and kept struggling for new meanings in life with a passion and love that he conveyed to others and which by far outlived his political vision.

Remembering the havoc of my childhood and adolescence has made me sort out the negative and positive legacies. It has helped me see my parents as loving, complex, confused, and imperfect. Most of all, memory has given me a sense of continuity I lacked. In our fast-paced world we must make hard and fast choices without clearly visualizing their far-reaching consequences. Belonging to a particular culture tells us who we are and what our origins are. Following a set of beliefs, be they religious, political, or philosophical, determines how we should act. A life without a firm tie to a particular culture, language, ancestors, landscape, or permanent set of beliefs forced me to search for my own connections and to build my own palace of childhood memories. They link me to the generations that came before me and that will follow me. They are, as I discovered on the pages of this memoir, a family heritage of ideas, accomplishments, tragedy, and dreams.

Plattsburgh, New York, 1988–1995